For John and Diana
Some help for
society-watching.

love

gene

Colombo 1982

Caste and family
in the politics of the Sinhalese
1947–1976

Caste and family in the politics of the Sinhalese 1947–1976

JANICE JIGGINS

K.V.G. de Silva & Sons Colombo Limited
Branch: Serendib Gallery

Published in Sri Lanka by K.V.G. de Silva & Sons Colombo Ltd
415 Galle Road, Colombo 4, Sri Lanka
in association with the Syndics of the Cambridge University Press
The Pitt Building, Trumpington Street, Cambridge CB2 IRP
Bentley House, 200 Euston Road, London NW1 2DB
32 East 57th Street, New York, NY 10022, USA
296 Beaconsfield Parade, Middle Park, Melbourne 3206, Australia

© Cambridge University Press 1979

Printed in Great Britain by
Western Printing Services Ltd, Bristol

Contents

Tables

MAPS

CHARTS

Preface

The interpretation of Sinhalese political dynamics given in this book is put forward with some confidence; it is equally certain that the results of the general election of August 1977 herald the beginning of a new era. This is not to say that the nice calculations of interest described here – the interactions, loyalties, and identities which have influenced Sinhalese politics since Independence – have been all at once overthrown or discarded; on the contrary, the composition of the new United National Party Cabinet indicates that considerations of caste support retain some importance. But both the overwhelming nature of the UNP's landslide victory and the fundamental constitutional changes which the new Prime Minister, Mr J. R. Jayawardene, brought about so swiftly, mark the abandonment of Westminster-style parliamentary politics in Sri Lanka.

For the first time in the island's electoral experience a single party gained an absolute majority of votes at the polls, giving it nearly 83 per cent of the seats in the National State Assembly. The major partner to the defeated United Front government, Mrs Bandaranaike's Sri Lanka Freedom Party, was reduced to eight seats with approximately 31 per cent of the votes, only two sitting MPs, both Cabinet members, being returned. The other two partners to the United Front – the Communist Party and the Lanka Sama Samaja Party – standing in association with left Independents and some former left-wing members of the SLFP in a United Left Front, took less than 7 per cent of the poll and returned no candidates whatsoever.

Not only did the UNP gain a plurality in aggregate; it won a majority of votes in all but two Tamil-speaking provinces, and out of its 156 candidates, 126 won with an absolute plurality. Even more significantly for the arguments of this book, the UNP captured the SLFP's electoral heartland in Uva Province, Central Province, and North-Central Province (the SLFP returning no member for the first two and only three for the North-Central Province), and ousted the left vote in the coastal Western Province and in Sabaragamuwa. The whole-hearted swing in the Sinhalese areas is indicated, too, in the Moslem representation, which re-emerged strongly in support of the UNP, ten out of eleven Moslem MPs being returned for the UNP.[1]

The elimination of most of the Sinhalese opposition at the polls has consequences beyond party, however, for it leaves the Tamils, newly joined in the Tamil United Liberation Front, as the official opposition, symbolising the increasing confrontation between the ethnic groups; a constant reminder of the fears and hostility which broke out into violent communal rioting shortly after the elections.[2] Some settlement has to be made but no one is pretending it will be easy, nor that it can be made without modifying the concept of the island's polity as Sinhalese and Buddhist, which the Bandaranaikes' SLFP has articulated so forcefully in the years since Independence.[3]

Mr Jayawardene has sought and been granted powers to move Sri Lanka away from Westminster parliamentary practice towards an executive Presidency with features drawn from both the American and the French experience. The President is to be directly elected as sole executive authority and to have powers to appoint both the Prime Minister and the Cabinet, choosing from members of the National State Assembly who will continue to be directly elected on a constituency basis. Drawing on a principle adopted in the 1972 constitution, the President's decisions and acts will not be subject to judicial review. Mr Jayawardene himself became the first President under the new constitution on 1 January 1978, and will serve a six-year term.

It is argued by the UNP that such a move is necessary to secure an island-wide consensus for policies over the longer term, beyond party factionalism and what has been dubbed the 'political *thathumaru* system' (*thathumaru* refers to a traditional agricultural labour-sharing arrangement). It is to be hoped that the powers and position of a President elevated beyond the parliamentary and party pressures of Sinhalese nationalism will also allow a statesmanlike settlement to be reached between the Tamils and the Sinhalese.

J.J.

July 1978

Select glossary of Sinhalese terms and list of abbreviations

Adigar	traditional Kandyan office and title: chief minister
ANCL	Associated Newspapers of Ceylon Ltd; also known as Lake House, the site of its major publishing business
Appuhamy	respectful form of address (m), as to well-off shopkeepers, etc.
ayurvedic medicine	traditional system of medical knowledge and practice, still widely used
bana hall	preaching hall, attached to Buddhist temple
Bandara	deferential form of address (m) to traditional notable
Bhasha Peramuna	Language Front
Batgam caste	originally, foot-soldiers. Also known less respectfully as the *Padu*
Berawa caste	drummer caste
bhikkhu	Buddhist monk
chena	jungle or scrub cleared for short-term cropping and then abandoned
CJC	Criminal Justice Commission
CNC	Ceylon National Congress
CP	Communist Party – Moscow-oriented
Dingiri Hamuduruvanē	specifically Kandyan deferential form of address (f) to a 'Lady of an ancestral house'
Dissawe	traditional Kandyan office and title: governor of a province
Durava caste	toddy-tapper caste
gē	suffix appended to *Goyigama* family names indicating that the person is descended from that particular house or lineage

gedera nāma	name indicating descent from a particular house or lineage
Goyigama caste	cultivator caste
Hamuduravo	deferential form of address (m); Kandyan usage. Abbreviation: *Hamu*: familiar/affectionate form of address used with first names
Hamumahataya	deferential form of address (m); maritime usage
Hena caste	washer caste
Hunu caste	lime-burner caste
JVP	Janatha Vimukthi Peramuna – People's Liberation Front
kachcheri	district administration centre
Karava caste	fisher caste
Lake House; Lake House Group	terms used to denote ANCL
LPP	Lanka Prajathanthrawadi Party – Ceylon Democratic Party
LSSP	Lanka Sama Samaja Party (Trotskyist) – Ceylon Equal Society Party
Maha Nayake Thero	high clerical officer within a Buddhist *nikaya*; fully ordained monk of more than ten years' standing
MEP	Mahajana Eksath Peramuna – People's United Front
MSC	Member of the State Council
mudalali	indigenous entrepreneur or trader in the process of becoming wealthy
Mudaliyar; Gate *Mudaliyar*; *Maha Mudaliyar*	high-ranking traditional officers
mudiansē nāma	name indicating inherited traditional title(s)
Muhandiram	traditional Kandyan title and office: one of the officers of the palace
nayake	clerical officer within a *nikaya*; a fully ordained monk
Navandanna caste	artificer caste
NI	no information
nikaya	sect of Buddhist monks

nindagam	traditionally, land belonging to the king and granted to individuals
Peramuna	Front, as in Bhasha Peramuna
Radala	collective term for members of Kandyan *Goyigama* noble families
rajakariya	king's service: forced services to the state
Rate Mahatmeya	traditional Kandyan office and title: principal officer of a county
Rodiya caste	small caste, nearest in Sinhalese society to an outcast community
Salagama caste	cinnamon-peeler caste
Sangha	the community of Buddhist monks
Sangharamaya	place of study belonging to the *Sangha*
SLFP	Sri Lanka Freedom Party
SLFSP	Sri Lanka Freedom Socialist Party
SMS	Sinhala Maha Sabha – Great Council of the Sinhalese
swabhasha	mother tongue (Sinhala or Tamil)
thathumaru	traditional form of agricultural labour-sharing
Theravada	one of the two major schools of Buddhism
UF	United Front
Unnahē	respectful form of address (m), as to skilled craftsmen, etc.
UNP	United National Party
Vahumpura caste	jaggery-maker and domestic service caste. Also known less respectfully as the *Hakuru*
Valawē Hamuduruvanē	deferential form of address (f) to a 'Lady of an ancestral house'
valauwwa	house of a local notable
varṇa	a fourfold hierarchy of castes, in which status and power are differentiated, based on classical Hindu theory
vihara	Buddhist temple
viharadhipati	chief monk of a temple
viharagam	land and villages granted to *viharas*
vinaya	rules for the maintenance of discipline among members of the *Sangha*
VLSSP	Viplavakari Lanka Sama Samaja Party – Marxist offshoot of the LSSP

I

Introduction

I first went to Sri Lanka* to study the *bhikkhus'* (Buddhist monks) involvement in national politics. From the early years of the nineteenth century Buddhist monks had been active in rousing the Sinhalese to awareness of their Buddhist heritage. I wanted to discover the nature of the continuity lying beneath the years of colonial rule and the slow, peaceful emergence to formal Independence in 1947 which would explain the paradox of 1959. In that year the man who had articulated and shaped, first in his Sinhala Maha Sabha (Great Council of the Sinhalese) and then electorally in the Sri Lanka Freedom Party, the aspirations the *bhikkhus* had so long championed, was shot dead by a Buddhist monk.

The event seemed the more inexplicable because of the way it was treated in the academic literature, which described Sri Lanka in terms of its constitution and the structure of its Westminster-style parliamentary democracy. In this distinctly exterior view of the island, S. W. R. D. Bandaranaike's electoral landslide at the general election of 1956 was seen merely as a notable example of a general observation: that indigenous leaders tend in time to replace the westernised, bourgeois elites confirmed in power by departing colonial rulers.

Some flavour of the dynamics of contemporary Sinhalese society is to be found in the writing on ancient Sri Lanka, but as scholarship approaches the last few hundred years the Sinhalese disappear behind the activities and concerns of their colonial rulers, first the Portuguese, then the Dutch, and finally the British, till we can find the Sinhalese only behind the presence of military men, administrators, missionaries, and planters, whose energies and loyalties rarely were concentrated on the island, being claimed at least equally by imperial economies and directives, or by the higher authority of the Christian Church.

Most of the chroniclers are too busy telling us of the acts, amendments, reforms, and councils of the British to spare much thought for

* Ceylon became Sri Lanka under a new constitution proclaimed in 1972. The term 'Sri Lanka' is used throughout.

the impact of their rule on the daily lives of the villagers, or to describe how tradition was superseded or in turn absorbed the new ways. Then, as the years pass, we begin to hear of lawyers educated at the British Inns of Court, of merchants grown rich on government carting or provisioning contracts; we see new families emerge and take their place beside the old and aristocratic families in the seats of the Legislative Council. We catch glimpses of a solid middle class emerging, largely professional, and we become familiar with the major figures of post-Independence Sri Lanka as they patiently debate the stages to constitutional maturity. Yet the literature remains oddly gentle, urbane, comfortable. A picture emerges finally of a polity governed under a Westminster-type two-party consti-tution, with an independent judiciary, regular elections, and periodic exchange of power between groups recognisable as parties, where the freedom of an energetic and outspoken press is encouraged, the whole underpinned by a welfarist economic liberalism, sustaining a well-fed, healthy, and increasingly literate population. As Sir Charles Jeffries, who as Deputy Under-Secretary of the Colonial Office was at the heart of the Independence negotiations, has commented, Ceylon was regarded as 'the prototype and model for the new Commonwealth of the latter part of the 20th century'.[1] Many Sinhalese echoed these sentiments, and with Sir Oliver Goonetilleke asserted that as far as parliamentary government and political stability went, Sri Lanka was 'the best bet in Asia'.[2]

The reality of the 'prototype' gained credence in my mind the first day I spent in Colombo, the capital city. It was getting shabby, not yet blessed (or desecrated, depending on one's point of view) by the international hotels which have been built in the last few years, but in the autumn of 1969 it looked prosperous and settled, with a gleaming white neo-classic Town Hall, and an imposing sandstone Parliament gracing the wide open space known as Galle Face Green which stretches along the sea front. Stuccoed colonial buildings, cavernous mahogany-and-teak hotel lobbies, and a famous emporium purveying fine goods in continuing Victorian splendour – these were solid evidence of an absorbed western tradition and stability. The seal of reassurance was set by the red ex-London Transport double-decker buses that roared and boiled their way along the tree-lined streets.

I began to read through the haphazard collection known as the National Archives, then temporarily housed at Vidyodaya University to which I was nominally attached. Formerly one of two leading centres of higher learning for the *bhikkhus*, it had not as yet succeeded in transcending a monkish, narrowly scholastic tradition that imposed on its students large doses of learning by rote and the memorising of lecture notes. The

Archives were largely inaccessible due to the slow process of cataloguing, but the staff were unfailingly helpful. I began reading the notes and reports of Government Agents, Revenue Officers, and Special Commissioners from the earliest years of the British administration, trying to get a feel for their problems and a reflected outline of the world as the Sinhalese saw it. Mostly I concentrated on the problems that arose between the administration and the Buddhist laity and *Sangha* (community of Buddhist monks), partly matters of a practical kind, as this or that edict threatened or was felt to threaten religious interest. More serious problems arose because British understanding of their rights and obligations towards the 'heathen rites and beliefs' of the Buddhists was incomprehensible to the *Sangha*, which clung to the precedents of ancient times and its own definitions of the special relationship between the king, the *Sangha*, its members, and their temporalities.[3]

I spent nearly a year reading about the *bhikkhus*, visiting their temples, interviewing *viharadhipatis* (chief monks of the temple) and lay Buddhists active in the years leading to 1956. The National Museum Library yielded rich veins of interest in the records of Executive and Legislative Council debates. Lake House (Associated Newspapers of Ceylon Ltd) newspaper archives gave insight into old scandals, described the *personae* and the detail in recurring complaints and litigation. In the continuity of public utterance, old newspaper reports gave shape to the policies and aims of the various pressure groups, and flesh to the claims of the chief temples to speak authoritatively. I travelled about the country, checking on the extent of temple revenues and temporalities against returns given to the Public Trustee in recent years, and against the acreages and other assets recorded in the nineteenth century by the Commissioners appointed at different times to investigate and define these matters.

I learned a great deal and acquired a sense of the life of the country that was not to be found in any academic book or scholarly article: I was beginning to be able to see the universe as a Sinhalese Buddhist might see it, and to define it in his terms and priorities. But by the end of 1970 I had realised two things of importance to my further studies. One was simply that, as a woman, my ability to become close to the monks and their way of life was limited; certain avenues of investigation were not open to me, and the strangeness of a female research student was too great to establish a useful rapport with many of those I wished to interview or work with.

The second was the discovery that there was no defined, direct institutional relation between the power and influence of the Buddhists and the secular centres of power. The relationship was wholly personal, based on family and caste loyalties and antipathies, a loose nexus whose lines of demarcation were often fluid and rarely primarily doctrinal, ideological, or indeed rational from an external point of view. The relationship appeared often irrational, that is, if one defined the political structure as it was defined in the prototype, and assessed its inner working according to its familiar formal outline. The problem of analysis became infinitely more fascinating; no longer a question of something miraculously akin in Sinhalese and British natures that ensured the easy transplant of Westminster to Galle Face Green, but a question of how and why the framework suited the indigenous society, a question of the style of the Sinhalese way of doing things. How did the formal structure and its constitutional provisions contain and accommodate traditional loyalties, and what were those loyalties? Did they operate within parties and cabinets, or spill over in family blocs and caste groupings? Were electorates aware of these personal characteristics in their representatives, and were they ever a necessary and/or sufficient condition of their support?

In 1971 I began to pursue these questions, talking to Government Agents and Civil Servants, and listening to university students as they tried to get employment; I went again to the villages and up-country towns, but this time to listen to teachers, co-operative store owners, village headmen, kachcheri clerks, and police sergeants. I sat on many hospitable verandahs, listening to family histories. I heard of intercaste and intracaste feuds and rivalries, of alliances sealed by marriage, of the lesser and the great, till the web became familiar to me. I began to see Sinhalese society as it had appeared to the 4.5 million who entered into Independence, as a parochial, closely known society, when its leaders were visible, their allegiances understood in terms of their family history, and when it was enough to ask, 'Where are you from, what is your village?' to establish an intimate profile of a man's antecedents, his rank, his influence. Among students, this knowledge was less certain, partly an affectation of their new knowledge, but mostly because in twenty-five years the Sinhalese population had doubled and had become increasingly mobile geographically. This enormously important demographic burst had loosened and was beginning to break the tight established order, so that ties and relationships were less well known and more difficult to establish correctly. As I later realised, this change was beginning to be reflected in attitudes to parties and party leaders as the *persona* of caste-and-kinship became of less importance, and secular characteristics (party image as defined ideologically, for example) became primary in many situations.

I carried out some preliminary fieldwork to see if my initial interpretation was valid, and to ascertain if certain methods of enquiry were practicable and trustworthy. I moved from Vidyodaya and became affiliated to the beautiful Peradeniya campus in the hills around Kandy, the last capital of the Sinhalese kings. By this time I had become aware of the deep concern of the young for their own future, and had listened attentively to their various critiques of the hitherto ruling parties which, they felt, were incapable of leading the country to prosperity and were incapable of providing jobs for the 60 per cent of the population who were under twenty-six years old in 1969.[4] They distrusted the radical pronouncements of Mrs Bandaranaike's left-wing SLFP-led United Front which had gained power in the 1970 general election[5] as merely the necessary electoral sayings of a socially traditionalist and conservative elite living comfortable bourgeois lives in the capital. Many of the young feared that the United Front would prove unwilling to act radically to solve the problems of rural unemployment.

The insurgency which broke out in April 1971, largely among the young, took the government by surprise in its ferocity, and the fact of its occurrence came as a shock to a nation which had experienced no widespread police or military activity since the early years of the British conquest. Any number of explanations and justifications followed, from the class analyses of the left to Mrs Bandaranaike's own assessment that the majority were misguided youths who had been led astray by criminals and subversive elements.[6] For my own part, I was sure that a major impulse had been provided by the social dynamic between the castes. The continuing depressed status of two of the largest up-country castes, combined with the political frustrations of the south- and west-coast fishing caste (denied adjustment within the existing political parties despite, since 1956, an increasingly populist stance by governments proclaiming the 'age of the common man') formed a core of disaffection to be exploited by the insurgent leaders. Delineated in these terms, the bitterness among the insurgents, the fears of the political and social elites, and the brutality of the repression by the armed services and the police become a reflection of the social psychology of the movement, unaccounted for either in the explications of the Communist and Maoist left, or by overdue reliance on the supposed ideology of the insurgents themselves.

The year 1971 was a tragic and disturbing year, but not uninstructive to an outsider. Events exposed the inadequacy of the purely constitutional model. The vulnerability of the political system was not simply the vulnerability of all open parliamentary systems to armed violence; the response of the parties, their leaders and their rank and file, and the various extra-parliamentary groups that make up the body politic, revealed something of the underlying tensions among the Sinhalese, not overtly expressed in the structure of the constitutional prototype.

Towards the end of 1971 and in the early months of 1972 I embarked on a programme of extensive fieldwork among the electorates of Sabaragamuwa. The interest and curiosity of nearly everyone I met made these trips both stimulating and demanding, as my thoughts were time and again discussed knowledgeably and vociferously by those who gathered round. One is struck on such occasions by the oral traditions of the Sinhalese, where facts remembered and opinions reiterated from generation to generation remain present and alive, and set a standard for current events and personalities. Perhaps it is the tradition of listening to the *bhikkhus* in the *bana* (preaching) halls, perhaps it is the climate, so inimical to careful preservation of paper, that makes precious strict remembrance. Certainly their tales, if not always historically accurate, were richly illustrative and seemed to indicate that the Sinhalese view politics as a splendid arena for the absurdities and futilities of life; abundant in shrewd character sketches, realistic if not cynical toward large promises, tolerant of ostentation, and unsentimental about the common lot of man, their tales were neatly turned for good-humoured scorn at some ill-adept politician, and yet justly admired the clever tricks of the triumphant manipulator.

I give as examples the following verses:

> *Ūth kupadiyā*
> *Māth kupadiyā*
> *Gamē kupādiyata chandē denda!*
> (He's a blackguard
> I'm a blackguard
> So vote for the village blackguard!)

> *Apē Ammā langa enavā*
> *Hāl sēru deka denavā!*
> (Our 'Mother' is coming along
> She gives the two measures of rice!)

'*Apē Ammā*' refers to Mrs Bandaranaike – 'our Mother' – and illustrates the affectionate and familiar identity of the SLFP to the ordinary people of the village. The second line hints at the attempt during her 1960 government to cut the second measure of rice given to every household at a subsidised price, emphasises her promise to restore the full two measures (cut to one in 1966 by Dudley Senanayake) if elected in 1970, and underscores the reciprocal trading of votes for material benefit.

I left Sri Lanka in the summer of 1972 but returned for nine months

in 1973 in time to witness the extraordinary mourning for Dudley
Senanayake (three times Prime Minister) on his death in April, and the
fascinating by-election at Dedigama which followed.[7]

The story that is told here is of discovery, and of an enlightenment that
is possible only when one has received the privilege of entering the lives
of a people. To all those who gave me goodwill, their friendship, and a
gentle understanding of my frequent bewilderment, my thanks.

The importance of caste and family

This book is not intended to be a general political history of modern
Sri Lanka[8] but a description of two elements that interact with modern
political ideologies, parties, and platforms, and a tentative analysis of
their role within a parliamentary system. Those two elements are caste
and family. It is generally supposed among scholars and among the
Sinhalese themselves that caste is 'very important'. However, as is not the
case in India, where caste has been the subject of extensive and detailed
study, caste studies in Sri Lanka have been largely confined to anthropologists' village studies. Few writers on the politics of Sri Lanka have
attempted to describe (indeed, few have even mentioned) the interaction
of caste and politics at either the village, the constituency, or the national
level, often merely indicating a few instances where caste factors have
intervened, then resting content with a short section asserting their general
importance. The reticence on the part of Sinhalese scholars is more
understandable, for caste, like sex in Victorian society, is a 'taboo' subject,
and rarely spoken of openly. A great number of allusive phrases exist,
both in Sri Lankan English and in Sinhala, to describe the various caste
groups and their respective hierarchical status. Thus 'the fishing interest'
refers to the *Karava* caste of the south and west littoral and *okkoma nädä*
(all kinsmen) can indicate that the speaker is referring to his own caste
group. Writing of the 1947 elections, H. A. J. Hulugalle, for many years
a close observer of the political scene, expresses the typical embarrassment
of the westernised, educated, urban Sinhalese: 'This (caste) is not a subject
which educated Ceylonese like to talk about, especially if they have been
to schools in which there is a good mixture of races, religions and castes,
though everyone seems to know to which caste a friend belongs.'[9]

The village Sinhalese will rarely speak openly to urban Sinhalese on
caste matters, still less if that stranger is thought to have a caste interest in
the outcome of his enquiry. Sinhalese sociologists have been constrained
in their own work precisely by the accusations and counter-accusations of
bias and ulterior motive that have attended their attempts to clarify even

the historical aspects of caste. Investigations of the kind described in this book are perhaps possible at the present time only for an outsider. Reticence in public discussion must not be taken for lack of interest, however; few topics generate so much heat as the precise status or affiliation of this or that person or group.

Family and kinship are, of course, closely related to discussions of caste, and family membership, ancestry, and marriage alliances rouse as much interest as caste affiliation, but they are openly spoken of and are the subject of exhaustive enquiry and much gossip. Such matters can, and often do, stand as a surrogate for discussion of caste, for many members of the different caste groups retain a caste-distinct name, and lineage can make plain a person's caste without actual reference to it.

Diaries, documents, and memoirs which are intended to 'prove' the descent and status of a particular family are extremely popular, and are published in limited editions and circulated to 'bona fide' members. An example from 1911 begins with a foreword by the editor: 'It is perhaps correct to say that there is nothing which stirs up so much animosity and bitterness among the Sinhalese people as a whole, as questions of caste, class and family.' The foreword ends:

My chief object in placing before my kinsmen a portion of the information which I have collected during the last twenty years is to show them, as far as lies in my power, the truth about ourselves . . . This book is strictly for private circulation. All copies are numbered and a register is kept of the parties to whom copies are issued. It is earnestly requested that it may not be allowed to reach unworthy hands.[10]

Parties and programmes

The leaders of the two major political parties of the Sinhalese, the United National Party of the Senanayake clan, and the Sri Lanka Freedom Party of the Bandaranaikes, have all been *Goyigama*, the highest in status and numerically the largest caste, and they have all come from upper-class families, the Senanayakes being a low-country family of good background who accumulated wealth and rose to the highest status under the British, and the Bandaranaikes/Ratwattes being of feudal descent from the most powerful families of the traditional Kandyan aristocracy. In the following chapters I shall be following the implications of these identities, but it is perhaps as well to begin here by briefly outlining the history of the various parties and their major political programmes.

The UNP was formed in 1946 by the merger of the Ceylon National Congress and the Sinhala Maha Sabha (SMS) of S. W. R. D. Bandaranaike, and with the support of other minor political elements and individuals willing to adopt its general outlook. The Ceylon National Congress had completed its main task of winning self-government for Sri Lanka, and a new vehicle was needed to carry the country into Independence. The only political parties which hitherto had been constituted as, and functioned as, recognisably modern parties were the minority Lanka Sama Samaja Party (Trotskyist) and the Communist Party (Marxist). The UNP was formed as a coalition of interest with an island-wide appeal to fight the first general election of 1947. Its inspiration and figurehead was D. S. Senanayake, long active in the political struggle for Independence, and widely known to the people for his irrigation schemes and agricultural projects which had opened up vast new tracts for cultivation and settlement from the 1930s onwards. A large number of independent candidates stood in 1947, but the UNP took over from the departing colonial power without great difficulty, winning forty-two seats in a Lower House of ninety-five elected members (a further six being appointed by the Governor-General), and formed a government with D. S. Senanayake as Prime Minister.

In 1951 S. W. R. D. Bandaranaike led his Sinhala Maha Sabha out of the UNP, when the government refused to adopt a number of resolutions passed by the SMS at its annual sessions at Madampe. These included the adoption of Sinhala as the official language and the recognition of Buddhism as the religion of the Sinhalese. In September 1951 S. W. R. D. formed the Sri Lanka Freedom Party, translating into political terms the appeal he had made under the SMS for a new Sri Lanka based on the aspirations of the Sinhalese, Buddhist masses. He promised the overthrow of the westernised, English-educated elites of Colombo, and the revival of the traditional virtues and values of the Sinhalese villager.

S. W. R. D.'s defection removed only six supporters from the UNP's strength in parliament. A more serious blow occurred in 1952 when D. S. Senanayake fell from his horse whilst riding on Galle Face Green and died. His son, Dudley Senanayake, who had worked with D. S. in the State Council preceding Independence, took over the leadership of the UNP, and went to the polls in April 1952 on a platform which promised to continue to uphold the 'ideals' of his father. It would be realistic to suppose that, over and above the affection people had felt for D. S. as the 'Father of the Nation', the most important element in the son's appeal as far as the mass of the people were concerned was his continuance of the food subsidies. These had been introduced some years earlier at a time when Sri Lanka had ample foreign reserves and domestic resources to buy food, chiefly rice, on the world markets and to distribute it at a much reduced price to every household on a weekly ration. By 1952 rice was offered at less than a third of its imported cost; in the financial year 1951–2 one-third of government expenditure went into transfers and subsidies on a range of goods and services, with food subsidies as the largest single item.[11] In 1952 the UNP captured fifty-four seats, to the SLFP's nine. But Dudley suffered from a prolonged period of ill-health, and he resigned from the premiership – and at that time also from active politics – in October 1953. His uncle, Sir John Kotelawala, Leader of the House and Minister of Transport, took over, after a short struggle with J. R. Jawardene, then Minister of Finance.

The events leading up to the next general election in 1956, when the SLFP came 'from nowhere' to sweep the polls on a landslide, have been well documented elsewhere; suffice it to say that they related increasingly to a conflict of style and identity, Sir John being all for an open, western-ised society, and S. W. R. D. playing on the traditionalist sentiments of the mass of the people, moving the political game for the first time away from the caucus politics of the Colombo elites to mass-based electioneering and populist policies. S. W. R. D. joined forces with an offshoot of the LSSP led by Philip Gunawardene, who had a strong trade union base, and with the Sinhala Bhasha Peramuna, or Language Front, led by W. Dahanayake, which was pressing for the adoption of Sinhala as the official language. The Mahajana Eksath Peramuna – People's United Front – won fifty-one seats, the SLFP alone taking forty-three; the UNP were left with a rump of eight.

S. W. R. D.'s appeal was expressed in terms very like those now used by his widow, Mrs Sirimavo Bandaranaike. To illustrate both the emotional flavour of the message and the continuity of the tradition which S. W. R. D. established I will quote briefly from the broadcast to the nation made by Mrs Bandaranaike after winning the elections in 1970:

The victory that was won yesterday is not my victory or that of my party. It is the victory of the men and women of this country, of the common people . . . The forces that have brought me to this high office, which I have today with deep humility accepted, were not set in motion by the tears of a weeping widow. They were created by the agony and the anguish of the forgotten millions scattered throughout this country, who suffer in silence, without a roof over their heads, or four walls to call their own; without one proper meal to nourish or sustain them, without the bare essential amenities of a decent life . . . There are many problems which the Government will be called upon to face in the next five years. The great social revolution led by my late husband which began in 1956, must be taken on its proper course to its logical end. Many radical reforms will have to be initiated. Massive development projects will have to be launched.[12]

She ended with the traditional Buddhist blessing: May the blessings of the Triple Gem be upon you.

Such was the message and the appeal of the SLFP in 1970 – and it drew its resonance from S. W. R. D.'s campaign in 1956. In contrast to the smart cars and modern-style dress of the UNP campaigners, S. W. R. D. appeared as a slight figure who walked to election meetings, and who wore the village cloth and shirt; a Buddhist who promised radical social change and the redistribution of economic opportunity.

The redistribution programme had two prongs, one industrial and the other agricultural. On the industrial front, S. W. R. D. followed a programme of nationalisation, including the ports and bus transport, backed by the introduction and expansion of wide-ranging schemes for health insurance, sickness benefit, etc., for public sector and government employees. Yet within three years he lost the support of Philip Gunawardene and his faction, and their withdrawal from the MEP in 1959 led to its collapse and the formation of a purely SLFP government. The agricultural programme rested on the introduction of an improved Paddy Lands Act, designed to provide a modicum of secure tenure and to remove the inequalities of, and the presumed restraints on, production imposed by traditional forms of land tenure. This measure was applied in only a few areas in the first instance, but even so it proved inoperative in many cases, and its weaknesses led to new legislation. The initial reaction to the 1958 Act was a flood of (illegal) evictions. It was amended twice, in 1958 and 1959, but remained a weak and defective instrument.

The redistributive economic programme went hand in hand with the adoption of Sinhala as the official language (Official Language Act, 1956) and the switch from English to *swabhasha* – the national languages – as the medium of instruction in the schools. New avenues of advancement and access to the bureaucracy were for the first time offered to the mass of the people. But here, too, S. W. R. D. met with disaster. The Tamils, who form the largest minority group in the island, viewed his policies as communalist if not actively anti-Tamil, and their campaigns against the Official Language Act led to rioting and violence. The Act was amended in 1958 when the Tamil Language (Special Provisions) Bill was introduced providing for the 'reasonable use' of Tamil.

Increasingly under pressure from the LSSP and CP and their trade unions, governing under a state of emergency following the language riots, and having failed to secure any significant changes for the small cultivator, S. W. R. D.'s revolution seemed to be losing direction. Furthermore, his parliamentary majority was being eroded; shortly after Gunawardene led his group out of the MEP, he was joined by six SLFP members of parliament. Three months later, S. W. R. D. was assassinated.

Was his failure simply that he had aroused forces that he could not control, and that the people as well as the different pressure groups expected too much in too short a time? The answer to this depends in part on how one characterises the nature of the 'revolution' of 1956. We know what sentiments he had appealed to, we know what class of people formed his active supporters – the village schoolteacher, the temple monk, the doctors who practised *ayurvedic* (traditional) medicine – we know what interest groups his actual policies, when in power, were designed to appease or reward, but the 'common man', the heart of Bandaranaike's success in 1956 and the key to his lack of solid achievement when in power, has not yet been sufficiently described.

It is clear that S. W. R. D.'s appeal was directed at the non-*Goyigama* and at those of the *Goyigama* who were less advantaged. As will become apparent in later chapters, he set his sights on the votes of those who previously had not voted in what they saw as a contest between elites, or who had voted for their patron or a local notable. He secured the vote of the lower castes and the lower-class *Goyigama*.

D. S. Senanayake had entered Independence with a basically Sinhalese–*Goyigama* and Tamil–*Vellava* administration, but he had associated members of the smaller castes with the government with an air of a great aristocrat extending personal patronage. In this manner he brought in such men as George E. de Silva (*Hena*), R. S. S. Gunawardene (*Hunu*), L. A. Rajapakse (*Salagama*), U. A. Jayawardene (*Navandanna*), N. H. Keerthiratne (*Batgam* – as Junior Minister), and N. U. Jayawardene (*Durava*). It seems that the pattern altered radically with S. W. R. D.'s success in 1956, however, when for the first time a party made an electoral appeal to the lower castes through the language of democratic socialism and Sinhalese Buddhist nationalism. Electors felt for the first time that they had an effective alternative party of government to the Senanayake caucus and their elite interests. In G. V. S. de Silva's vivid phrase, at the 1956 elections the 'dumb could speak'.[13]

Senator S. Nadesan wrote on Bandaranaike's death:

a deep social revolution brought Mr Bandaranaike to power. The millions of ordinary men and women hitherto courted at election time and abandoned as quickly as possible thereafter – came into their own as a factor in political life, conscious of their own dignity as effective human beings and as Ceylonese. The grip of a few families on the sources of power was broken.[14]

While this conclusion proved to be unduly optimistic, the Senator's perception of the '1956 revolution' is significant, as suggesting that

Bandaranaike's contemporaries were shrewdly aware of the social as well as the political implications of his efforts. From time to time S. W. R. D. himself hinted at the underlying forces behind his success. In the Convocation Address to the University of Sri Lanka, Peradeniya, in 1957, entitled indicatively 'The Age of the Common Man', he philosophised thus:

Harmonious conflict is a concept that has a great deal of meaning for me. Conflict is very essential to life. Out of conflict alone does progress come; but it must be conflict that does not militate against a harmony above it. I have always felt that it was possible, and the people of this country have made it possible now for me to put my theories into practice. I have made efforts recently, I have experimented recently in the ultimate good sense and sanity of mankind. I have experimented with it in this country, and, believe me, with considerable success.[15]

If one understands the Bandaranaike years from the 1956 election in these terms, as a bold social and political experiment, then a number of S. W. R. D.'s actions – or lack of activity – which puzzled and angered some of his colleagues and soi-disant supporters become explicable.

The 1956 election had seen a convergence of vociferous sentiment and interest, with each faction claiming to be the 'architects of the revolution'. Each expected to be rewarded by position, patronage, or legislation, but S. W. R. D., in the event, handed out few rewards except under pressure. The lay Buddhist leaders received little. Of the more prominent, only N. Q. Dias received an appointment, and then only as Director of Cultural Affairs. The '*Swabhasha* Twins', F. R. Jayasuriya and K. M. P. Rajaratne, received nothing. Bandaranaike's language settlement, too, disappointed the more intransigent Sinhala-Only campaigners.[16]

His treatment of the left was not less casual. Philip Gunawardene was only a last-minute inclusion in the 1956 Cabinet.[17] Throughout, Bandaranaike followed a policy of appeasement, faced with militant trade union strikers who felt that, in their interpretation, the 'socialist revolution of 1956' was not progressing fast and far enough. By 1959 he was quite prepared to remove the 'father of socialism' in Sri Lanka from office; Philip Gunawardene and his colleague William de Silva left the Cabinet. A few months later, the Minister of Justice, M. H. W. de Silva, a respected *Karava* Buddhist leader, was also manoeuvred out of the Cabinet by Bandaranaike.

It is tempting to suppose that, assessing to his own satisfaction the true social sources of his political power, Bandaranaike felt he could do without the extremists of 1956. Talking of the '1956 issues' and his handling of them, at a time of tension just after the Declaration of Emergency in

1958, he himself declared: 'On the one side or the other, questions of race, culture, and religion are issues on which mischievous persons, even those who may be bona fide utterly mistaken and fanatical – men of straw who, otherwise, do not count for anything – can still create unrest and a feeling amongst masses of the people.'[18]

Others commented on these 'men of straw'. Senator S. Nadesan noted in 1959: 'Mr Bandaranaike came to power with the help of extremist and obscurantist forces. They thought that in him they had at last found a champion and that through him they would be able to exercise decisive power.'[19] D. K. Rangnekar, writing in 1960 shortly after Bandaranaike's death, put it thus:

Mr Bandaranaike was fully aware of the explosive nature of these forces and there was guile in his technique of appearing to appease labour. He knew the real nature of the conflict between the privileged and the underprivileged class and he realised that the latent feelings of the various communities, classes, and groups had to be brought into the open rather than suppressed. He was confident that in time he could give these forces a sense of direction.[20]

Time was denied him, and we are left to speculate on how S. W. R. D. would have consolidated his revolution. He himself was always conscious that his plans would need 'bags of time', a phrase he used constantly. He was accused, in his three years as Prime Minister, of spinelessness and inactivity, characteristics earlier noted by his one-time colleague, Bernard Aluvihare: 'It is in political action that he has earned for himself the charge of inconsistency: he is supine.'[21] Many of the actions he did take distressed his colleagues and his critics. Almost the first exercise of his new powers after the elections was his nomination of Asoka Karunaratne of the *Batgam* community as an appointed MP. Later he was to include Asoka Karunaratne in the Sri Lanka delegation to a Commonwealth Parliamentary Conference. H. R. Premaratne, also of the *Batgam* community, was made Director of Public Works over the head of V. C. de Silva, a *Karava*, who expected the post as next in line to the outgoing Director.

Many of Bandaranaike's contemporaries did not doubt that he had set out deliberately to create an alternative power base to the Senanayakes, unable to challenge them at the national elite level, by appealing to populist forces in the countryside who hitherto had been neglected and excluded from active participation in the political process. Using the language both of modern ideology (democratic socialism) and of traditionalist sentiment (Sinhalese Buddhist nationalism), he manipulated traditional identities and relationships to secure power within the contemporary political framework.

The sudden death of S. W. R. D. left the parties in a state of some uncertainty, and at the March 1960 elections a large number of Independents and small factional groups stood for election. The UNP took sufficient seats to form a minority government with the tacit support of the Tamil Federal Party, but lost the vote on the Address of Thanks. At the July 1960 elections the SLFP returned to power with Mrs Bandaranaike at its head. Her victory was regarded as largely a sympathy vote, and signified a willingness on the part of the 'common man' to press on with the 'revolution'. Most of the 'extremists' of the left splinter groups and the Sinhalese–Buddhist fanatics were defeated. The UNP, for its part, campaigned against the 'forces of disruption', and gained strength from the resumption of active leadership by Dudley Senanayake, who had returned as the head of the party in February.

The broad outlines of the character of the two main Sinhalese parties were thus established by 1960. They have been reinforced by the economic policies carried out by the UNP from 1965 to 1970 and by the SLFP-led United Front of Mrs Bandaranaike from 1970 to 1977.[22] Though economic issues and policies are of significance in winning (or losing) votes, they chiefly seem to be influential in hardening party support; economic matters are seen to be of importance in relation to the class image of the parties, and specific measures, such as the promise or provision of jobs to the low-paid or unemployed, seem not to disturb the conformism of hard-core party loyalty but rather to reinforce the party image. (The exception is the 'rice issue'; both parties have been tempted to promise increases in the weekly ration, or to reduce the subsidised price. In 1965 Dudley Senanayake embarked on a programme designed to achieve rice self-sufficiency and cut the ration. Mrs Bandaranaike before the 1970 elections campaigned hard on the promise to 'restore the full ration'.) Hard-core party loyalty seems to reside in a number of factors: the caste basis of the electorate and the caste of the candidate; deference to traditional or other leaders; the past performance of candidates; and the services rendered to the electorate or interest group by the parties. The last two factors in general appear to be increasing in importance, and in some cases supersede traditional social relations and attitudes.[23]

Except in 1956 the swing between the two major parties has been relatively small in terms of votes, and governments have frequently been formed on a minority (for example, the UNP took more votes than the SLFP, the major party of the United Front, in the 1970 elections); Sri Lanka follows British practice in electing the 'first past the post', and slight shifts in voting patterns have been sufficient to produce quite dramatic swings in terms of seats. Though this has put governments in very strong legislative positions, it has always been less certain that the government of the day has been able to convince the country at large of the wisdom or popularity of its parliamentary programme. Thus the UNP government thought to win over the 'Buddhist vote' when it was re-elected in 1965 by making the *poya* (day marking the moon's quarters), and the pre-*poya* the rest-days of the week; the consequent disruption, especially to international trade, irritated many people, and the gesture angered the Catholics, helping to turn a few of the important coastal electorates against the government. The most notable example of the consequences of first-past-the-post election has been the capture by the United Front of over two-thirds of the seats in 1970, leaving the UNP with a legislative rump, which failed to reflect its true strength in the country. The government had the necessary two-thirds majority to alter the constitution: the Lower House was convened as a constituent assembly and recommended that Sri Lanka become a republic within the Commonwealth. The Upper House was abolished and the parliamentary term of the Lower House extended to run five years from the promulgation of the new constitution in 1972.[24]

There is no doubt that the UF's pre-election promise to restore the 'full ration' of rice to every household, even though the country could scarce afford the gesture, together with its less explicit support of land reform and nationalisation of foreign-owned estates, helped it to win the votes of the radical young, and of those landless labourers of the countryside who had not directly benefited from the UNP's 'green revolution' approach to national food self-sufficiency. None the less, the UF's open-handed populism did not overwhelm the voters, and a solid 38 per cent turned out for the UNP.

Some reflections on broader issues

Analysis and discussion of the theoretical implications of Sinhalese caste behaviour in the political arena should logically appear after the presentation of the material which forms the substance of this book, but it might be useful if I were to direct the reader towards concepts and problems which have emerged from studies of caste in India that may help to illuminate the Sri Lankan experience.

The process of 'Sanskritisation' has been described as an 'idiom of mobility'; André Béteille has drawn attention to one aspect of this process which sheds some light on S. W. R. D.'s success in 1956. He writes:

Its symbols and values are essentially those of the traditional order. At a time when a modernist elite is trying to push the country towards a secular and

Westernised social order, it is not unlikely that those wh
occupied a fairly low social position may set themselves up
traditional values. Unable to cope with the process of W
pace of rapid social change, such people may well throw
traditionalist or even revivalist movements and parties. It r
that the defence of the traditional order should become th
who had in the past been denied a position of honour with

He notes that this applies particularly to the upper strata among the back-ward classes.

His description can be read for Sri Lanka, with the UNP standing as the modernising force expressing its views in westernised symbols and behaviour, and with the SLFP mediating traditionalist sentiment. S. W. R. D. captured the demands of the lower castes and lower-middle classes of the village for a place within newly independent Sri Lanka, and in the SLFP created a vehicle which promised real mobility.

Some years ago Myron Weiner noted one of the most significant changes brought about by modern political practice in a parliamentary system operating within caste society – the politicisation of social relations. 'Politics has become the avenue for personal advancement in a society in which commercial activities offer little status and administrative posts are relatively few in number.'[26] He was writing of India, but even in Sri Lanka, where certain commercial castes claim high status and adminis-trative posts proliferate, it is none the less true that politics are becoming both a direct and an indirect source of status, authority, and advancement independent of traditional constraints and attitudes. In her study of a highland Sinhalese village conducted over a number of years, Robinson has noted that the party men in the village now deal directly with the outside authorities, and no longer need the 'brokerage' of traditional leaders. Party affiliation has become a critical factor in intravillage inter-actions. Leadership, alignment, perception of economic status, the bases for co-operation, 'conflict situations', have all been radically altered by the increasing contact with the state bureaucracy, and by higher levels of regional political participation.[27]

Though it would not be true to say that the political battle is now between ideological groups of a modern kind (despite the fact that the SLFP characterises itself as 'democratic socialist', and the UNP as 'modernising and rightist', and the LSSP and the CP as dogmatic Marxists of one kind or another; and despite the fact that all the parties make their appeal in the language of modern economic doctrines and secular political statements), none the less there has been a shift towards a kind of political authority independent of traditional relations. Broadly

...aking, political power at the elite level in Sri Lanka shifts from one alliance of caste groups to another, within a very narrow range of caste-acceptable allies; more differentiated political organisations and institutions have been slow to develop. Again speaking broadly, power at the elite level is derivative of family and caste, but there is a much less certain relationship at the level of local politics and in the sectors of the economy where traditional social attitudes have no customary role.

The urban trade unions are clearly organisations where the caste-family–status–power identities are very diffuse and weakly related. It might be thought that the LSSP and CP similarly formed examples of independent political organisations, but, as will be made clear, their support and their leadership are quite strongly linked to caste issues and identities. In sum, the emergence of independent and effective sources of power is a matter on which there is still a considerable lack of clarity with regard to Sri Lanka, but none the less there are signs that some voters are seeking alternative modes of expression to the traditionally based parties now in existence.

Finally, it ought to be emphasised that Sri Lanka's history of Independence has been quite different from India's in one important respect: there has been a regular interchange of power between parties; despite the fact that S. W. R. D. won the 1956 elections on a landslide, the UNP emerged as the largest single party (though not with a majority of seats) at the March 1960 elections; despite taking over two-thirds of the seats at the 1970 elections, Mrs Bandaranaike's United Front lost twelve out of the thirteen by-elections held over the next seven years. The size of the majority at election time has thus been no guarantee of long tenure in office, no once-and-for-all legitimisation of a party or its policies. Morris-Jones has written of the Indian voter that he tends to see the competition not as between parties to become government but between government and others: 'Even if he is displeased with what government has done, who else but government is in a position to do things for him? From this point of view, the question turns out to be, not why the Congress collects many votes, but why anyone else collects any.'[28] In Sri Lanka, no government over the last thirty years has held such a commanding position, and the questions are: on what basis is the electorate casting its vote to bring about such reversals? What is the composition of governments? What is the nature of the parties' support?

2

Description of castes

Few political studies have been made of caste in Sri Lanka; though Bryce Ryan's book, published in 1953, opened the way, subsequent students seemed to be anthropologists and the like, concentrating on village minutiae and unwilling to look at the wider implications of caste. Historians and political scientists, on the other hand, while usually including some mention of caste and politics, seemed to feel it was safer and more tactful to eschew detailed probing.[1] None the less, there seems to be general agreement with Ryan that caste among the Sinhalese is 'a self-contained emergent arising from diffuse Indian influences and historically unique situations'.[2] Further, it is agreed that a number of the castes originated as immigrant groups, but there is little agreement as to the nature of Sinhalese caste prior to their impact, either among historians or within the currently existing castes who put forward discrepant claims of descent and relative status. Nor is it known how many distinct castes there are, some students counting sub-castes as part of a larger grouping, others differentiating between the smallest subdivisions. Some of the castes are geographically dispersed, others concentrated within a few villages; some keep themselves within caste-distinct villages, others co-exist, or function in close interaction with a variety of castes. While it is generally acknowledged that the largest caste is also the highest in status, there is little unanimity regarding the precise status of the other castes, ranking being particularly confused among the more depressed of these.

It is clear that, contrary to the Indian experience, what is almost wholly lacking as an accepted referent is the idea of a single encompassing, universal, and primordial hierarchy, conceptualised in *varṇa* (fourfold Hindu classification). Status claims are made with reference to precedent, historical antecedent, and current circumstances. Absent, too, is any group recognisable as analogous to the Brahmins. Sinhalese caste has developed under the mantle of Buddhism, whose precepts discount social differences. The Buddha neither condoning nor denouncing caste, it is the religious organisation of the Theravada school of Buddhism that in

practice has adapted to the secular social structure, rather than vice versa.[3]
These peculiarities of Sinhalese caste have led Louis Dumont to dismiss
its title to be a 'system'.[4] Certainly the idealised religious hierarchy mani-
fest in Indian society is absent, and the dynamic of caste in Sri Lanka,
while recognisably similar to descriptions of caste interaction in parts of
India, is not constrained within the configurations of the Hindu caste
system.

It is important, too, to grasp the environmental dimensions of Sinhalese caste: first, that Sinhalese society is numerically small, though the
population is fast expanding; secondly, no part of the island is very distant
from any other part, nor are the conditions of life for the mass of the
villagers enormously divergent. Consequently, the society possesses an
intimacy, found perhaps in a large Indian district or small region, that
enables members of the same nominal caste to recognise each other as part
of the same community, at times to act together, and to display a common
response as a group to the demands and attitudes of other castes.[5] Their
chief families are known to members of the caste throughout the island,
and, to varying degrees, each major caste has representatives in public life
who offer patronage and seek to wield influence on its members' behalf.

The castes' names denominate prestige categories which are traditionally related to the functions formerly performed by the families of the
caste group. The Sinhalese use the term *jāti* (hereditary group) to refer
both to caste groups other than their own, and to sub-groups within their
own caste. The more important distinctions of gradation within a caste
are related, in the Sinhalese tradition, to lineage and family ties. Thus,
among the *Goyigama* the aristocrats are called *vangsa adipati* (nobles of
pedigree), and those of lowest status are referred to as *vangsa näti minissu*
(men without a pedigree). In addition, extra stature is allowed to those
who held feudal office under the Sinhalese kings, and whose names today
still preserve the traditional titles. Such titles are referred to by a variety
of phrases, such as *vasagama* or *mudiansē nāma*. Further indications of
status are given by the *gedera nāma*, the name which indicates that one is
descended from the 'house of so-and-so'.

The most significant ties of kinship are those of the lineage – of the
house. Kinship and property descend in both the male and female lines,
and marriage is held to establish a kinship bond not only between the
husband and wife but between the kinsmen by marriage. Marriage is thus
traditionally very much viewed as an alliance; it is sometimes used to
reinforce the circle of kinship by renewing bonds of descent which have
grown weak and to bring back distant relatives into close relationship.
Blood kin and marriage kin are referred to in Kandyan usage by the

single Sinhalese word *nädäyo* (kinsmen); the intermingled relationship network is often referred to as the *pavula*, which in its most limited sense indicates the domestic family, or even simply 'wife', but which also bears the wider connotations of 'kindred', and indicates the group which is expected to act together and to relate in all matters of public and private importance. All members of the *pavula* are in theory, and generally in practice, of similar status and caste.

The essentially feudal rather than religious structure of Sinhalese caste is thus closely reflected in, and related to, caste nomenclature, marriage alliances, and lineage.[6]

Caste under the British

Given its feudal setting in the Kandyan highlands, and its strong commercial identification in the south and west, how did the role of caste in public affairs alter, or become subsumed under the procedures and customs imposed by the British colonial powers? How did its principles mesh with the concepts of civic justice and individualism favoured by the new administration? Did the British consciously favour any caste or castes?

As a colonial power, it seems the British accepted the divisions present among the Sinhalese, and though establishing a judicial and administrative system that held all men equal under the law, were content to operate through the existing elites and leadership in the practical exercise of their power. Beyond the abolition of *rajakariya* (king's service) on the recommendations of the Royal Commissioners, Colebrooke and Cameron, in 1832, few further steps were taken that had the direct intention of altering existing relationships among the Sinhalese.[7] Their chief instruments of contact with the indigenous population were the *Mudaliyars* (holders of a traditional office) and the Kandyan chiefs.[8] Mostly of the highest caste, often descended from former ruling families, these officers took to an education in English and the prestige of office as the obvious channel by which to maintain some semblance of influence. They were landowners in a modest way, and, though they apparently did not greatly take to the new opportunities in commercial agriculture with the opening of the coffee estates, they commanded not insignificant economic resources.

Other castes were not discriminated against and benefited from the expanding economic opportunities, some individuals to such good effect that they were appointed, not without opposition, to positions hitherto regarded by the highest caste as their sole prerogative. For example, Gregory de Zoysa, of the *Salagama* caste, was made *Mudaliyar* in 1845, and in 1853 a member of the *Karava* caste from Moratuwa was appointed *Mudaliyar* of the Governor's Gate.[9] The estate sector provided one avenue of advancement. Though the larger tea and rubber estates became chiefly the concern of Europeans, some Sinhalese participated with profit in rubber and tea smallholdings, while coconut, a traditional garden crop of the Sinhalese, came to be cultivated by some families on large estates. But it was not only the growth of the estate sector that provided increasing economic opportunity; the opening up of new areas that needed provisioning and developing, and the expansion of the service industries provided a wide range of commercial activity for those willing or able to exploit it. Whereas the de Mel family (*Karava*) became influential coconut-estate owners, the de Soysa (*Karava*) family fortunes are said to have been founded on a carting contract between Kandy and Colombo. Not untypically, the de Soysa money was reinvested in commercial landholding, chiefly coconut and rubber, and in urban property. Indeed, until very recent times, the de Soysa family still owned a large block of desirable property between Galle Road and Thurstan Road, at Alfred Place, in what is now the residential heart of Colombo. Even members of the depressed castes obtained agencies, or slowly began to move into the modern economy, as mechanics to others' lorry fleets, or in ship chandling or general merchandising. The Mathew family (*Vahumpura*) and W. E. Bastian (*Vahumpura*), for example, accumulated considerable wealth in these sectors.[10]

Though not consciously, the British influence spread a growing rivalry among the castes. Mention of this greater unease in intercaste relations appears from time to time in the colonial records. Sir Hugh Clifford, Governor, wrote of the first election for the 'Educated Ceylonese' seat in the Legislative Council of 1910: 'The first election of a representative of the educated Ceylonese was fought purely on caste lines, a high caste Tamil being chosen with the aid of the high caste Sinhalese vote, caste prejudice thus proving to be a stronger passion than racial bias.'[11] With the gradual adoption of elective procedures in national institutions and for administrative office, and with a widening franchise, caste became increasingly a matter for political concern. Indeed, the Ceylon National Congress executive committee felt compelled to issue on 10 July 1924 a resolution to all its branches and associates strongly deprecating 'the attempt now made in certain constituencies to introduce considerations of caste and religion in connection with the election of members to the Legislative Council as fundamentally opposed to the principles and policy of the National Congress and inimical to the political progress of the country'.[12]

By the time the Soulbury Commission arrived in 1944 to report on, and to recommend, further constitutional development, caste had become established as an acute and legitimate political concern. During its hearings, Sir Frederick Rees describes how representatives of the 'fisheries interest'[13] asked for a separate Ministry:

They stated that the industry received scant attention from the Government while agriculture[14] was loaded with favours – free distribution of seed paddy and fertilisers, introduction of improved agricultural implements ... etc. Had assistance of this kind been given to the fishing industry, the Island would long ago have become independent of imported fish on which billions of rupees a year were now spent. It was asserted that the industry was the victim of religious and caste prejudices: the strict Buddhists objected to the taking of life which is involved; while the Goigama caste, which practically monopolised the Legislature, did not wish the Karava caste, to which the fishermen mainly belonged, to prosper and become a menace to its ascendancy.[15]

The Soulbury constitution, which was accepted finally, with amendments, as adequate to launch Sri Lanka into Independence, met its first test at the polls in 1947 in the absence of much of the experience which makes a Westminster style of party government workable. Understandably, caste voting filled the gap. As Ludowyck observed:

The presence of a large number of Independents, no less than 181 – was the surest indication that to the majority of people in the country there were no political issues at stake, but, as constituencies had been delimited, those with a fair chance of securing a bloc of caste votes appeared on the hustings, postponing the decision to make any political decision until it was clear who was likely to be in power and how some profit was to be gained from taking sides.[16]

Not surprisingly, not a few of the early members of the legislature were representatives of the *Goyigama*, and thus of the traditional feudal order; holders of rank and title such as P. B. Bulankulame *Dissawe* – Governor – (Anuradhapura 1947); T. B. Polhiyadde *Dissawe* (Horowupotana 1952); and H. B. Rambukwella *Dissawe* (Minipe 1952). Singer has further distinguished those in parliament, the legislative elite, between 1924 and 1948, as broadly Ceylonese; disproportionately Christian; mostly high-caste; highly urbanised; highly western-educated; largely engaged in western-type occupations; and of the highest economic and social class.[17] (In contrast, by 1964 the legislative elite had become overwhelmingly Sinhalese; heavily Buddhist; somewhat lower-caste; largely rural; generally less western-educated and more *swabhasha*-educated; engaged in more traditional occupations; and very largely from the middle economic and social classes.)

One facet of intercaste rivalry in particular became prominent in the latter part of the British administration. The Kandyan/low-country split, which in caste terms was essentially that between the aristocratic *Goyigama* families of the hill country, and the low-country *Goyigama* and the chief castes of the maritime provinces, had received definition in 1815 when the last surviving Sinhalese kingdom surrendered the lands of the Kandyan hill country to the British. The people of the low country, it was felt, had been influenced during the long years of colonial rule by western, Christian, and commercial ideas and activities, whereas the Kandyans prided themselves on embodying the virtues of Sinhalese traditionalism. As the Sri Lankans won increasing degrees of self-government, the Kandyans became aware that under any system of popular franchise, the low-country Sinhalese might outnumber them. Thus, when the Ceylon National Congress was founded it faced the opposition of the Kandyan Association, formed one year previously in 1918 by J. A. Halangoda, a staunch leader who expressed the up-country concern over constitutional reform proposals championed by the CNC.[18] A small but important Kandyan group upheld the cause within the CNC itself for a few years, but withdrew in 1924 to form the Kandyan National Association.[19]

The Kandyans have been remarkably successful in preserving their interests. From the time of the first State Council till 1956 the proportion of Kandyans among new recruits to the legislature rose steadily. In 1956–9 under S. W. R. D. Bandaranaike, on the other hand, the Kandyans and low-country Sinhalese entered the legislature on an approximately 1 : 1 basis. But by 1970, when on total population figures the low-country Sinhalese outnumbered the Kandyan Sinhalese by a ratio of approximately 3 : 2, the distribution of seats between the up-country areas and the low-country areas favoured the Kandyans in an approximate ratio of 3 : 2, thus:

Area	Population	Ratio	Seats allocated	Ratio
Low-country	4.5 m.	3	54	2
Kandyan	3.0 m.	2	73	3

The disproportionate representation of the Kandyans has been reflected in the choice of Cabinet members, too; it has been especially marked in Mrs Bandaranaike's administrations, and, after the elections in 1970, the Cabinet breakdown was as shown in table 1.

This brief review indicates the kinds of pressures that were present, and the intensity of feeling among certain castes that their interests would not be commensurately represented after Independence. It suggests, perhaps,

TABLE 1 *Representation of Kandyans by caste and race in the 1970 Cabinet*

Sinhalese:	*Goyigama:* Kandyan	8
	Goyigama: low-country	5
	Salagama	2
	Karava	2
	Vahumpura	1
Moor		1
Tamil		1
Burgher[a]		1
Total		21

[a] Descendant of Sinhalese–Dutch intermarriage.
Source: derived from list of twenty-one Cabinet Ministers in Mrs Bandaranaike's United Front government at May 1970. Ceylon Daily News, *Seventh Parliament of Ceylon, 1970* (Colombo, ANCL, 1970), p. 7.

the potential that existed for exploiting caste sentiment, possibly not overtly, but in the guise of appeals to economic interest or 'underprivileged' status.

Status, occupation, and location of major caste groups

It is generally agreed that the highest caste in status among the Sinhalese is the *Goyigama*. Traditionally associated with peasant agriculture, this caste group also claims the historical prerogative to provide the chief office-holders of the state. The fact of *Goyigama* dominance at all levels of office-holding is assumed and largely accepted; the sufficiency of caste as a justification for a claim to power and prestige is taken as natural by the *Goyigama*, but no longer necessarily so by other castes. There are at least nine sub-castes, and a number who call themselves *Goyigama*, though the others do not always recognise their claim. The *Goyigama* caste is largely Buddhist, and the *Siyam Nikaya* (*Siyam* sect), which claims to speak for the *Sangha* in national matters, recruits solely from the *Goyigama*. Found throughout the island, the community's major internal division is geographic, between the *Radala* Kandyans (*Goyigama* of noble family) and the aristocratic families of the low country. This division is broadly reinforced by their respective economic resources, the Kandyan families since 1815 becoming relatively impoverished traditional landholders of *nindagam* (king's land).[20] Many of the low-country aristocracy have maintained or enhanced their economic position via cultivation of commercially productive land in tea, coconut, and rubber.

Though numerically the largest caste, the number of *Goyigama* families involved in trade, commerce, or industry of a sizeable scale is not preponderant. The community is involved in four main categories of business: *mudalali* (indigenous accumulators of wealth) trading entrepreneurship; rupee company business; family firms; and, more recently, merchant banking and credit finance.[21]

For example, in the first category, all the 134 Panchikawatte *Mudalalis* listed as members of the Mudalali Association are *Goyigama* (though some may have become accepted as such *pari passu* with their economic rise).[22] The Panchikawatte *Mudalalis* by and large control the entire motor-spares trade and a sizeable share of the transport business in the island. They and their retail outlets are important in secondary banking as significant sources of credit.

In the second category, a breakdown of the directors of rupee companies by caste reveals a substantial *Goyigama* participation.

TABLE 2   *Directors of rupee companies by caste and race, 1971*

Sinhalese:	Goyigama	76
	Karava	67
	Salagama	10
	Durava	2
Burgher		22
Moor		8
Parsee		2
Borah		14
Tamil		54
European		88
No information		35
Total		378

Source: Handbook of Rupee Companies, 1971 (Colombo, Colombo Brokers' Association, 1971); identities mine.

In the third category, it is notable that the majority of the large Colombo-based family businesses are *Goyigama*; for example, Associated Newspapers of Ceylon Ltd, until recently one of the most powerful press and allied industrial groups in the island;[23] Gunasena's Ltd, engaged in similar activities; Maliban's Ltd, producing biscuits and confectionery; and McCallum Ltd, involved in book-trading and brewing.[24]

Merchant banking and credit finance have prospered with the growth of the modern economic sector after Independence. The pioneer has been N. U. Jayawardene of the *Durava* community, and he remains the leading merchant banker in the island, but the majority of real estate, finance houses, and credit firms are now owned by *Goyigama* families. Of the thirty-four merchant banks (including hire-purchase) in existence in 1973, twenty-nine were *Goyigama*.

The *Karava*, *Salagama*, and *Durava* castes of the western and southern coastal areas have a distinctive caste structure. One author claims that their caste structure owes its form directly to South Indian practice, whereas that of the Kandyan kingdom is an indigenous and ancient evolution of Sinhalese culture.[25] In his view, it is the intrusion of the one into the other that has produced the peculiarities of Sinhalese caste and its particular nuances of intercaste behaviour. The castes of the south and western littoral claim to be of high status and stand in lateral rather than subordinate relationships to the *Goyigama*. Being situated largely in the maritime provinces, numbers became converts to Christianity under colonial rule, so that the *Karava* are divided into Christian and Buddhist wings, and the *Salagama* and *Durava*, though largely Buddhist, both contain a number of influential Catholic families. The *Karava* Christians are geographically concentrated north and south of Colombo between Chilaw and Moratuwa, while the *Karava* Buddhists live further to the south. A number have emerged as important lay Buddhist leaders, geographically drawn from an area in and around Panadura, an influential centre of *Sangha* activity. Their influence reaches as far as Ambalangoda, and to Galle and Matara in the area known as the 'deep south'.

All three castes are of great importance in trade, commerce, and industry, out of proportion to their numerical size.[26] *Karava* economic interests are extensive. (See table 2.)

The main economic activities of the caste are traditionally fishing and carpentry, and large numbers are still engaged in these industries.[27] The older *Karava* families, such as the de Mels, the Pierises, and the de Soysas, are heavily involved in the estate-owning sector, chiefly in coconut and rubber. They follow a pattern of accumulation rather than entrepreneurship. The entrepreneurial *Karava* are of more recent emergence, and are largely Christian. They control important and extensive commercial and trading groups such as Mackwoods Ltd, Brown's Group Ltd, Richard Peiris Ltd, and J. L. M. Fernando's Group. In addition, a number of smaller families have gone into retail trading throughout the island and have an important base in the Kandyan area.[28]

Salagama families, whose traditional occupation was cinnamon-peeling, like the *Karava* acquired important plantation interests, chiefly in the Western Province. For example, the Rajapakses, originally from Balapitiya, owned the coconut land bought by the British for what is now known as the Bandaranaike International Airport. Like the *Karava*, the *Salagama* estate interests in general have not moved into commercial entrepreneurship. *Salagama* commercial enterprise in recent times began with Sir Cyril de Zoysa who started the South Western Bus Company and became a rupee millionaire in his lifetime. He acquired the British Leyland agency, and moved into the manufacture of car batteries and motor spares, rubber goods, etc. Such enterprise saw the formation and growth of Associated Motorways, for example. Later, under C. P. de Silva, Minister of Lands and Land Development in S. W. R. D. Bandaranaike's government, the community benefited both by the dry-zone colonisation schemes and by large-scale construction and development projects.

The *Durava* community's economic influence is bound up with the rise of N. U. Jayawardene. He joined the Government Service as a clerk and rose to be Governor of the Central Bank in 1952. When he was removed from office in 1954 he went into commerce to become the leading merchant banker in the island. He remains the pivot of *Durava* economic strength. The community owns important tracts of urban property; for example, in Colombo the *Durava* own the stretch of Galle Road between Galle Face Hotel and High Street, Wellawatte, and a large part of Thimbirigasaya – arising out of their employment by the British as masons and bricklayers. The firm of D. D. Fonseka and Co. prospered in this manner. Another prominent *Durava* businessman, Arunadisi *Mudalali* of Union Place, Colombo, became a rupee multi-millionaire via the cigarette distribution monopoly of Ceylon Tobacco Co. Ltd. A number remain in their traditional occupation of toddy-tapping in the coconut lands of the south and west, while some who have migrated to the towns remain as distinct groups in Colombo and Matara.

The groups described so far have been of high status, but the relative ranking of other castes is not as clear. At the bottom end clearly must be placed the small numbers of *Rodiya*. Much more important among the depressed castes by virtue of their large numerical size are the *Vahumpura* and the *Batgam*. (The *Batgam* are known also, though more derisively, as the *Padu*, and the *Vahumpura* as the *Hakuru*.) The *Batgam* popularly are said to have been the foot-soldiers and sword-bearers of the ancient kings, though they themselves claim to have been palanquin-bearers of high status. The *Vahumpura*'s traditional occupations are jaggery-making and domestic service, though the caste itself claims that they came to Sri Lanka with Mahinda as his personal attendants and as guardians of Buddhism, when he brought the Bo-tree sapling and Buddhism to the island. *Vahumpura* communities are concentrated in the villages around the town of Kegalle, stretching to Ratnapura, and the *Batgam* community in the villages between Kegalle and Matale. Both are strongly grouped in the North-Western Province, in and around Balagalla and the town of Kurunegala, and in Sabaragamuwa. The *Vahumpura* are also grouped in pockets inland from the south coast.

Both castes are largely Buddhist and have been fiercely nationalist since they came into the limelight in 1956. They are both economically weak. Though the *Vahumpura* community has had important trade interests it has lost these either to the *Karava* or to Indian trading groups. Both have thrown up a number of wealthy individuals (for example, D. L. F. Pedris, Cyril Mathew and Semage for the *Vahumpura*, and N. H. Keerthiratne for the *Batgam*), but though such prominent rich men have at times claimed to speak and act on behalf of their communities, none of them in practice has been an effective community leader in quite the manner of, say, N. U. Jayawardene. Neither community possesses the interrelated elite families and well-ordered internal structures of the *Karava*, *Salagama*, or *Durava* castes, and their group identity is amorphous and incohesive. Rather than face caste confrontation or the forceful assertion of their caste identity, there is evidence that a number of these castes have chosen regional migration and, over time, the assumption of *Goyigama* status in their new surroundings.[29]

In between the *Goyigama* and the *Vahumpura* and *Batgam* fall a number of numerically tiny castes with traditional ritual or service status, such as the *Hena* (washers), *Hunu* (lime-burners), *Berawa* (drummers), and *Navandanna* (goldsmiths); their rank *vis-à-vis* the *vasagama Goyigama* (those with inherited traditional titles) is inferior, but the relationship, especially of the skilled craftsmen castes, to the lesser *Goyigama*, is less clear, and is often locally determined.

Now, if the identities described above are accurate, albeit somewhat sweeping, summaries of relative caste position, then a number of queries arise. Are the castes' economic strengths represented commensurately in politics? Does the House of Representatives reflect the numerical strength of the communities? What would the effect be, in a formal representative structure in which numbers count, of a caste, or castes, awaking to a depressed status and seeking redress through the power of the vote? Does the geographic distribution of the castes have implications for the delimitation of constituencies? Do candidates seek a caste vote, and do castes try to send a community leader to parliament?

Unlike the case in India, no census of castes has been taken in this century in Sri Lanka, but the localism and intimacy of Sinhalese society might permit one to arrive at least at an approximation of the distribution of the population among the castes. Thereafter the geographic distribution of the various communities would have to be considered more carefully in the light of the major revision of electoral boundaries in 1959 (and 1976). Only then could the central political questions begin to be answered.

3
Preliminary investigations

The span of this study, from Independence to the early 1970s, comprises years of dramatic demographic change. The rate of population growth increased rapidly after Independence, largely as a result of a sharp reduction in the death rate following a comprehensive DDT programme of malaria control after the devastating epidemics of 1934–5, and, to a lesser extent, 1944–5.[1] From 1945 to 1950, the death rate was cut from 21.5 per thousand to 12.4 per thousand, and by 1955 this was down to 10.8 per thousand. By 1960, the death rate had declined further to 8.6 per thousand. The effect has been a doubling of the population, creating a remarkably youthful age structure, and a great discontinuity in generational experience. Of the 8.9 million Sinhalese alive in 1970, about 6 million were born after 1946.[2]

One might expect that the sudden increase in population *per se*, and more people competing for limited and only slowly increasing economic resources, would intensify intercaste rivalry, and render more acute the lower castes' sense of deprivation. More specifically, one might guess that the castes residing in the more heavily populated areas would begin to feel inadequately represented in terms of the number of members their votes could elect, compared to the more sparsely inhabited electorates. A further speculation is prompted by the precise geographic prevalency of malaria. For Newman's study reveals that malaria, both endemic and epidemic, was more vicious in certain areas than in others; that the fall in death rates subsequent to malaria eradication was greatest in those areas where malaria had been most prevalent; and that the resulting crude rate of natural increase was highest in those same areas.[3] It happens that these areas by and large coincide with areas of *Batgam* and *Vahumpura* concentration, i.e. the districts of Kegalle, Ratnapura, Matale, Kurunegala, Anuradhapura, and Hambantota. The devastating effects of malaria and the subsequent sharp increase of population thus would have seriously altered the numerical relationship of the castes in those areas, possibly with far-reaching shifts in social and political behaviour. As will become

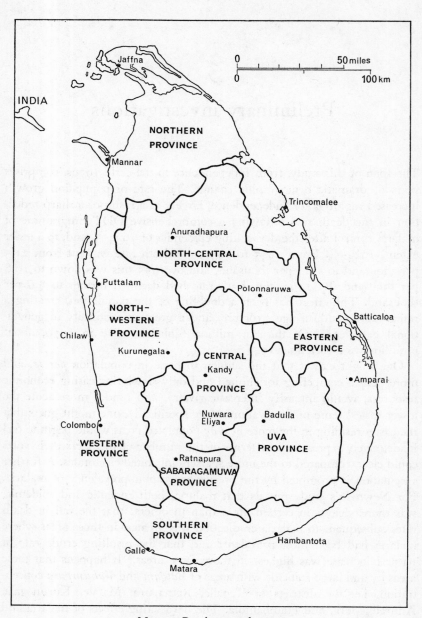

Map 1   Provinces and towns

TABLE 3 *Electorates by Sinhalese province under the 1959 Delimitation*

Western Province	44 Kundasale	107 Dambadeniya
1 Colombo North	45 Teldeniya	108 Polgahawela
2 Colombo Central	46 Minipe	109 Kurunegala
3 Borella	47 Walapane	110 Mawatagama
4 Colombo South	48 Hanguranketa	111 Dodangaslanda
5 Wattala	49 Hewaheta	
6 Negombo	50 Gampola	North-Central Province
7 Katana	51 Nawalapitiya	112 Anuradhapura
8 Divulapitiya	52 Kotmale	113 Medawachchiya
9 Mirigama	53 Nuwara Eliya	114 Horowupotana
10 Minuwangoda	54 Maskeliya	115 Mihintale
11 Attanagalla		116 Kalawewa
12 Gampaha	Southern Province	117 Kekirawa
13 Ja-ela	55 Balapitiya	118 Minneriya
14 Mahara	56 Ambalangoda	119 Polonnaruwa
15 Dompe	57 Bentara–Elpitiya	
16 Kelaniya	58 Hiniduma	Uva Province
17 Kolonnawa	59 Baddegama	120 Mahiyangana
18 Kotte	60 Ratgama	121 Bibile
19 Dehiwela–Mt Lavinia	61 Akmeemana	122 Passara
20 Moratuwa	62 Galle	123 Badulla
21 Kesbewa	63 Habaraduwa	124 Sorantota
22 Kottawa	64 Weligama	125 Uva Paranagama
23 Homagama	65 Akuressa	126 Welimada
24 Avissawella	66 Deniyaya	127 Bandarawela
25 Horana	67 Hakmana	128 Haputale
26 Bulathsinhala	68 Kamburupitiya	129 Moneragala
27 Bandaragama	69 Matara	
28 Panadura	70 Devinuwara	Sabaragamuwa Province
29 Kalutara	71 Beliatta	130 Dedigama
30 Beruwela	72 Mulkirigala	131 Galigomuwa
31 Matugama	73 Tissamaharama	132 Kegalle
32 Agalawatte		133 Rambukkana
	North-Western Province	134 Mawanella
Central Province	96 Puttalam	135 Yatiyantota
33 Dambulla	97 Nikawaratiya	136 Ruwanwella
34 Laggala	98 Yapahuwa	137 Dehiowita
35 Matale	99 Hiriyala	138 Kiriella
36 Rattota	100 Wariyapola	139 Ratnapura
37 Wattegama	101 Bingiriya	140 Pelmadulla
38 Akurana	102 Chilaw	141 Balangoda
39 Galagedera	103 Nattandiya	142 Rakwana
40 Yatinuwara	104 Wennapuwa	143 Nivitigala
41 Udunuwara	105 Katugampola	144 Kalawana
42 Kandy	106 Kuliyapitiya	145 Kolonne
43 Senkadagala		

Source: Report of the Delimitation Commission, SP xv (Colombo, The Government Press, 1959).

clear, these three consequences of radical demographic change do seem to have produced corresponding movements in voting behaviour.

Nobody knows exactly the distribution of the total Sinhalese population among the castes, though it is generally assumed that the *Goyigama* are the largest single group. Ryan settles 'for at least one half',[4] and many *Goyigama*, in conversation, justify their caste's social and political supremacy by reference to a supposed absolute numerical superiority. However, it is also agreed that the *Vahumpura* and *Batgam* are very large, and members of these castes would question why their power of number in an electoral system had not brought them benefit. As for the socially cohesive and commercially powerful castes of the south and west, particularly the *Karava*, they would at times attribute their political frustration to their small numbers, concentrated as they were into relatively few electorates.

Interviews

Since the estimates of caste size seemed to vary according to the status of the informant, a survey was carried out among each of the major castes. Interviews were conducted in each of the seventeen predominantly Sinhalese districts (i.e. excluding Jaffna, Trincomalee, Mannar, Vavuniya, and Batticaloa). The estimated total population for 1970 was taken from the Registrar-General's estimate based on Census figures for 1963, adjusted for births, deaths, migration, and underenumeration. The ethnic breakdown between Sinhalese, Sri Lankan Tamils, Moors/Malays, Indians, and others was based on the 1963 Census figures corrected for the estimated population for 1970. The number of interviews in each district was chosen in proportion to the percentage size of the Sinhalese population in that district compared to the total Sinhalese population. Within the number arrived at, the interviews were distributed equally among the major caste groups in that district. Each respondent was asked to estimate the breakdown between the castes for the total Sinhalese population in the following categories: *Goyigama*, *Salagama*, *Karava*, *Durava*, *Batgam*, *Vahumpura*, others. These estimates were then averaged. The survey was undertaken on neither a random nor a quota basis, nor was any correction made to compensate for respondents' innumeracy, though care was taken to ensure that each response was internally consistent. Finally, twenty respondents in Colombo from each of the *Goyigama*, *Karava*, *Salagama*, *Durava*, *Batgam*, *Vahumpura*, *Hena*, *Hunu*, *Navandanna*, and *Berawa* castes were asked to indicate the size of their own community. The replies again were averaged. The results are summarised in table 4.

TABLE 4 *Distribution of caste groups: estimated figures, mid 1970*

Race	Caste	Population (m.)	Total
Sinhalese	*Goyigama*	4.50	
	Salagama/Karava/Durava	0.80	
	Batgam/Vahumpura	3.00	
	Others	0.60	8.90
Sri Lankan Tamils			1.40
Moors/Malays			0.75
Other Sri Lankans			0.05
Indian Tamils			1.40
Total population			12.50

This result seemed to modify the *Goyigama*'s over-estimates, and to make less justifiable their supremacy on numerical grounds alone. It also emphasised the position of the *Karava, Salagama,* and *Durava,* and made their economic visibility the more notable. *Goyigama* acquaintances were surprised at the apparent size of the *Vahumpura* and *Batgam* and were inclined to disbelieve the figures. It is interesting to note here a comment by Sir Frederick Rees, who was in Sri Lanka between 1944 and 1945, that the *Batgam* then estimated their community to number 'some 400,000 and the *Vahumpura* caste a million; together, over one-third of the total Sinhalese community'.[5]

Matale

The *Goyigama/Batgam/Vahumpura* relationship clearly needed further clarification, and to this end a methodology of caste enumeration that often has proved disappointing in the Indian context – the identification of castes via the household names given in such public documents as electoral rolls – was adopted. The accuracy of such an identification was cross-checked with those who had local knowledge, such as the MP and village headmen, and local administrative officials at the kachcheri. In the event, this approach proved feasible, if tedious and excessively time-consuming for anything but a localised study.

The exercise was carried out in Matale District to the north of Kandy; specifically, the area covered by the Matale District Revenue Officer's Division. An examination of the household lists (1971) for that Division yielded, on the basis of the *gē* names, supported by the experience of the officers of the DRO, the totals in table 5.

TABLE 5   *General classification of population by caste in Matale DRO's Division (not including Matale Urban Council)*

Caste[a]	Number
Goyigama	22,874
Hakuru (Vahumpura)	8,833
Sadel (Rodiya)	30
Navandanna	990
Padu (Batgam)	14,105
Panna[b]	1,001
Rada (Hena)	972
Kinnara (kind of Rodiya)	340
Nakethi (Berawa)	1,325
Karava	500
Non-Sinhalese	891
Total	51,861

[a] The caste designations are those used by the source. The caste names in brackets indicate the more usual or larger term for the given caste community.
[b] A minor caste: weavers.

In this area, then, the *Goyigama* form approximately 44 per cent, the *Batgam* approximately 27 per cent, and the *Vahumpura* 17 per cent of the population, the last two castes together accounting for the same proportion of the population as the *Goyigama*.

Here was evidence of a significant deviation from the assumed norm; it seemed likely that a similar relationship between the *Goyigama* and non-*Goyigama* existed in other areas of lower-caste concentration. What were the political implications? It seemed probable that the nature and intensity of caste influence would to a large extent rest on the delimitation of the relevant electorates. Had these been carved out to include particular caste interests, and to break up certain blocs of castes where they might, potentially, challenge a *Goyigama* hegemony? Or perhaps caste-distinct electorates had been deliberately created? Could caste be shown to have been a consideration at all?

Electorates

The Order-in-Council of 1946 specified that

where it appears to the Delimitation Commission that there is in any area of a province a substantial concentration of persons united by a community of interests, whether racial, religious, or otherwise, but differing in one or more of these respects from the majority of inhabitants in that area, the Commission may make such division of the province into electoral districts as may be necessary to render possible the representation of that interest.[6]

In effect, this enabled the Commissioners to make provision for ethnic (Indian Tamil), religious (Roman Catholic and Moslem), and non-*Goyigama* representation, chiefly through the creation of multi-member seats, and the manipulation of 'area weightage' in favour of the sparsely-populated rural areas. Seats were allotted to each province on the basis of the number of resident persons, as enumerated in the 1931 Census, but additional seats were added on the basis of one for each thousand square miles in the province. These arrangements gave disproportionate representation to the Kandyan Sinhalese of the hill districts, an element that was considered to bring a desirable conservatism to the inaugural years of Independence.[7] Electoral demarcation endeavoured to give a voice to the 'underprivileged castes' in certain areas, for example in a number of constituencies in Sabaragamuwa, and in at least two cases, dual-member seats enabled caste-distinct areas to return caste representatives.[8]

The Delimitation Commission appointed in 1959[9] sought to achieve a greater equality of citizens per seat within each province. Under legislation in 1948 and 1949 the majority of the Indian Tamils largely working on the tea estates in the up-country areas had been disenfranchised. As the number of persons as well as the area continued to determine the number of seats allotted to each province, the effect was to reinforce the over-representation of the Kandyan areas. On an island-wide population basis, the Kandyan Sinhalese would have had 51 seats and the low-country Sinhalese 76. In fact, after the 1959 Delimitation, the low-country Sinhalese could count on 54 seats and the Kandyan Sinhalese on 73.[10] In party terms, these provisions disadvantaged the left-wing parties, the CP and LSSP, who had made their base in the more heavily urbanised areas of the south and west coasts. In caste terms, they were biased against those castes resident in the densely populated areas of the south and west while they gave a greater opportunity of expression than hitherto to the larger of the underprivileged castes of the Kandyan areas.

No provision was made for communal interests as such, but a number of multi-member seats gave representation expressly to Sri Lankan Tamils and Moors wherever they were present in sufficient concentration. As for caste, the Commissioners wrote strongly in answer to requests for special representation: 'While we have every sympathy with them, yet we consider it a pernicious policy to carve out separate electorates for them, thereby perpetuating their alleged under-privileged status, when it is everyone's desire that class distinctions should disappear.'[11]

TABLE 6 *Population, citizenship, area weightage: 1959 Delimitation*

Province	Total population	Total no. of citizens	No. of electoral districts on basis of 75,000 persons	Area weightage	Average no. of citizens to be obtained per electoral district	Total no. of electoral districts
Western	2,547,500	2,392,200	34	1	68,438	35
Central	1,552,600	1,000,700	21	2	43,508	23
Southern	1,258,700	1,237,100	17	2	65,110	19
Northern	664,300	638,600	9	4	49,123	13
Eastern	496,200	487,300	7	4	44,300	11
North-Western	1,000,900	977,700	13	3	61,106	16
North-Central	275,100	270,600	4	4	33,825	8
Uva	549,900	359,300	7	3	35,930	10
Sabaragamuwa	1,016,100	850,300	14	2	56,686	16
Total	9,361,300	8,213,800	126	25		151

Source: Report of the Delimitation Commission, SP xv (Colombo, The Government Press, 1959).

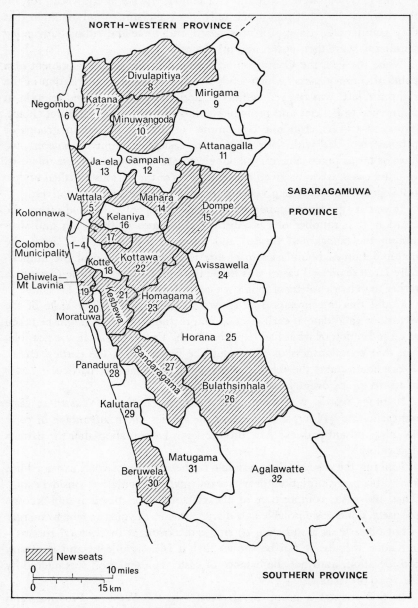

NORTH-WESTERN PROVINCE

Negombo
6

Katana
7

Divulapitiya
8

Mirigama
9

Minuwangoda
10

Attanagalla
11

Ja-ela
13

Gampaha
12

Wattala
5

Mahara
14

Dompe
15

Kolonnawa

Kelaniya
16

Colombo
Municipality

1-4

17

SABARAGAMUWA

PROVINCE

Kotte
18

Kottawa
22

Avissawella
24

Dehiwela—
Mt Lavinia

19

21

Homagama
23

Moratuwa

20

Kesbewa

Horana   25

Panadura
28

Bandaragama

27

Bulathsinhala
26

Kalutara
29

Matugama
31

Beruwela
30

Agalawatte
32

New seats

0   10 miles

0   15 km

SOUTHERN PROVINCE

Map 2   Electoral districts in the Western Province, 1959

This reasoning struck a number of non-*Goyigama* as equivocal, for, on the contrary, they felt that it was only by caste-distinct representation that they could make their problems heard and force the ruling *Goyigama* families to share their power and privileges.[12]

None the less, the Commissioners conceded that the development of a political consciousness 'which tends to what is called a polarisation of the right and left' was not yet completed, and that caste, race, and religion in preference to policies and principles still could determine electoral choice. Thus, wherever 'economic community of interest of certain groups of peoples coincided with their religious or caste community of interest, we have as far as practicable carved out electorates to represent those interests. In other cases, we have given concentrations of the various so-called under-privileged classes, a strong voice in the choice of their representatives.'[13]

It was tempting to suppose that, expressed openly, this had meant the creation of a number of caste-distinct electorates in the south and west among the *Salagama*, *Karava*, and *Durava*, and, in the hill areas, the manipulation of boundaries to ensure that representation of the numeri-cally large depressed castes was made through members of the *Goyigama* rather than by members of their own communities.

Could this interpretation be shown to be plausible? The caste of the victorious candidate at each election before and after 1959 might be taken as an indication of what had happened at the Delimitation. It was possible, too, that consciousness of caste could be discerned in the parties' choice of candidates, and the relative support for candidates of particular castes in an electorate, over a series of elections.

In other words, was there caste voting at elections? Was there caste representation? How, if at all, had the parties taken advantage of caste loyalties and antipathies? And did the 1959 Delimitation alter the pattern discernibly?

Linking the caste of the candidate to the number of votes cast for him, and to his party affiliation, provokes only general, tentative considerations. Since the caste composition of the electorates discussed is not known precisely, nor is caste isolable as a discrete factor, the picture which emerges is not of caste as a sufficient or single determinant in electoral success – but none the less it can be shown that it is a significant and necessary consideration, and that the balance of caste representation was altered by the 1959 provisions.

In this chapter a group of electorates in the Western Province, and thereafter a number in the deep south, will be considered, and finally, the sparsely populated electorates in the North-Central Province that have been subject to colonisation from the south.

TABLE 7   *Candidates at general elections: Ja-ela*

Year[a]	Candidate	Caste	Party	No. votes	No. registered voters	Total no. votes per caste	
1947	D. P. Jayasuriya[b]	G	UNP	11,133	51,274	G	11,133
	P. N. Siriwardene	S	–	8,406		S	10,319
	Stanley Mendis	S	LSSP	1,913			
	F. Nettisinghe	NI	–	777			
1952	D. P. Jayasuriya[b]	G	UNP	18,212	55,368	G	19,237
	L. W. Panditha	D	CP	6,308		S	5,790
	S. Stock Anthony	S	–	5,790			
	D. F. Hettiaratchyge	G	–	1,025			
1956	Stanley de Soysa	S	MEP	24,381	61,091	G	19,728
	Paris Perera	G	UNP	19,132		S	24,381
	Don Martin Jayamahamudalige	G	–	596			
July 1960[c]	Paris Perera	G	UNP	13,622	34,002	G	24,520
	D. Oliver Jayasuriya	G	SLFP	10,898		S	2,308
	Stanley de Soysa	S	LPP[d]	2,308			
	D. G. B. Joseph	NI	MEP	234			
1965	Paris Perera	G	UNP	21,867	43,432	G	35,717
	D. Oliver Jayasuriya	G	SLFP	13,850			
1970	Paris Perera	G	UNP	21,657	52,066	G	21,657
	Shelton Amarasekera	S	SLFP	19,762		S	21,928
	Peter Mendis	S	–	2,166			

[a] Single-member seat for each year.
[b] Full name: Gate *Mudaliyar* Don Pantleon Jayasuriya, whose family had been closely associated with the colonial establishment.
[c] March 1960 election not included.
[d] Lanka Prajathanthrawadi Party.
NI No information.
Source: figures taken from *Results of Parliamentary General Elections in Ceylon 1947–1970* (Colombo, Dept of Elections, 1971).

TABLE 8   *Candidates at general elections: Negombo*

Year[a]	Candidate	Caste	Party	No. votes	No. registered voters	Total no. votes per caste	
1947	H. de Z. Siriwardene	S	UNP	10,174	55,642	S	10,174
	W. S. Fernando	K	–	9,218		K	9,218
	A. L. J. C. D. Rajchandra[b]		–	6,169			
1952	A. N. D. A. Abeysinghe	S	UNP	22,721	60,617	S	22,721
	Hector Fernando	K	LSSP	9,396		K	15,999
	M. B. G. Kurera	K	–	3,396			
	C. M. Fernando	K	–	3,207			
	K. C. D. Senanayake	G	–	459			
1956	Hector Fernando	K	LSSP	20,892	67,060	S	4,589
	T. Quintin Fernando	K	UNP	18,212		K	39,104
	Tudor B. Gunasekera	S	–	4,589			
July 1960[c]	T. Quintin Fernando	K	UNP	14,469	32,569	K	21,577
	M. B. G. Kurera	K	SLFP	7,108			
1965	T. Quintin Fernando	K	UNP	22,056	37,900	K	28,822
	M. B. G. Kurera	K	SLFP	6,766			
1970	Denzil Fernando	K	UNP	20,457	44,284	K	36,377
	Justin Fernando	K	SLFP	15,920			

[a] Single-member seat for each year.
[b] A member of the Bharatha, an Indian ethnic group and a mercantile community, resident largely in and around Colombo.
[c] March 1960 election not included.
Source: figures taken from *Results of Parliamentary General Elections in Ceylon 1947–1970*.

TABLE 9   *Candidates at general elections: Mirigama*

Year[a]	Candidate	Caste	Party	No. votes	No. registered voters	Total no. votes per caste
1947	D. S. Senanayake	G	UNP	26,762	55,474	G 37,435
	Edmund Samarakkody	G	LSSP	10,673		
1952	John E. Amaratunga	G	UNP	27,447	56,728	G 44,949
	James Peter Obeysekere	G	SLFP	17,502		
1956	V. Wijewardene (Mrs)	G	MEP	38,193	63,440	G 49,863
	John E. Amaratunga	G	UNP	10,896		
	H. P. Jayawardene	G	–	399		
	A. A. Stanley Dias	G	–	375		
July 1960[b]	W. Wijayasinha	G	SLFP	15,424	37,086	G 29,634
	W. D. Senanayake	G	UNP	13,934		
	E. A. Jayasinghe	NI	–	345		
	Tilaka Kulasekera	G	MEP	276		
1965	S. Obeysekere (Mrs)	G	SLFP	17,872	44,575	G 38,106
	W. Wijayasinha	G	UNP	17,028		
	K. P. P. Karunanayake	G	–	1,956		
	M. K. W. Fonseka	G	–	1,015		
	B. Ratnayake	G	MEP	235		
1970	S. Obeysekere (Mrs)	G	SLFP	24,872	50,721	G 44,421
	W. S. Karunaratne	G	UNP	19,549		

[a] Single-member seat for each year.
[b] March 1960 election not included.
Source: figures taken from *Results of Parliamentary General Elections in Ceylon 1947–1970.*

TABLE 10   *Candidates at general elections: Wattala*

Year[a]	Candidate	Caste	Party	No. votes	No. registered voters		Total no. votes per caste
July 1960[b]	D. Shelton Jayasinghe	S	UNP	11,633	30,201	G	11,623
	A. D. J. Leo	G	SLFP	11,529		S	11,633
	W. S. Perera	NI	MEP	287			
	D. J. Weerakody	G	–	94			
1965	D. Shelton Jayasinghe	S	UNP	17,649	38,456	G	14,076
	A. D. J. Leo	G	SLFP	14,076		S	17,649
	D. G. B. Joseph	NI	MEP	184			
1970	A. D. J. Leo	G	SLFP	21,856	48,875	G	21,856
	D. Shelton Jayasinghe	S	UNP	19,667		S	19,667

a Single-member seat for each year.
b March 1960 election not included.
Source: figures taken from *Results of Parliamentary General Elections in Ceylon 1947–1970.*

TABLE 11   *Candidates at general elections: Katana*

Year[a]	Candidate	Caste	Party	No. votes	No registered voters		Total no. votes per caste
July 1960[b]	Wijayapala Mendis	S	UNP	10,846	31,019	S	10,846
	Hector Fernando	K	LSSP	10,802		K	10,802
1965	Wijayapala Mendis	S	UNP	16,469	37,264	S	16,469
	Hector Fernando	K	LSSP	13,682		K	13,809
	Santiago Fernando	K	MEP	127			
1970	H. C. de Silva	S	SLFP	22,370	43,074	S	33,959
	Wijayapala Mendis	S	UNP	11,589			

a Single-member seat for each year.
b March 1960 election not included.
Source: figures taken from *Results of Parliamentary General Elections in Ceylon 1947–1970.*

TABLE 12 *Candidates at general elections: Minuwangoda*

Year[a]	Candidate	Caste	Party	No. votes	No. registered voters	Total no. votes per caste	
July 1960[b]	M. P. de Z. Siriwardene	S	SLFP	16,327	36,957	S	16,327
	S. F. de Silva	K	UNP	11,202		K	11,202
	K. K. D. H. de Silva	NI	MEP	537		G	289
	R. M. S. Ratnayake	G	–	289			
1965	M. P. de Z. Siriwardene	S	SLFP	19,095	44,025	S	19,095
	S. F. de Silva	K	UNP	16,827		K	16,827
	Vajira Marasinghe	NI	MEP	276		G	205
	D. S. Jayasinghe	G	–	205			
	G. Piyasekera	NI	LPP	142			
	R. A. D. W. Ratnasekera	V	–	94			
1970	M. P. de Z. Siriwardene	S	SLFP	24,904	48,875	S	42,970
	Bennet Gunasekera	S	UNP	18,066			
	Dharmasiri Wijetunga	V	–	252			

[a] Single-member seat for each year. [b] March 1960 election not included.
Source: figures taken from *Results of Parliamentary General Elections in Ceylon 1947–1970*.

TABLE 13 *Candidates at general elections: Divulapitiya*

Year[a]	Candidate	Caste	Party	No. votes	No. registered voters	Total no. votes per caste	
July 1960[b]	Lakshman Jayakody	G	SLFP	15,049	32,755	G	25,359
	Percy Jayakody	G	UNP	10,310			
	Amarapala Ariyatillaka	NI	–	214			
	D. S. Simon	NI	–	182			
1965	Lakshman Jayakody	G	SLFP	17,637	39,613	G	33,343
	Wimaladharma Jayakody	G	UNP	15,567			
	W. H. C. Amarasekera	S	LPP	266			
	Wiswamithra Jayakody	G	MEP	139			
1970	Lakshman Jayakody	G	SLFP	23,772	44,080	G	38,373
	Ariyaratne Jayatilake	G	UNP	14,601			
	Sri C. S. Dagonna	V	–	252			

[a] Single-member seat for each year. [b] March 1960 election not included.
Source: figures taken from *Results of Parliamentary General Elections in Ceylon 1947–1970*.

Looking first at that part of the Western Province to the north of Colombo, new electorates were created at Katana, Wattala, Minuwangoda, and Divulapitiya (nos. 7, 5, 10, 8). These were carved out of the old constituencies of Ja-ela and Negombo. In addition, the old electorate at Attanagalla was split, part going to Mirigama, and part of its southern borders being included in the new electorates of Dompe (no. 15) and Mahara (no. 14). Mahara and Dompe also took from Ja-ela, Kelaniya, and Gampaha. The caste geography of these areas is mixed, with *Karava* and *Salagama* forming the predominant non-*Goyigama* castes, though a few pockets of *Vahumpura* exist, notably in the southern and eastern villages of Divulapitiya and Minuwangoda, and in the south-western parts of Mirigama that were, till 1959, part of Attanagalla. The details of voting and the caste and party of the candidates are given in tables 7–13. It is clear that where electorates have a mixed caste population, caste-community interest has been used as a basis of support by opposing parties.

The population of Ja-ela electorate was much altered by the Delimitation, but this has made no great impact on the caste of the candidates. The seat has been won most consistently by a *Goyigama* for the UNP; the SLFP has come closest to winning the seat with *Salagama* candidates, Stanley de Soysa wresting it briefly from the UNP in the 1956 landslide. In that election Stanley de Soysa apparently distributed a pamphlet criticising those who were trying to raise the caste issue against him.[14] Negombo, one of the most famous centres of the fishing industry in the island, has had mostly *Karava* candidates; since 1956, every candidate has been *Karava*, in contrast to the pre-1959 practice when a *Salagama* won in 1947 and 1952. We may speculate that part of its *Salagama* interests were hived off in acknowledgement of the overwhelming 'community of economic interest' of the *Karava*, and distributed among the new electorates of Wattala and Katana. Mirigama has been overwhelmingly *Goyigama* in its candidates, the vote swinging to the SLFP from 1956.

Wattala since 1960 has seen close contests between the *Salagama* candidate of the UNP and the *Goyigama* candidate of the SLFP. Katana and Minuwangoda are both of interest in that in 1970 the losing party changed the caste of its candidate to that of the winning party, and in the case of Katana, won the seat. Both Minuwangoda and Divulapitiya have had *Vahumpura* candidates, drawing support, presumably, from their villages hived off from Attanagalla at the Delimitation, but none have drawn any sizeable vote. Divulapitiya has put up *Goyigama* candidates for both the UNP and the SLFP; Lakshman Jayakody for the SLFP has substantial family interests in the area, owning considerable coconut acreage.

TABLE 14 *Caste of major party candidates before and after 1959, Western Province*

Electorate	Before	After
Ja-ela	*G/S*	*G/S*
Negombo	*S/K*	*K*
Mirigama	*G*	*G*
Gampaha	*G*	*G*
Attanagalla	*G*	*G*
Kelaniya	*G*	*G*
Wattala	–	*S/G*
Katana	–	*S/K*
Minuwangoda	–	*S/K*
Divulapitiya	–	*G*
Mahara	–	*G*
Dompe	–	*G*

The effects of the 1959 Delimitation on these constituencies can be summarised as in table 14. Before the Delimitation it seems the *Goyigama* could count on returning four candidates; after the Delimitation the *Karava* gained one electorate specific to them, the *Salagama* gained the opportunity to win four, as opposed to two, and the *Goyigama* were returned to seven, leaving them, as before, with a 'net margin' of two.

In other words, one can cautiously say that the demarcation of new electorates to secure the representation of caste-specific interests does not seem to have been at the expense of the *Goyigama*. How much calculation was involved in the 1959 deliberations, and how much awareness has there been on the part of voters and parties to produce such returns? This particular analysis does not admit of an answer to these questions, and they will be raised again in the next chapter.

Turning to the Southern Province, the area covered by Ambalangoda, Balapitiya, and Bentara–Elpitiya (nos. 55–7) has a mixed caste population, but the three strongest castes are the *Goyigama*, *Salagama*, and *Karava*. There are numbers of *Vahumpura*, but nowhere are they concentrated except in the villages in and around Karandeniya.

Up to the Delimitation, the one large two-member seat of Ambalangoda–Balapitiya returned *Salagama* and *Karava* candidates, with the *Vahumpura* polling substantial numbers of votes. I. D. S. Weerawardana writes of the 1956 election: 'One Independent candidate came forward ... almost entirely on the caste issue. A pamphlet in support of this candidate stated that there were at least 13,000 voters of his caste in the constituency ... The pamphlet urged the caste-group to return a son of

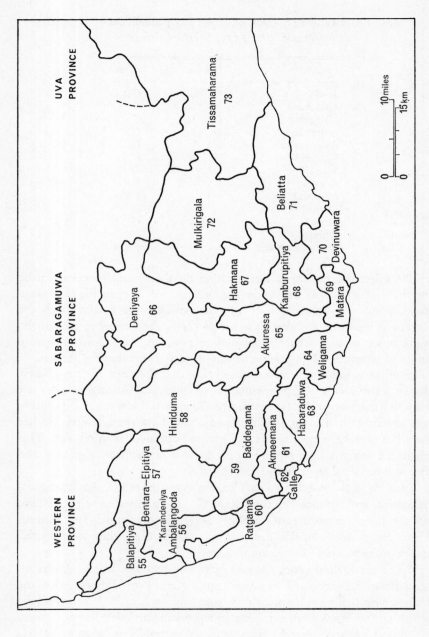

WESTERN PROVINCE

Balapitiya
55

Bentara—Elpitiya
57

•Karandeniya
Ambalangoda
56

Ratgama
60

Galle
62

Akmeemana
61

Baddegama
59

Hiniduma
58

Habaraduwa
63

Weligama
64

Akuressa
65

Kamburupitiya
68

Devinuwara
70

Matara
69

Deniyaya
66

SABARAGAMUWA
PROVINCE

Hakmana
67

Mulkirigala
72

Beliatta
71

Tissamaharama
73

UVA
PROVINCE

10 miles
15 km

Map 3   Electoral districts in the Southern Province, 1959

TABLE 15 *Candidates at general elections: Ambalangoda–Balapitiya*

Year[a]	Candidate	Caste	Party	No. votes	No. registered voters	Total no. votes per caste	
1947	P. H. W. de Silva	K	LSSP	37,650	104,843	K	57,170
	Arthur de Soysa	S	UNP	26,764		S	30,691
	P. de S. Kularatne	K	–	17,520		V	10,088
	P. A. Premadasa	V	–	9,086		G	3,105
	Stanley de Zoysa	S	–	3,927			
	S. Abeygunawardena (Mrs)	G	–	3,105			
	K. T. E. de Silva	K	–	2,000			
	D. J. Prematilleke	V	–	1,002			
1952	Ian de Zoysa	S	UNP	37,901	92,398	K	50,748
	P. H. W. de Silva	K	LSSP	33,803		S	57,749
	A. H. E. Fernando	V	–	18,657		V	18,657
	M. H. Saddhasena	K	–	16,945			
	M. P. de Zoysa	S	SLFP	12,496			
	W. A. de Silva	S	–	6,017			
	S. de S. Goonetilleke	S	–	1,335			
1956	M. P. de Zoysa	S	MEP	45,626	100,326	K	45,565
	P. H. W. de Silva	K	MEP	43,769		S	68,585
	S. I. A. de Zoysa	S	UNP	22,959		V	12,811
	Sammie Ranasinghe	V	–	12,811			
	N. C. D. de Silva	K	–	1,796			

[a] Two-member seat for each year.
Source: figures taken from *Results of Parliamentary General Elections in Ceylon 1947–1970.*

TABLE 16 *Candidates at general elections: Ambalangoda*

Year[a]	Candidate	Caste	Party	No. votes	No. registered voters	Total no. votes per caste	
July 1960[b]	P. de S. Kularatne	K	UNP	10,034	28,618	K	21,294
	P. H. W. de Silva	K	MEP	8,045			
	P. W. Wilfred de Silva	K	LSSP	3,215			
1965	M. H. Saddhasena	K	UNP	15,433	35,335	K	29,241
	P. de S. Kularatne	K	SLFP	13,808			
1970	L. C. de Silva	K	LSSP	22,356	40,103	K	34,084
	M. H. Saddhasena	K	UNP	11,728		V	544
	U. D. Kulasinghe	V	–	544			

[a] Single-member seat for each year.
[b] March 1960 election not included.
Source: figures taken from *Results of Parliamentary General Elections in Ceylon 1947–1970.*

TABLE 17   *Candidates at general elections: Balapitiya*

Year[a]	Candidate	Caste	Party	No. votes	No. registered voters	Total no. votes per caste
July 1960[b]	Lakshman de Silva	S	SLFP	13,812	34,384	S 24,970
	V. T. de Zoysa	S	UNP	10,841		
	J. Munasinghe	S	–	317		
1965	L. C. de Silva	K	LSSP	16,615	41,823	K 16,615
	R. L. de Silva	S	UNP	16,519		S 16,683
	J. Munasinghe	S	–	164		G 130
	P. L. V. Gunawardene	G	–	130		
1970	P. D. W. de Silva	S	LSSP	22,659	45,682	S 38,210
	R. T. de Silva	S	UNP	14,431		
	E. M. M. Wijerama	S	–	951		
	J. Munasinghe	S	–	169		

[a] Single-member seat for each year.
[b] March 1960 election not included.
Source: figures taken from *Results of Parliamentary General Elections in Ceylon 1947–1970.*

TABLE 18   *Candidates at general elections: Bentara–Elpitiya*

Year[a]	Candidate	Caste	Party	No. votes	No. registered voters	Total no. votes per caste
July 1960[b]	Albert Kariyawasam	G	SLFP	18,349	41,412	G 30,711
	R. G. Samaranayake	G	UNP	12,362		
	J. D. A. Jayasekera	NI	–	819		
1965	R. G. Samaranayake	G	UNP	22,085	52,449	G 44,341
	Albert Kariyawasam	G	SLFP	21,084		
	J. P. Gajanayake	G	MEP	1,172		
1970	Albert Kariyawasam	G	SLFP	29,801	59,022	G 52,510
	Rupasena Karunatillaka	G	UNP	22,709		

[a] Single-member seat for each year.
[b] March 1960 election not included.
Source: figures taken from *Results of Parliamentary General Elections in Ceylon 1947–1970.*

the caste to Parliament.'[15] Sammie Ranasinghe received in fact 12,811 votes. At the 1959 Delimitation, however, the Karandeniya area was split between the three new electorates; subsequently only one *Vahumpura* candidate stood in any of the three: U. D. Kulasinghe in Ambalangoda in 1970. He received only 544 votes.

In effect, each electorate seems to have become caste-distinct in its representatives, and the voting seems to have become concentrated along more obviously party lines, swinging between the UNP and the left. In Ambalangoda, for example, where all candidates since 1960 have been *Karava* (with the exception in 1970 mentioned above), P. de S. Kularatne stood successfully in 1960 as the UNP candidate. By 1965 he had joined the SLFP but lost the election to the UNP, the implication being that it was party rather than the person or caste of the candidate that was decisive. Similarly, in Balapitiya, where all candidates have been *Salagama*, with the exception of L. C. de Silva in 1965, the contest has become virtually a straight two-party affair, between the UNP and the LSSP. Though largely *Salagama*, the constituency as it emerged in 1959 had a very sizeable *Karava* minority. L. C. de Silva, a *Karava*, won by a very narrow margin in 1965 and in 1966 was unseated by an election petition issued by the defeated UNP *Salagama* candidate.[16] In 1970 he moved to adjoining Ambalangoda, which has put up mostly *Karava* candidates, and won the seat for the LSSP. In Balapitiya itself, the seat was won by P. W. de Silva, *Salagama* LSSP, and Colvin R. de Silva's son-in-law. In Bentara–Elpitiya all candidates have been *Goyigama*, the vote swinging between the UNP and the SLFP.

By eliminating the possibilities for caste contest that seemed to arise in the old two-member Ambalangoda–Balapitiya seat, the Delimitation opened the way for caste-distinct representation recognised by all parties in their choice of candidates, and presumably thus enabled elections to be fought along clear party lines. In so doing, the Delimitation appears to have eliminated the potential for caste-specific *Vahumpura* representation. It is notable that both the SLFP, and more particularly the Trotskyist LSSP which claims to define the population along class rather than caste lines, have chosen candidates of suitable caste.

The radicalism of the south also stands out clearly; it is in the densely populated, urbanised, westernised, and entrepreneurial electorates that the CP and LSSP have concentrated their effort and won their support since the 1930s and 40s. The anti-*Goyigama* frustrations of the *Karava*, *Salagama*, and *Durava* have been exploited by the CP, and to a lesser extent by the LSSP, to their advantage.

Matara, on the edge of the less-populated deep south, where the land

TABLE 19   *Candidates at general elections: Matara*

Year[a]	Candidate	Caste	Party	No. votes	No. registered voters	Total no. votes per caste	
1947	H. D. Abeygoona-wardena	D	CP	11,970	39,930	D	17,249
	W. Gunaskera	D	–	5,279		G	2,661
	G. Weeratunga	G	–	2,661		K	442
	K. K. D. Silva	K	–	442			
1952	M. Samaraweera	D	CP	11,861	41,166	D	22,646
	E. B. Senaratne	D	–	10,785		G	2,265
	S. P. de Silva	K	–	2,565		K	2,565
	Yapa S. Rajapakse	G	–	2,265			
1956	M. Samaraweera	D	MEP	18,571	47,068	D	25,913
	D. H. P. Gunawardene	D	UNP	7,342			
	E. H. P. Gawrapala	NI	–	4,894			
July 1960[b]	M. Samaraweera	D	SLFP	13,105	30,640	D	13,105
	C. J. Wijayawardhena	G	UNP	10,200		G	10,200
1965	B. Y. Tudawe	D	CP	15,207	37,399	D	29,494
	M. Samaraweera	D	LPP	14,287			
1970	B. Y. Tudawe	D	CP	20,764	41,751	D	35,344
	S. K. Piyadasa	D	UNP	14,580			
	E. P. Wijethunga	S	–	160			

[a] Single-member seat for each year.
[b] March 1960 election not included.
Source: figures taken from *Results of Parliamentary General Elections in Ceylon 1947–1970.*

becomes dry and the roaming buffalo herds produce some of the best curd in the country, emphasises the effects of the Delimitation already indicated.

The preponderant non-*Goyigama* caste in the area is *Durava*, though numbers of *Karava* are also present. At the Delimitation some part of the electorate passed to Devinuwara. The chief party contest has been between the UNP and the CP, the CP deriving a large part of its influence from Dr S. Wickremasinghe, formidable leader of the CP, whose home area it is. I. D. S. Weerawardana describes how in the 1956 election 'it was alleged that the Communist Party candidate... was chosen on caste grounds'.[17] It is clear that at every election (except 1960 when M. Samaraweera crossed to the SLFP and no CP candidate stood) the CP has chosen a candidate from the main non-*Goyigama* caste of the area. Though the UNP at nearly every election has also picked a *Durava* candidate, it is clear that caste alone has not been able to pull support from the radical party.

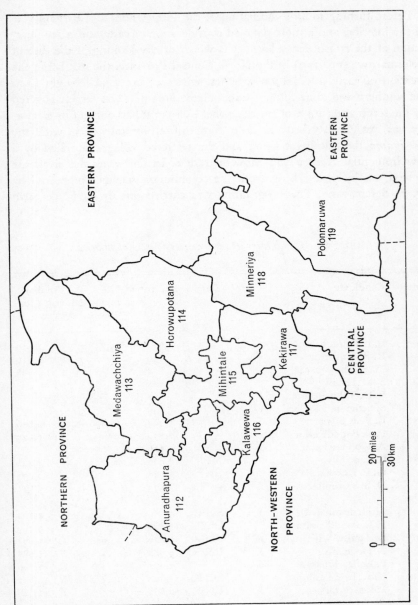

Map 4   Electoral districts in the North-Central Province, 1959

Before turning to an examination of the *Vahumpura* and *Batgam* vote in the interior, and a more detailed consideration of caste and party inter-action at the constituency level, it is worth briefly looking at the case of Polonnaruwa (no. 119) in the North-Central Province, the seat being the creation of early colonisation schemes, when settlers were brought from the southern wet zone into an unpopulated area that was largely covered by the scrub and jungle of the dry zone. In 1947 it had only a tiny elector-ate, as yet undisturbed in caste composition by intruders, with the *Goyigama* the dominant caste, and the scattered villages supplied by a few influential *Karava* and Moslem traders. In five years the electorate trebled, an increase arising from the colonisation schemes pioneered by D. S. Senanayake. The programme was carried out by C. P. de Silva

TABLE 20   *Candidates at general elections: Polonnaruwa*

Year[a]	Candidate	Caste	Party	No. votes	No. registered voters	Total no. votes per caste	
1947	P. L. Bauddhasara	G	–	1,604	5,838	G	2,479
	R. B. Wijeratne	G	–	830		b	926
	M. S. Abubucker[b]		–	818		K	68
	S. M. Ismail[b]		–	108			
	P. D. S. Jayasekere	K	–	68			
	S. Seneviratne	G	–	45			
1952	C. P. de Silva	S	–	5,498	15,796	G	2,856
	P. L. Bauddhasara	G	–	2,856		S	5,627
	A. Goonasekara	S	–	129			
1956	C. P. de Silva	S	MEP	10,072	26,727	G	4,427
	G. L. Kotelawala	G	UNP	3,948		S	10,072
	D. S. Kuruppu	G	–	479			
July 1960[c]	A. H. de Silva	S	SLFP	9,489	17,654	G	2,177
	P. L. Bauddhasara	G	UNP	2,177		S	9,489
1965	Leelaratne Wijesinghe	K	SLFP	7,840	22,938	G	3,673
	A. H. de Silva	S	LPP	5,988		S	5,988
	P. L. Bauddhasara	G	–	3,673		K	7,840
1970	K. A. L. Wijesinghe	K	SLFP	11,927	27,452	S	10,802
	Merril de Silva	S	UNP	10,802		K	11,927

[a] Single-member seat for each year.
[b] Moor.
[c] March 1960 election not included.
Source: figures taken from *Results of Parliamentary General Elections in Ceylon 1947–1970*.

(*Salagama*) as Director of Land Development, and the sudden appearance of a sizeable *Salagama* vote in Polonnaruwa is widely attributed to his bringing in members of his own community from the south as colonists. The 1953 Census showed 20 per cent of the population as 'Southern Low-Country'. Neither in 1952 nor 1956 was the election hotly contested, and even in the excitement of 1956, only just over half the electorate voted. What began as a personal vote for C. P. de Silva seems to have ended in a confirmed preference for the SLFP, C. P. de Silva being a leading member of the SLFP-led MEP in 1956. At the Delimitation the electorate was split into two to form Minneriya and Polonnaruwa, and C. P. de Silva moved to the new electorate, winning in 1960 for the SLFP. In 1964 he led his supporters in the House of Representatives into opposition to the SLFP and stood in 1965 for the LPP, part of the UNP's electoral grouping. He won again in 1965, but in 1970, standing for the UNP label, lost to the SLFP.

In Polonnaruwa meanwhile, the seat passed to C. P. de Silva's brother standing for the SLFP. But in 1965 and 1970, as his brother moved with him to the UNP, the seat stayed with the SLFP though the candidate was *Karava*. (*Karava* had moved into the area with the growth of colonisation, expanding the early trading interests, though I do not think that the *Karava* form an identifiable base of party support in this instance.) The implication of the Minneriya and Polonnaruwa results is that over time caste and personal following became a less sure basis of support, the vote remaining with the more radical party and failing to follow the lead of C. P. de Silva into the UNP.

Sufficient indication has been given to establish a clear link between the caste of candidates, their electoral success, and the caste population of the electorate, and to show that the major parties follow caste in their choice of candidates. Though these examples are drawn only from those electorates which display these characteristics most obviously, and, doubtless, in other areas caste is not as pressing an issue, none the less the general importance of caste, its distribution and numerical strength, as necessary considerations in electoral analysis, seems well established.

When it comes to weighing up the effects of Delimitation, it is less easy to be certain. It seems likely that the Commission took note of the social composition of the electorates much more closely than is admitted in the Delimitation Report. Tentatively, it seems that wherever possible the creation of a caste-distinct electorate around the 'communities of economic interest' formed by the *Karava*, *Salagama*, and *Durava* of the south and west coasts was balanced by the creation of an electorate able to be represented by a *Goyigama*. And though, in this chapter, the outcome of the intention to give a voice to the 'so-called under-privileged' castes has not been traced in detail, the data shows how effectively the opportunity for *Vahumpura* caste representation through a member of their own community was removed in these areas.

4

Sabaragamuwa:
a study of a caste vote in a traditional area

The constituency data brought forward in the last chapter raised many questions, the answers fraught with difficulties of analysis and interpretation. Here the questions are studied in more depth, essentially by sharpening the focus to a specific area and establishing more exactly its caste geography. The role of the *Vahumpura* and *Batgam* in particular needed to be examined further, to discover how substantial a 'voice' they had been allowed, and more generally, whether the exercise of the vote by these numerically large communities, in a system where numbers matter, through an era of increasingly 'popular' politics appealing to the 'common man' against the elites, had altered their awareness of participation and brought any political benefit to them. How did they categorise the parties? In what terms did parties appeal for their support?

Sabaragamuwa Province curls round the edges of the Kandyan highlands, embracing the mountainous regions arising from the plains of the Southern and Western Provinces. Divided into the two administrative districts of Kegalle and Ratnapura, the province has sixteen electorates, roughly 10 per cent of the total. The areas immediately about Kegalle are accessible, the main road to Kandy from Colombo passing through Dedigama, Galigomuwa, Kegalle, Rambukkana, and Mawanella over gently rising hills. Further south, in Ruwanwella and Dehiowita, the hills are steeper, covered by tea and rubber estates. Their eastern boundaries are less easily accessible and sparsely populated.

Ratnapura District is mountainous, with the famous Adam's Peak range bordering the north. A secondary ridge runs across the district roughly north to east. The eastern side is classified as a dry zone, an area which extends to the south-east plain. The hill areas are mainly under tea and rubber cultivation. Large parts of the district are still poorly provided with roads and are relatively inaccessible.

Both districts have patches of jungle, forest, and scrublands, sparsely populated and unapproachable by car. However, there are a number of well-sited and comfortable Rest Houses, and these formed bases from

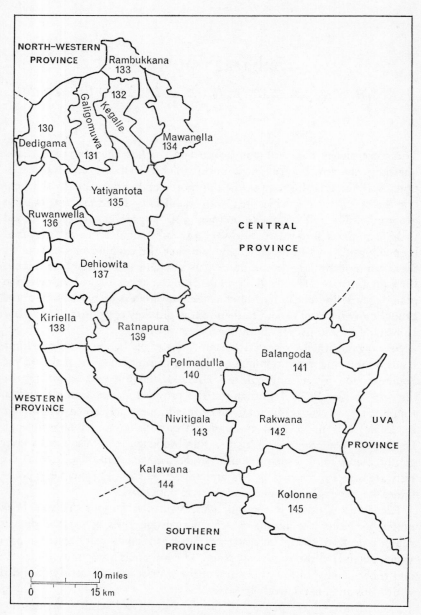

NORTH–WESTERN
PROVINCE

Rambukkana
133

132

Galigomuwa

Kegalle

130
Dedigama

131

Mawanella
134

Yatiyantota
135

Ruwanwella
136

CENTRAL

PROVINCE

Dehiowita
137

Kiriella
138

Ratnapura
139

Pelmadulla
140

Balangoda
141

WESTERN
PROVINCE

Nivitigala
143

Rakwana
142

UVA

PROVINCE

Kalawana
144

Kolonne
145

SOUTHERN

PROVINCE

0   10 miles
0   15 km

Map 5   Electoral districts in the Province of Sabaragamuwa, 1959

which to explore. Both Ratnapura and Kegalle are served by frequent buses, and though this is not a mode of transport I would recommend to anyone wishing to arrive in comfort or tranquillity, the conversation at the bus stands, roadside halts, and in the buses themselves was as revealing of people's daily worries, and the attitudes of voters to their leaders, as such conversations are in this country.

Sabaragamuwa was chosen for a number of reasons, not least because it is an area of *Vahumpura* and *Batgam* concentration, and, in certain electorates, the Delimitation Commission had expressly tried to give them representation. In addition, considerable background data as to the major families and the political history of the province was available to form a framework in which to set the new information. Furthermore, Dudley Senanayake had stood at Dedigama for the UNP since 1936 (except for a brief period of retirement between 1956 and 1960), and Dr N. M. Perera of the LSSP had been Member for Ruwanwella from 1936 to 1960 (except for a short break between 1943 and 1947) and had taken Yatiyantota (which is part of the Ruwanwella electorate) since its creation in 1959. What was the social basis of this stability in support for these two leading national figures of such radically opposed party images and ideologies? And then, Sabaragamuwa had been an area of heavy insurgent fighting: would the traditional social relationships and their interaction with, and expression via, the political structure provide insight into the bases of insurgent support?

TABLE 21   *Constituencies in Kegalle and Ratnapura Districts, 1959*

Kegalle		Ratnapura	
Dedigama	130	Kiriella	138
Galigomuwa	131	Ratnapura	139
Kegalle	132	Pelmadulla	140
Rambukkana	133	Balangoda	141
Mawanella	134	Rakwana	142
Yatiyantota	135	Nivitigala	143
Ruwanwella	136	Kalawana	144
Dehiowita	137	Kolonne	145

First it is necessary to sketch in the basic political data for the area since Independence. The 1945 Delimitation had divided Sabaragamuwa into ten seats, including a two-member seat at Balangoda. In 1959 representation was increased to sixteen seats, each district having eight, as shown in table 21.

At the time of the Delimitation of 1959 the total population was 1,016,000 persons of whom 850,300 were citizens. Of the citizen population, 675,298 were Kandyan Sinhalese, 128,743 were low-country Sinhalese, 25,913 were Sri Lankan Moors, and 15,204 were Sri Lankan Tamils. The non-Sinhalese formed just under 15 per cent of the total provincial population, but it was not evenly spread throughout the province. For example, in Kegalle the Sri Lankan Moor population in 1959 was estimated at 13 per cent. The Moors are heavily concentrated in Mawanella, with sizeable numbers in Ruwanwella, and a few in both Dehiowita and Dedigama.[1]

TABLE 22 *Kegalle District: percentage distribution of votes by parties, 1947–70*

Party	1947	1952	1956	March 1960	July 1960	1965	1970
UNP[a]	51.2	56.7	31.1	39.3	46.0	51.6	43.5
SLFP[b]	–	13.0	50.1	25.6	33.9	29.3	36.1
LSSP	23.5	21.3	10.9	23.6	17.0	18.4	19.9
CP	–	–	–	1.7	–	–	–
MEP	–	–	–	3.6	0.4	–	–
Ind.	25.3	9.0	7.9	6.2	2.7	0.7	0.5
Total	100.0	100.0	100.0	100.0	100.0	100.0	100.0

[a] UNP in 1965 includes MEP and SLFSP.
[b] SLFP in 1956 = MEP.
Source: calculated from *Results of Parliamentary General Elections in Ceylon 1947–1970.*

TABLE 23 *Ratnapura District: percentage distribution of votes by parties, 1947–70*

Party	1947	1952	1956	March 1960	July 1960	1965	1970
UNP[a]	52.2	63.9	33.2	29.4	38.7	45.0	37.8
SLFP[b]	–	14.7	51.6	21.9	41.7	35.9	39.6
LSSP	21.5	21.4	14.9	15.0	11.7	11.0	16.4
CP	–	–	–	3.9	–	–	5.3
MEP	–	–	–	17.7	6.0	–	–
Ind.	26.3	–	0.3	12.1	1.9	8.1	0.9
Total	100.0	100.0	100.0	100.0	100.0	100.0	100.0

[a] UNP in 1965 includes MEP and SLFSP.
[b] SLFP in 1956 = MEP.
Source: calculated from *Results of Parliamentary General Elections in Ceylon 1947–1970.*

The percentage distribution of votes by parties from 1947 has been as shown in tables 22 and 23. The UNP has consistently drawn over 30 per cent of the votes in both districts, the lowest percentage being cast in 1956, but the Bandaranaike landslide in that year has not permanently undermined the UNP's strength. In 1956 the SLFP/MEP seems to have received some 20 per cent of the UNP vote, and, under the no-contest arrangements between them, some 10 per cent of the LSSP's vote. In March 1960 it is clear that the uncertainty surrounding the leadership of the SLFP following S. W. R. D.'s death devastated the SLFP vote which spread itself uncertainly among the parties. By July 1960 confidence had presumably been restored, and the majority returned to the SLFP. The LSSP percentage share shows clearly the nation-wide decline in their electoral support. It is noticeable, too, that the SLFP does not command a majority share of votes by itself, and, except in 1956, has needed the support of the LSSP and CP to defeat the UNP.[2]

Comparing the two districts, the influence of Dr N. M. Perera (LSSP MP for Yatiyantota) and of Dudley Senanayake (UNP MP for Dedigama) on the voting in Kegalle district is apparent. Note also the higher percentage polled for the UNP in 1965 in both districts, reflecting the massive campaign mounted by the UNP in that election. In addition, the role of Asoka Karunaratne, *Batgam* UNP candidate for Rambukkana, who left Mrs Bandaranaike's government in 1964 to join the UNP, was, if not decisive, of considerable importance.

It is interesting that the proportion voting for the UNP has remained relatively stable, particularly since the percentage voting has increased dramatically at each election.[3] In 1947 the national turn-out was barely above 50 per cent. Sir Ivor Jennings put forward the view that, as a contest between the predominantly *Goyigama* ruling class (and *Wellawa* caste in Tamil Jaffna), many of the electorate simply did not bother to vote.[4] In 1952 and 1956 roughly 70 per cent voted. There is no hard data to explain the persistence of UNP support, but it is clear both that the basis of alignment has fluctuated over time, and that generational movement has occurred.

Part of the significance of 1956 in Lanka's political history is that it demonstrated that it was indeed possible to change governments; it appeared at the time to be a fundamental dethronement. Elections undoubtedly began to matter to the electorate, and in both March and July 1960 some 75 per cent of the electorate voted. The percentage turn-out shows no sign of declining; in 1965 it had climbed to 82 per cent and by 1970 to 85.[5]

These percentages undoubtedly can be read as reflecting the increasing politicisation of the electorate, roused by the possibilities indicated for the first time in 1956. They are also a reflection of demographic changes in the age structure of the population, and the lowering of the voting age to eighteen years under the 1959 Delimitation. Yet it cannot be said from the voting figures that a discernible 'young vote' has emerged: the new voters appear to be dividing among the major parties proportionately. This is the more surprising in that the youthfulness of the population is extreme. By 1969, 60 per cent of the total population of 12.5 million were under 25 – and 45 per cent of the 14- to 25-year age group were out of school but wholly unemployed.[6] One could *a priori* expect a significant swing to the left, given the well-documented voting behaviour of young people in similar circumstances elsewhere, yet there has not been any dramatic erosion of the UNP's electoral support.

The swings towards and away from the UNP in terms of votes have been small – in Kegalle, for example, a 2.5 per cent swing to the UNP in 1965 and a 3 per cent swing away from the UNP in 1970. What are the characteristics of this stability, and what are the elements that are swinging the vote?

To answer these questions it was necessary to discover the caste distribution geographically and numerically between the communities. This could be done by correlating the population of each village in an electorate with estimates of caste size and location obtained in interviews. The villages in each electorate were taken to be those listed in the 'Alphabetical and Numerical Lists of the Villages in the Province of Sabaragamuwa', compiled and issued by the Department of Census and Statistics in Colombo, July 1963. (The Lists were corrected up to February 1961.) The village populations were taken from the Census returns of 1963. The matching of village to population was made tedious by the fact that the villages are listed alphabetically in one document but under District Revenue Officers' Divisions in the Census returns.

The proportions as between low-country and Kandyan Sinhalese, and between Sinhalese and Moors were taken from the Delimitation Report, 1959. The voting figures and the turn-out at each election were taken from the *Results of Parliamentary General Elections in Ceylon 1947–1970*, issued by the Department of Elections, Colombo, 1971.

The identification of the castes within each village was obtained by interviews both in Sabaragamuwa and in Colombo. Interviewees were selected in no statistically controlled manner; village council chairmen, party organisers, members and ex-members of parliament, Buddhist monks, and other special-interest representatives formed the major types of informant. At first rather haphazard, the technique was perfected over a period of several months. Doubts as to the accuracy of this approach were allayed as the data began to cross-check and dovetail; in most cases the response was detailed, perceptive, and ready. A number of interviews were conducted for each electorate, each respondent being asked to go through a list of villages in his area and to state the major caste groups he knew to be resident there. He was further asked to estimate the numerical and percentage size of each community in the electorate as a whole. Finally, he was asked to describe how he thought each caste had tended to vote at the general elections of July 1960, 1965 and 1970.

One important deficiency in this approach could not be overcome: the town populations were ignored altogether as being unidentifiable in caste terms via this kind of approach. None the less, it seemed probable that by not including the town population some distortion in favour of the *Goyigama* could arise. Since there was some drift to the towns from the surrounding countryside, and since those seeking town work would tend to be largely the depressed, landless, and unemployed, such populations would tend to include a high proportion of the non-*Goyigama* and the low-status *Goyigama* groups. In turn, this could lead to an under-representation of these groups in any study which looked at the villages alone. Local information tentatively suggested that in Ratnapura, for example, the incoming population was largely drawn from the lower-status villages.

The study began with a trial run in Kalawana and Kolonne at the southern and eastern end of the province. Before 1959 this area had been covered by the two-member seat at Balangoda and by Nivitigala.

After the Delimitation, Balangoda became a single-member seat, and new electorates were carved out at Kalawana, Rakwana, and Kolonne. Nivitigala had been a largely *Goyigama* area of some 90,000 registered voters, though with numbers of *Vahumpura, Navandanna, Berawa,* and a few Moslem and Tamil traders. After the Delimitation Nivitigala continued to return *Goyigama* members, areas of *Vahumpura* concentration being hived off into Kolonne and Kalawana. Kolonne has subsequently returned *Vahumpura* members and Kalawana *Goyigama* members, though with *Vahumpura* members polling substantially.

In 1947 Balangoda was won by a *Goyigama* and a *Vahumpura*, with two Indians standing as representatives of the trading interest and the largely Indian estate population; the latter were thereafter deprived of the vote. In 1952 *Vahumpura* and a *Navandanna* stood against *Goyigama* competition; in 1956 the first three places were taken by members of the *Berawa, Navandanna,* and *Vahumpura* communities, only one *Goyigama* standing. From 1960, candidates at Balangoda have been mostly

Goyigama, and *Goyigama* have been returned at each election. The *Berawa* vote was hived off to the new seat at Rakwana, which has been held by V. T. G. Karunaratne of the drummer caste for the SLFP in 1960 and 1970; he was narrowly defeated in 1965 by 333 votes by a *Goyigama* UNP candidate.

I. D. S. Weerawardana writes of the 1956 elections:

A certain minority caste was in the majority in the Balangoda two-member constituency and was a sizeable minority in many of the constituencies of the Central Province and Sabaragamuwa. A Minister of the UNP government who belongs to this caste sent a personal letter (as a pamphlet) to these constituencies urging the people to vote for the UNP candidates on the ground that the UNP had eschewed caste considerations.[7]

In 1947 and 1952 Balangoda returned *Goyigama* and *Vahumpura* members, in 1956 a *Berawa* and a *Navandanna*. The substantial minority castes in the area are the *Vahumpura, Navandanna,* and *Berawa.* As there was no *Vahumpura* Minister prior to 1956, it is possible that Weerawardana, mistakenly, is referring to N. H. Keerthiratne, *Batgam* Minister in the UNP government. (There was one *Batgam* candidate at Balangoda in 1965, T. G. Gunadasa, who received only 113 votes.) The *Berawa* are decisive in Rakwana under V. T. G. Karunaratne, but that seat was not created till after 1956. Weerawardana probably refers to Sir Ukwatte Jayasundera, *Navandanna,* who was elected Secretary to the UNP under D. S. Senanayake and appointed Minister of Justice.

Kalawana and Kolonne are both very poorly served by roads. Kalawana is bounded to the south and west by the primeval Sinharaja Forest, connected by road to Nivitigala but with the main north–south link to Rakwana still incomplete. Kolonne has to its south-east the rivers and tributaries which, since the 1950s, have been developed under the major irrigation schemes of the Uda Walawe Project. It is crossed in the north by the Balangoda road from Ratnapura via Pelmadulla. Two other roads run north-west to south-east to the coast at Ambalantota, via Embilipitiya in the south-east of the electorate. The lower road runs across Kolonne to the fantastic Bulutota Pass to Madampe in Rakwana, and thence to Pelmadulla and Ratnapura. The higher road follows the course of the Rakwana Ganga to the north-eastern side of the electorate and thence to Madampe.

In both cases, the 1959 Commissioners pointed out, the provincial average used in determining representation was low, the areas then being poorly developed, inaccessible, and sparsely populated. As they stated, 'the development of these areas would be greatly accelerated after they receive the undivided attention of a separate Member of Parliament'.

TABLE 24 *Percentage distribution of Sinhalese population by caste in Kalawana and Kolonne, 1972*

	Caste				Total
	Goyigama	*Batgam*	*Vahumpura*	*Others*[a]	
Kalawana	55	–	38	7	100.0
Kolonne	32	–	59	9	100.0

[a] Includes, chiefly, *Hena, Berawa*, various types of potter castes, *Navandanna*.

TABLE 25 *Caste and party of winning candidates in Kalawana and Kolonne*

	July 1960		1965		1970	
	Caste	Party	Caste	Party	Caste	Party
Kalawana	*G*	SLFP	*G*	UNP	*G*	CP
Kolonne	*V*	UNP	*V*	UNP	*V*	LSSP

A series of interviews indicated that the population was distributed among the castes as shown in table 24. Compare table 24 with table 25. On the face of it, there seems to be a clear relation between the balance of caste and the caste of the winning candidate. But the caste–party relation is exceedingly unexpected, the UNP commonly being held to be the 'party of the *Goyigama*', and the left being supposed to represent depressed-caste interests. The identification of the major parties with particular caste interests is often used as a general explanatory factor for voting behaviour in certain areas. H. A. J. Hulugalle has written of the 1947 elections:

The Left parties won the coastal strip from Wellawatte to the South with a single exception. They also made inroads into the Kelani Valley up to Ruan-wella. Caste distinction no doubt played some part in the election ...

The United National Party suffered from the fact that its leaders had been in power for a long time, and that they came in the main from the 'goigama' caste which comprises sixty per cent of the population. The Marxist parties, being parties of protest, had an appeal not only to those with low incomes or none but also to many members of the minority castes who felt that the UNP did not give them sufficient recognition or political opportunity.[8]

Bryce Ryan writes similarly: 'The "Left" vote is highly concentrated in the narrow belt along the coast in which the non-Goigama high castes are dominant ... Very few agricultural peasant areas ... are Left ... It is the protest vote of the caste.'[9] And if the caste of candidates standing for the LSSP and CP in such areas is abstracted from the data presented in this and the previous chapter, it is clear that the caste basis of the left's support is reflected in the choice of candidates.

TABLE 26   *Caste of candidates of LSSP and CP in 17 electoral districts, 1947–70*

	Goyigama	Salagama	Karava	Durava	Vahumpura	Batgam	Total
LSSP	4	2	8	1	2	1	18
CP	–	–	1	2	–	–	3
Total	4	2	9	3	2	1	21

(Constituencies of the coastal strip: Mirigama, Negombo, Wattala, Katana, Minuwangoda Ja-ela, Moratuwa, Wellawatte–Galkissa, Chilaw, Ambalangoda, Balapitiya. Non-littoral constituencies: Kegalle, Kaduganawa, Kolonne, Polonnaruwa.)

Robinson has presented, in fascinating detail, a picture of the effect on village life of the progressive identification of parties with the various castes and status delineations within the village. With the SLFP from 1956 deliberately canvassing the support of the depressed castes, the lower castes of the village have become 'at least partially' reintegrated into village society. She adds: 'their acceptance is conceptualised largely in political terms'.[10]

In Kalawana and Kolonne, the reversal of expected party–caste labels is explained by the interaction of national events with the local political environment. In Kalawana in 1960 the SLFP candidate won by a margin of only 474 votes. Local opinion suggested that he was able to draw a considerable part of the non-*Goyigama* vote, following the triumph of S. W. R. D. in 1956 which seemed to provide for the first time a national party which, ideologically, was closer to their economic and social position. But by 1964 Asoka Karunaratne of the *Batgam* community had moved into opposition to Mrs Bandaranaike's government following the lead of C. P. de Silva, and in 1965 he, and D. L. F. Pedris of the *Vahumpura* community, campaigned nationally for the return of the UNP. In the adjoining electorate of Kolonne, the leading *Vahumpura* family were campaigning actively for the UNP. The national example of the two leaders of depressed communities and the local pressure from Kolonne apparently were sufficient to swing the *Vahumpura* to the UNP candidate, who took nearly 46 per cent of the vote. None the less, not all the *Vahumpura* felt that either party – the SLFP or the UNP – would represent them satisfactorily, and the Independent *Vahumpura* candidate received some 16 per cent of the votes.

It was felt strongly that the swing between the SLFP and UNP was largely the result of the depressed community seeking a party of greatest benefit to them, influenced in their assessment by national events and the behaviour of prominent depressed-caste politicians. In 1970 the party of the winning candidate was the CP – what looks at first like a radical and unstable departure. In part it was attributed in the electorate to the young who had become eligible to vote since 1960 – the number of registered voters having increased by half over the base figure in ten years. The older activists pointed to the greater 'party, policy, ideology' emphasis of the young in their assessment of electoral choice, since they had been brought up in a welfarist economy and had more open access to education and job opportunity. Their political heat was generated by frustration, while the older activists' perspectives were formed by the experience of traditional social oppression and lack of economic and educational opportunity.

In part it was felt that Cyril Mathew's temporary break with the UNP in neighbouring Kolonne affected the *Vahumpura* in Kalawana, too. A relation of the family, Mrs Soma Mathew, lost at Kolonne in 1970, standing as an Independent *Vahumpura* and receiving only eighty-five votes. There was considerable feeling that in Kalawana at least, a caste-distinct representative was of no advantage, and that it was better to be represented via the most radical party.

The CP candidate was Sarath Muttetuwegama, son-in-law of the national LSSP leader, Colvin R. de Silva. Linked by marriage to a prominent politician, locally too he had family influence. His father had been the *Rate Mahatmeya* (principal officer) of Kalawana, a respected member of the local (*Goyigama*) elite. It was felt by this distinction that he scored on a number of counts, not necessarily compatible logically. On the one hand, he was known to the prominent *Goyigama* families and had access to them, and, it was felt, through his family background he would know how to operate in Colombo circles. On the other hand, he was known to be at odds with the more conservative members of his family, and in his radicalism was seen by some as a symbol of the overthrow of entrenched privilege and tradition by the new generation of leftists, a most suitable representative for those who wished to combine their traditional social inclinations with an expression of defiance and hopes for change.

The history of Kolonne electorate is dominated by the Mathew family, leading members of the *Vahumpura* caste hierarchy in the area. Long the supporters of the UNP, Cyril Mathew won the seat in 1960 and his son in 1965. (For an elucidation of the Mathews' support for the UNP, see pp. 99–100.) But the *Vahumpura* have not followed the family's lead

unreservedly. In 1960 and in 1965 the LSSP candidate has taken a substantial part of the *Vahumpura* vote, challenging the UNP closely, and in
1970 winning the seat by a comfortable margin from C. Nanda Mathew
for the UNP.

The *Vahumpura* followed the UNP lead of the Mathews partly because
the UNP has posed as the protector of Buddhism in the area, specifically
of the extensive *viharagam* (lands granted to Buddhist temples) of the
ancient Sanchapala *Vihare* (Buddhist temple) in Pallebedde Wasama,
against the land-takeover proposals advocated by the LSSP. The
Vahumpura claim in their own community's traditions to be the appointed
guardians of Buddhism, assigned this role at the time of Mahinda's bringing Buddhism to Lanka, and in Kolonne many still honour the position of
the *Sangha* as landlord.

Notwithstanding the concern to protect the Buddhist lands and villages,
others of the *Vahumpura* have felt aggrieved by the supposed failure of
the UNP to protect the *chena* lands of the community in the fertile river
basins under irrigation development, and against the demands of settlers
brought in as colonisation schemes proliferate. Traditionally, the
Vahumpura in the area have practised two, if not three, types of cultivation, growing paddy along the narrow valley bottoms irrigated by the
streams running off the central highlands; *chena* cropping on the slopes
of the valleys (clearing the jungle for one or two seasons' cultivation of
cereals and vegetables to obtain the rich, if short-lived, fertility of the
jungle soil); and sometimes in suitable areas cultivating the hillsides on a
more regular basis for small fruit gardens. Though there have been a
number of minor irrigation works carried out in the area since the 1930s,
the major change has been brought about by the development of the Uda
Walawe, a large-scale, long-term project which over the last twenty years
has opened considerable land to paddy cultivation, hitherto reserved for
chena. Associated with the irrigation project, large settlement projects
have been developed to provide lands for the landless Kandyans squeezed
over the years by the development of the estates, and to ease the over-
crowding of the densely populated south. Perhaps inevitably, those of the
local population without recognised and documented legal title have lost
access to areas which they regarded as theirs to cultivate by traditional
right. Lacking an effective 'voice' to represent their position to the new
bureaucracies set up to administer the development, they turned to the
UNP. Possibly their understanding of what the party could accomplish
on their behalf has been over-expectant and unrealistic, but they are
presently somewhat disenchanted with the UNP's ability to act in a
protective role. Among the *Goyigama*, the UNP was felt to be able to

rely on the support of the old-established *Goyigama* families living in *nindagama* in the fertile paddy-growing areas.

What seems to have been decisive in 1970 was the disenchantment of some part of the *Vahumpura* with a community leader who could not secure for the caste their traditional cultivable lands. As in Kalawana, for the depressed castes and the lower-status *Goyigama*, the party with the most radical ideology has come to seem the most advantageous representative.

Encouraged by the results yielded in these two electorates a major investigation in the eight electorates of Kegalle was undertaken. It was expected that the fluctuation in caste distribution among the electorates would relate positively to the caste of candidates elected and to their party, and that, as in Kalawana and Kolonne, the depressed castes' move away from caste-distinct representation towards representation by the most radical candidate presented, would be apparent.

From interviews, the percentage distribution of castes was indicated as shown in table 27. The identity of winning candidates by caste and party in each of the electorates has been as shown in table 28.

TABLE 27 *Percentage distribution of Sinhalese population by electorates and caste in Kegalle District, 1972*

	Caste				Total
	Goyigama	*Batgam*	*Vahumpura*	*Other*	
Dedigama	56	26	12	6	100.0
Galigomuwa	48	30	16	6	100.0
Kegalle	46	22	24	8	100.0
Rambukkana	47	30	16	7	100.0
Mawanella	55	18	16	11	100.0
Yatiyantota	46	43	8	3	100.0
Ruwanwella	46	21	27	6	100.0
Dehiowita	47	29	19	6	101.0

Note that the LSSP electorates are those in which the *Batgam* and *Vahumpura* combined form a higher percentage of the population than the *Goyigama*. Note also that in Dedigama, where the *Goyigama* appear to be in an absolute majority, the seat has been taken by a *Goyigama* UNP candidate. In Galigomuwa, which has nearly an overall majority of *Goyigama*, and Mawanella, which has an absolute majority, the candidates have been *Goyigama*, and the voting has followed the national swings between the parties. Yet what is the background to the difference

TABLE 28 *Caste and party of winning candidates at elections in the Kegalle District, 1960, 1965, 1970*

	July 1960		1965		1970	
	Caste	Party	Caste	Party	Caste	Party
Dedigama	G	UNP	G	UNP	G	UNP
Galigomuwa	G	SLFP	G	UNP	G	SLFP
Kegalle	G	SLFP	G	SLFP	G	SLFP
Rambukkana	B	SLFP	B	UNP	V	SLFP
Mawanella	G	SLFP	G	UNP	G	SLFP
Yatiyantota	G	LSSP	G	LSSP	G	LSSP
Ruwanwella	G	UNP	G	UNP	G	LSSP
Dehiowita	G	LSSP	G	LSSP	G	LSSP

between Yatiyantota and Rambukkana, both of which have substantial *Batgam* communities, that the former should return an LSSP member, but the latter return members of the non-*Goyigama* communities representing alternatively the SLFP and the UNP?

It is worth briefly describing these electorates, indicating their idiosyncrasies, and drawing on the historical memory of constituents to illustrate certain facets of voting behaviour. Such explanations as those the people offered were frequently didactic in an ethical sense as well as immediately illustrative; others seemed coloured by the delight of the raconteur in his telling, yet those who were interviewed revealed a spontaneous and vivid consciousness of the difference between the *honda minissu* (men of good lineage; good, pure *vangsa* – pedigree) and the mere *väda ḳārayo* (working people). Such a consciousness necessarily informed their assessment of what was appropriate behaviour politically, and the view from the extremes was widely divergent. Among those of higher status a strong sense of drawing together in defence of a position that fewer and fewer were willing openly to justify was apparent, coloured by a melancholy for the 'old days' when they did not have to contemplate the now disturbing personal consequences of changes whose first benefits had passed to them alone, together with a regret that in their home areas they still had responsibilities and duties, but could exercise few of the rights and enjoy few of the concomitant privileges of inherited status. Finally, they often revealed a fastidious involvement in the manipulation of resources, which began with the shrewd and knowledgeable calculation of the social bases of their political survival.

Such were the sentiments of the elite families in this part of the old Kandyan kingdom, in strong contrast to the elite families of the *Karava* or *Salagama* of the coast, whose communities are seeking greater political visibility, and who are consciously energetic in enabling their members to 'get on'. Nor were these the feelings of those leaders among the *Goyigama* who welcomed social change, saw it indeed as inevitable, and who sought to quicken its pace via Marxist policies of one kind or another. Their analysis of the social order was phrased in terms of class, their rhetoric proclaiming the familiar economic rationale for land nationalisation. Their terminology was close enough to the reality of the depressed castes' lives to obviate crude references to caste. Their message was expressed in terms of class conflict; their programme promised direct economic gains to the landless labourer and the exploited rural working classes. Yet it was assumed that such policies, such a party image, were none the less skilfully directed to none other than the depressed castes.[11]

For their own part, many of the depressed castes saw their choice much less clearly. As a generalisation it is true to depict their political motivation as, initially, a feeling of excitement that the opportunity to vote for a member of their own community would afford them real social and material benefit. These expectations seem to have been fairly swiftly disappointed, as they realised the enormity of the attitudinal change that was necessary, perhaps even as a prerequisite before significant progress could be made in other spheres. S. W. R. D. Bandaranaike and his land-slide of 1956 for a time seemed to herald such a change, and released enthusiasm and hope among the Kegalle communities. Subsequently, events led them to think that for the time being their best channel of advancement was through the good offices of a high-caste representative, either one personally disposed to aid their progress, or one who, in his party and declared policies, might reasonably be supposed to enhance their welfare generally. Most recently, a number of their younger members have grown impatient both with a political system that in effect, whether for procedural or cognitive reasons, seems to deny them direct expression of their grievances, and with the slow approach advocated by their disillusioned elders as the only way to achieve change from within – that is, by using the structure of caste, indeed the very people within that structure whose high status they intend in many respects to devalue.

The perceptions of the *Radala* of Sabaragamuwa and how the game of politics was played among them will be described in more detail in a subsequent chapter, and the political outlook of the frustrated young *Vahumpura* and *Batgam* is set out in detail in the chapter on the insurgency of 1971. In this chapter, these communities are treated more generally as electors in the constituencies of Kegalle.

Dedigama is known as the stronghold of the Senanayakes. Held by Dudley from the days of the State Council for the UNP, he had inherited

it from Sir Francis Molamure who had won it uncontested in 1931.
Sir Francis had held his successful legal practice locally, was an outstand-
ing national political figure, and was connected to some of the leading
Radala families in the district, such as the Eknaligodas and Mahawela-
tennes. He was himself married to Adeline Meedeniya, daughter of
Meedeniya, *Adigar* of Kegalle, and whose sister was married to Dr Don
Richard Wijewardene, founder of the influential Lake House Group of
newspapers. Sir Francis was imprisoned for contempt of court following
a testamentary case in which he was a beneficiary, and the Senanayake–
Wijewardene family and political caucus moved to have Dudley elected.
It is now commonly believed that Sir Francis was imprisoned for mis-
appropriation of funds, but his conviction on a purely technical charge
explains why at the time he was able to re-establish himself in politics so
easily and rise to be the first Speaker of the House of Representatives
(1947). Dudley lacked both the personal stature and local influence of
Sir Francis, and as an outsider he always faced considerable opposition in
Dedigama. Local residents, significantly, up to the time of his death in
July 1973, addressed him by the deference title of '*Hamumahataya*' of
the maritime districts, rather than by '*Bandara*', the deference title of the
Kandyan tradition.

Opposition to Dudley is commonly asserted to be based on antipathy to
the *Goyigama*, originally roused in 1936 when Sir John Kotelawala's
supporters are supposed to have physically prevented voters from the
Batgam and *Vahumpura* villages reaching the polling booths. In 1936
Dudley was contested by N. H. Keerthiratne standing openly as the
representative of the *Batgam* community. Felix Dias Bandaranaike,
Minister of Home Affairs, etc., recently referred to the indignities devised
by the Senanayake/Kotelawala combine for the lower castes in 1936. It
seems, for example, that latrine buckets were emptied into N. H.
Keerthiratne's house.[12]

With the Delimitation of 1946 the *Batgam* and *Vahumpura* strongholds in Dedigama were incorporated into Kegalle, leaving Dedigama
till 1959 overwhelmingly *Goyigama*. Dudley's large majorities at the
elections of 1947 and 1952 reflect this. In addition, by 1947 N. H.
Keerthiratne had joined the UNP and was accommodated as the party's
candidate at Kegalle. Dudley's position weakened after 1959 when the
seat, to his disadvantage, was redrawn. Many of his *Goyigama* strongholds went to Galigomuwa, and a large chunk of the old Ruwanwella
electorate and of Kegalle were brought in, including many *Vahumpura*
and *Batgam* villages that were opposed to him.

The year 1956 is the only one in which Dudley did not contest at the elections, having temporarily retired from politics. The candidates for both the SLFP and the UNP were *Goyigama* of prestigious families with local influence in the district, and in caste or family terms there was little to choose between them.[13] Here we can see party as being decisive, for the vote followed the national landslide to the SLFP/MEP, the SLFP candidate drawing, for the only time, a large part of the *Goyigama* support.

After 1959 no minority-caste candidate has stood at Dedigama, the SLFP *Goyigama* candidates drawing most of their support. Dudley won the seat at every election, though with increasingly slender majorities. On his death the seat passed to his nephew, Rukman Senanayake.[14]

Galigomuwa was created in 1959, largely from the old Dedigama seat. It has been contested by P. B. Balasuriya for the SLFP who won in 1960 and 1970, and Mrs Wimala Kannangara for the UNP who won in 1965, the swing thus following national patterns, though the voting has been marginal. Mrs Kannangara (who unsuccessfully contested Dedigama for the UNP in 1956) has local influence through the medical practice of her husband. She estimates that in 1965 she was able to draw some part of the *Batgam* support from the SLFP following Asoka Karunaratne's association with the UNP on leaving Mrs Bandaranaike in 1964. A leading member of the *Batgam* community, Karunaratne won neighbouring Rambukkana in 1965 for the UNP. By 1965 Philip Gunawardene, the 'father of socialism' in Lanka, had also joined the UNP and she considers that his move, too, had some influence in drawing support to the UNP.[15]

Kegalle, where the *Batgam* and *Vahumpura* combined come close to the *Goyigama* numerically, follows the Sabaragamuwa pattern. In 1947 and 1952 N. H. Keerthiratne, a leading member of the *Batgam*, won the seat as the representative of the minority castes. In 1956 Keerthiratne moved to Mawanella and at Kegalle the SLFP *Goyigama* won against the UNP *Goyigama* candidate. In 1960 Keerthiratne stood again at Kegalle for the UNP, and lost by just under 2,000 votes to the sitting SLFP member, P. B. Kalugalle. Keerthiratne's campaign was hindered by the fact that his younger brother, Asoka Karunaratne, was working for the SLFP in Rambukkana, and was becoming the more prominent in their community. His defeat[16] is interpreted as signifying that the caste vote remained with the party that seemed the most apt to serve their material cause, rather than following their caste representative into the UNP whose image, in terms of its leaders and attitudes, was less acceptable to them.

In 1965 Nimal Karunatillake, journalist and press agent for Dudley

Senanayake though earlier a supporter of S. W. R. D. Bandaranaike, challenged Kalugalle but was narrowly defeated. It was alleged that his family were related to the *Batgam* on his mother's side, though he himself was accepted as *Goyigama*. This, together with Asoka Karunaratne's association with the UNP in 1965, was said to have swung part of the community back to the UNP. The UNP also sought to win over some of the *Vahumpura* by the distribution of *beedi* (cigarette) licences.[17] In 1970 the vote went again to Kalugalle by a margin of 10,000, against a *Goyigama* UNP nominee.

In general the SLFP vote in Kegalle is seen as an anti-feudal expression by the minority castes against the *Radala* families of the area who have supported the UNP. The desertion of Keerthiratne by his caste is partly a consequence of his identification with the UNP. More particularly, it is noteworthy that many of his caste felt that his personal success, his partial acceptance in elite circles in Colombo, and his wealth, removed him as a fitting representative of his community. Unlike the *Karava* community, the gap between the wealthy individual and the common lot of the caste members is large among the minority castes and, paradoxically, it is widely, and sometimes strongly, argued among them that too great a success, and the enhanced status and privileges that wealth brings, disqualifies an individual to speak on their behalf. The distance can become too great between them for ready sympathy and identification and, the lesser members felt, it took their would-be leaders irrevocably beyond the economic and social class of the majority of the community.

Rambukkana, created in 1959, provides further insight into the complexities of caste voting. The contest is dominated by the very substantial *Batgam* vote, led in 1960 by Asoka Karunaratne into the SLFP. It can be regarded as one of the few minority-caste-distinct electorates allowed by the Delimitation (though I have shown the nature of the 'strong voice' allowed them in other electorates in Kegalle: it is notable that despite the very high concentration of minority caste in the district, seven of the eight are represented by *Goyigama*). The vote, in part support for a leading member of the community, was seen also as a vote against the 'feudal establishment' personified by the *Goyigama* UNP candidate, A. E. W. Beligodapitiya.[18]

When Asoka Karunaratne left Mrs Bandaranaike's government he stood in 1965 as an LPP–SLFSP candidate, a group which had a no-contest agreement with the UNP in some electorates. Under the UNP administration he became Minister of Social Services. He himself calculates that he took a good bit less than half the *Batgam* vote in that election.[19] Two other *Batgam* candidates stood, one as an Independent receiving 1,448 votes and one for the SLFP receiving 2,500 votes less than Karunaratne. As UNP candidate he received a large part of the *Goyigama* support. In 1970, standing again for the UNP, his minority-caste support passed almost completely from him to the SLFP and he lost by 4,000.

He is aware that as a man of substantial means he is regarded as belonging to the 'upper classes' by his community and cannot claim to be a caste-community leader in the manner, say, of N. U. Jayawardene, Bernard Soysa, and the Venerable Mädihé Pannaseeha for the *Durava*. He offers further explanation of minority-caste electoral behaviour by stressing that, in his experience, some of the *Batgam* prefer to become 'absorbed' either by migration and assumption of *Goyigama* status in a new area (which process may take more than one generation and migration)[20] or 'assimilated and raised up' by the *Goyigama* into groups and associations more nearly free of caste. They feel awkward in the concerted assertion of their caste against traditional claims, and tend to avoid the conspicuous confrontations on caste lines of public politics.[21]

D. L. F. Pedris, similarly placed among the *Vahumpura*, and in 1967 appointed to the Senate under the UNP, confirms Karunaratne's understanding.[22] He points out that no member of either caste was ever elected to the State Council nor did the two castes ever exercise much political pressure before Independence, despite the grant of universal suffrage as early as 1931. Again, despite a widespread education system (and universal free education from 1945), few members of the *Batgam* or *Vahumpura* apparently benefited. D. L. F. Pedris appeared before the Soulbury Commission of 1944–5 to outline the situation of his caste, and to ask that special provision should be made in the new constitution to overcome their difficulties. Sir Frederick Rees later wrote:

Two castes among the Sinhalese – the Bathgama and the Wahumpura – complained of the disabilities under which they laboured. They were denied, they said, equality of opportunity. Schools were not built in their villages. Their young men, even if they got high marks in a written test, were not appointed Divisional Revenue Officers. Only a few of their caste were employed as peons and police constables ... Naturally they were asked why they had not exercised greater political pressure under a system of universal suffrage and why it was that no member of either of the castes had been elected to the State Council. They attempted to answer these questions by alleging that electoral areas had been deliberately delimited to prevent them from being represented and that their names were often wilfully omitted from the register. It is more reasonable to infer that the great majority of them lacked education and passively accepted their social status. As one witness admitted 'indigenous minds have to observe caste'.[23]

Thus many vote for a *Goyigama*, preferably one who does not belong
to the local traditional hierarchy, seeking 'liberation' from their largely
caste-determined circumstances via anti-establishment leftist policies and
parties. The possibilities of this path were first demonstrated by S. W. R. D.
who made a tremendous impression on the minority castes wherever he
appeared by his disregard of traditional formality. He is well remembered
in Rambukkana for his unprecedented manner of campaigning. Instead
of summoning Karunaratne to meet him, or more likely his agent, as he
sat at the Rest House or on the verandah of some local notable, S. W. R. D.
called personally at Karunaratne's house and talked man to man of the
problems of the electorate. Here was dignity and honour unknown before
and it won many to the SLFP cause.

The impact of Bandaranaike among the depressed castes is reflected
vividly in their speech. For them, he became *Apē Agamäthithumā* – *our*
political leader; and the SLFP became *Apē Ānduva* – *our* government.
The sense of identification was very strong, very personal. The people of
the area illustrate the sense of it by describing in scorn the behaviour of
fashionably dressed UNP men, maybe wearing golf shoes or carrying
silver-knobbed canes, who, after a stroll round the electorate with the local
notable, would retire to the Rest House or the notable's verandah, shout
'Boy!' to the servant, and drink whisky. So for them, the UNP candidate
would be remote, alien, arrogant, and upper class. In contrast Bandaranaike's supporters trudged to the remotest villages on foot, across country
where there were no roads, hitching up their sarongs to cross the muddy
paddy fields. At the end of an exhausting day they would retire to the
back of some local run-down clapboard hotel, and say to the customers:
'*Gahapan machan addiäk*' – 'Come, let's have a shot' – and the arrack
bottle would pass round. Thus the SLFP members seemed to the *Batgam*
and *Vahumpura* to be accessible, familiar, unpatronising fellows who
knew what village life was like.

However, it is clear that many of the younger members of these communities have become disenchanted and impatient with such slow parliamentary possibilities which, by and large, seemed to them to be more
potential than actual. It is no coincidence that of the four villages most
involved in the 1971 insurgency in Galigomuwa, for example, the two
largest were chiefly *Batgam*.

Mawanella stands as a further example of the complexities and
subtleties of manipulation of caste by parties and candidates and the
response of the electorate. In 1956 Keerthiratne stood for the UNP and
lost, while the SLFP candidate C. R. Beligammana, an aristocrat from a
local family, and married to Don Charles Wijewardene's daughter (D. C.

being the brother of D. R. Wijewardene of the pro-UNP Associated Newspapers of Ceylon – Lake House – combine) won convincingly.

In 1960 Beligammana stood as an Independent, effectively splitting the *Goyigama* vote, and the *Goyigama* SLFP candidate, P. R. Ratnayake, was closely pressed by the UNP *Goyigama* candidate. By 1965 Beligammana had passed firmly into the UNP and took the vote with massive *Goyigama* support by a margin of 5,000. However, by 1970 Beligammana was firmly established as the candidate of the traditional *Goyigama* establishment, and the vote followed the national swing to the SLFP.

Mawanella has a large Moslem community, and though with little chance of electing their own candidate, they have put forward nominees at the elections. The only election in which they are considered to have voted decisively is in 1965 for the UNP, following Dudley Senanayake's wooing of their support.

Yatiyantota is somewhat outside the pattern, having been created in 1959 for Dr N. M. Perera, national leader of the LSSP, with a huge *Batgam* population out of Ruwanwella which Dr N. M. Perera had represented since 1936. N. M. wins on the radical appeals of the LSSP to the *Batgam* community and his substantial personal following. In addition, the not inconsiderable Sinhalese contingent among the labourers working on the rubber estates in the electorate come under the Democratic Workers' Congress which consistently advocates left-wing policies. Unable to draw anything but negligible support from the *Batgam*, George Kotelawala (a nephew of Sir John), retains a solid though small UNP vote. Though Yatiyantota is delimited so as to produce a strong caste vote, this caste basis has been manipulated in the language of class politics, and the policies of the Marxists have found a ready hearing.

It is interesting that the Marxist *sahodarayā*, or brotherhood, has evoked no such sympathetic linguistic phrases as Bandaranaike and the SLFP. In Yatiyantota, the *Batgam sahodari* – comrades – would never refer to N. M. Perera as *Aiyā* (Brother), though they refer to Mrs Bandaranaike as *Sirimā Akkā*, Sister Sirimavo. See for example, the following drily humorous verse:

> *Sirimā Akkā langa enavā*
> *Hāl sēru deka denavā*
> (Sister Sirimavo is coming along
> She gives the two measures of rice).[24]

Now, the normal deference locative between a *Batgam* and a *Radala* such as Mrs Bandaranaike is *Valawē Hamuduruvanē* (Lady of the ancestral house), or the specifically Kandyan locative: *Dingiri Hamuduruvanē*. For the *Batgam* to characterise such a person so familiarly and affectionately is strongly indicative of their response to the SLFP and its leaders.

It is important to remember, too, that Sabaragamuwa, especially towards the south and east, was the heartland of Sinhalese feudalism, and the bastion remained unchallenged until the 1930s when the LSSP began to campaign on behalf of the 'backward classes' in the area. The LSSP's historic role is not forgotten today in Yatiyantota and Ruwanwella, and the affection for Mrs Bandaranaike is the greater among the depressed castes in the province as she is herself a *Radala*, from one of the great feudal families.

Ruwanwella, N. M. Perera's former stronghold, retains a large non-*Goyigama* population. The *Goyigama* UNP candidate won by small margins in 1960 and 1965, challenged by the LSSP. The LSSP candidate succeeded in 1970. The voting pattern is considered by the electorate as a consequence of the *Goyigama* vote lying largely with the UNP and the non-*Goyigama* with the LSSP, the swing between the two being determined by national events capable of moving a small part of the anti-establishment *Goyigama* and the preferences of the non-*Goyigama*. In Dehiowita, too, the LSSP is strong, the interpretation of their support following that of Ruwanwella. The electorate has a small *Karava* trading population, and in 1956 the UNP put up a *Karava* candidate. In 1960 the UNP put forward A. F. Wijemanne, of elitist family and married to J. R. Jayawardene's cousin (J. R. was second-in-command to Dudley and at his death, took over the leadership of the UNP). Wijemanne lost by a small margin; the UNP challenge was strong in 1965 too, and the LSSP candidate won again only with a narrow advantage. In 1970 the LSSP candidate increased his majority in the swing to the United Front nationally.

The previous chapter indicated the apparent caste bias to the *Goyigama* in terms of representatives; in this chapter the question has been, who benefits in party terms? Incautiously, one would conclude the UNP, the 'party of the *Goyigama*', but in these electorates at least one has been able to test this assumption a little more clearly. For though the SLFP's *Goyigama* candidates often have been no lower in status or more deficient in background than the UNP's, their image, policies, and social identity have been taken to favour the exploited and oppressed – the common man of Bandaranaike's speeches – and thus they have drawn the low-caste support which the UNP is able to command only infrequently and exceptionally.

In describing these relationships there is a risk of sounding too definite, as if all members of a caste acted in one way, determinately, prescriptively, indeed as if the relationship between caste, representative, and party were a simple, linear, one-to-one correlation. This, of course, is not true, and the attempts at description and analysis presented here must be taken as they are, crude first steps in the study of political change and alignment, and the evolution of party strength within a traditional society operating a sophisticated system of parliamentary democracy inherited from a quite different culture.

5

Consequences and implications
at the national level

The Delimitation of 1976

The *Report of the Delimitation Commission* of 1976 explicitly recognises the caste pressures indicated in the previous chapters, and also makes provision for population changes and ethnic claims in the emptier areas of the centre and east, and the high-density areas of population in the south and west. Colombo Central, Beruwela, Harispattuwa, Nuwara Eliya–Maskeliya, Batticaloa, and Pottuvil become multi-member constituencies, Colombo Central and Nuwara Eliya–Maskeliya returning three members and the others, two members. In the Colombo District, boundary changes have been made at Kaduwela and Dehiwela, and Colombo South has been divided into Colombo East and Colombo West. New electorates have been created at Ratmalana, Biyagama, and Maharagama. In the Central Province and Kandy District, changes have been made at Harispattuwa, Pata Dumbara, and Uda Dumbara. Most significant for the arguments of this book are the new electorates created at:

Wellawaya	Moneragala District	Uva Province
Aranayake	Kegalle District	Sabaragamuwa
Panduwasnuwara	Kurunegala District	North-Western Province
Anuradhapura East ⎫ Anuradhapura West ⎬	Anuradhapura District	North-Central Province
Tangalle	Hambantota District	Southern Province
Karandeniya	Galle District	Southern Province

The Report makes the point that it is not the absolute or overall number of a minority group that counts but whether or not they are concentrated in substantial numbers in a locality. It notes that minority groups not identified by race or religion 'are not always capable of easy identification'.[1] Paragraph 47 of the mimeographed press release on the Report goes on to say:

The 1959 Delimitation Commission took note of such groups in the so-called 'under-privileged concentrations' in certain Provinces in the delimitation of electoral districts. These arrangements have more or less been kept intact.

Representations were received from the Southern and Sabaragamuwa Provinces on behalf of certain other similar minority groups. The existence of substantial concentrations of such groups in these areas has made it possible for the Commission to accede to the requests made.

It is clear that the Commission was referring to Aranayake and Karandeniya, where substantial numbers of *Batgam* and *Vahumpura* reside – the latter also in Wellawaya, though the Commission does not specifically mention Uva.[2] Marginal changes to boundaries in the Kandyan highlands have removed or made negligible the lower-caste 'threat' to the upper-class *Goyigama*; this should be to the advantage of the UNP, but a number of the Kandyan *Goyigama* may choose to follow Mrs Bandaranaike into the SLFP. The SLFP, the CP, and the LSSP are left to compete in the 'non-*Radala*' electorates for the vote of the depressed castes.

Broader political considerations also came into play. Part of the price the SLFP had had to pay for securing the co-operation of the CP and LSSP in the formation of the United Front prior to the 1970 elections was the inclusion in the UF programme of fundamental constitutional reform of their demand that the inequality in the adult vote under the existing system of delimitation be rectified. Colvin R. de Silva (LSSP Minister of Constitutional Affairs), in a broadcast over the national radio on 10 September 1970, specifically listed the bias which favoured the remoter, up-country, rural areas as one of the shortcomings of the Soulbury constitution which the government intended to correct.

Yet of all the deficiencies identified in that broadcast, the existing system of delimitation was the only one which passed unchanged into the new constitutional structure. The method of delimiting constituencies had been specifically designed by the architects of the Soulbury constitution to counter the supposed radical urban vote, while the removal of the majority of the Indian estate workers from the electoral registers in the early 1950s (only slightly restored by the enfranchisement of some 300,000 under the Bandaranaike/Shastri Pact of 1960) further increased the value of the rural up-country vote at the expense of voters in the densely populated southern and western constituencies – the heartland of CP and LSSP influence. As events turned out over the years the SLFP had established itself precisely in those areas favoured by the Soulbury system of delimitation. It is not surprising, therefore, that the new constitution of 1972 which effected major changes in other directions should have observed the realities of its power base and left the existing system of delimitation unchanged: its survival reflected the dominant position of the SLFP within the UF and in parliament.

Once they had split from the UF, the CP and the LSSP freely criticised the government's failure to correct the bias. The government in fact increased it still further when it introduced in February 1975 the First Amendment to the new constitution which required the Delimitation Commissioners (appointed in August 1974) to take into account a new population criterion of 90,000 instead of 75,000 persons. The old limit would have expanded the National State Assembly membership from 151 to 220, an increase which the government rejected on grounds of cost. In the light of the 1971 Census figures, a new population criterion of 90,000 persons was judged to be reasonable, increasing the number of electorates to 143, which after adjustments for area weightage produced a total National State Assembly membership of 168. The First Amendment did not markedly change the pattern of distribution of seats, but it did increase the bias against the densely populated areas, the Western Province being most seriously affected. The CP and LSSP claimed that it was a measure 'detrimental to the interests of the working classes'.[3]

The Amendment also came under attack from the Moslems and the few thousand enfranchised Indian Tamils, since any increase in the average number of voters per electorate would tend to dilute their electoral strength in areas where they were concentrated – a tendency that did not pass unnoticed by the smaller Sinhalese castes. The Delimitation Commission sought to meet this criticism by the creation of the additional multi-member constituencies.

The left-wing parties and caste

It is curious that despite the CP's and LSSP's deliberate appeal to the lower castes of the highlands and the non-*Goyigama* coastal castes they are almost universally referred to as winning an *urban* and a *class* vote. It is by no means clear that the Marxist left's electoral strength can be validly characterised in such terms, however. At the 1970 elections, for example, which marked a massive swing to the United Front in terms of seats, nearly all the major towns were held by the UNP: Kandy, Negombo, Galle, Colombo North, one of Colombo South's two seats, two of Colombo Central's three seats. (Jaffna and Trincomalee in the north and east were both held by the Federal Party, at that time pro-UNP.)

Nor are the electorates which they can consider theirs predominantly urban. Taking the CP electorates in 1970, only Matara, Colombo Central, and Ratgama can be considered non-rural; of these, both Matara (B. Y. Tudawe – *Durava*) and Ratgama (M. G. Mendis – *Salagama*) have large *Durava* and *Salagama* caste votes. Of the remaining three CP electorates, Akuressa has been held by Dr S. A. Wickremasinghe since 1936, and he clearly has an overwhelmingly personal following. Sarath Muttetuwegama in Kalawana draws on a tradition of family influence in the area: his father was *Rate Mahatmeya* of Kalawana. Aelian Nanayakkara in Kamburupitiya benefits from the influence of Dr Wickremasinghe in the neighbouring electorate.

The LSSP electorates similarly draw on a caste vote or personal influence. For example, Colombo South, Bernard Soysa's electorate, has a large *Durava* vote. Yatiyantota and Ruwanwella, as has been shown, both have a large non-*Goyigama* vote and are influenced by Dr N. M. Perera's standing nationally. Similarly, Kolonne, Kiriella, and Dehiowita have large non-*Goyigama* populations. Agalawatte and Bulathsinhala are situated in the home areas of Anil and Mangala Moonesinghe's family; they are themselves grand-nephews of Anagarika Dharmapala, a renowned Buddhist and nationalist leader of the late nineteenth and early twentieth century. Mangala, in 1970 was elected the LSSP MP for Bulathsinhala; Anil passed Agalawatte to one of the leading LSSP politicians, Colvin R. de Silva, when he was unseated following an election petition. Panadura, Moratuwa, Kalutara and Ambalangoda, four south-coast towns, vote more or less consistently for the LSSP: all four have large *Karava* populations: all four LSSP candidates in 1970 were *Karava* (Leslie Goonewardene, Wimalsiri de Mel, Chomondeley Goonewardene, and L. C. de Silva). Leslie Goonewardene, MP for Panadura, in addition has much personal influence in the area. Vivienne Goonewardene, at Dehiwela–Mt Lavinia, gains support from the sizeable *Durava* population there through the influence of Bernard Soysa. At Borella, Kusella Abeyawardhena, herself *Karava*, gains votes from the small *Karava* and large *Salagama* population. In addition, as LSSP member she has the support of some of the Moslem population of Sri Lankan Moors through the Islamic Socialist Front. At Kottawa, adjacent to Avissawella which was Philip Gunawardene's seat, Philip's first cousin Chandra Gunasekera is the LSSP MP. Wilfred Senanayake at Homagama similarly benefited from the influence of Philip (who was a founder member of the LSSP). The LSSP MP for Deniyaya in 1970 (S. Dahanayake) was formerly a member of the SLFP and, at the last moment only, he switched to the LSSP ticket. P. W. de Silva at Balapitiya again draws on a caste (*Salagama*) vote, and also benefits from his relationship as son-in-law to Colvin R. de Silva. W. Neale de Alwis at Baddegama has no caste vote but has personal influence beyond the electorate as one-time Chairman of the Southern Province Planters' Association.

It is clearly not the case to say of the CP and LSSP simply that their support is largely urban and working class. First, the UNP has a solid base in the towns; secondly, a number of CP and LSSP electorates are non-urban; thirdly, in many cases, even in the towns, their vote may be seen as in fact a caste vote; and finally, it is clear that their support is to be found largely among the non-*Goyigama* or lesser *Goyigama* families.

Indeed, the leadership of the CP and LSSP reflects their non-*Goyigama* representation although the head of each is a *Goyigama*. Dr Wickrema-singhe, *Goyigama*, leader of the CP, is married to an Englishwoman; their daughter is married to a *Karava*. Pieter Keuneman, in 1970 Secretary to the CP, is a Burgher; he married first an Austrian then an English wife. B. Y. Tudawe is *Durava* and M. G. Mendis is *Salagama*. H. G. S. Ratnaweera, ex-editor of the party newspaper, *Aththa (Truth)*, is *Karava*. The President of the CP Youth League, Sarath Muttetuwe-gama, though himself *Goyigama*, is married to a *Salagama*. Of the LSSP Ministers in 1970, Dr N. M. Perera is *Goyigama*, but Leslie Goone-wardene is *Karava* and Colvin R. de Silva is *Salagama*. (Philip Guna-wardene, 'father of the revolution' and founder of the LSSP, was *Goyigama*, married to a *Hunu*.)

An interesting movement of important party members from the left into the UNP has occurred since 1956. Philip Gunawardene, Robert Goonewardene (and his wife Kusuma), and Lakshman Rajapakse, of the VLSSP, and Percy Wickremasinghe (Dr Wickremasinghe's brother) of the CP have moved. Nimal Karunatillake, I. M. R. A. Iriyagolla, K. M. P. Rajaratne and his wife Kusuma, and W. Dahanayake have similarly all shifted from the SLFP into the UNP. The significance is that they are all *Goyigama*, and were all members of the 1956 'revo-lution' who have moved into their 'natural' base, the UNP.

Neither the CP nor the LSSP has developed as a mass party, nor captured substantial votes among the urban working classes or small farmers and landless rural poor. (It is interesting that Philip Guna-wardene's MEP – an amalgam of personalities and Buddhist campaigners – both in July 1960 and 1965 polled approximately the same number of votes as the CP, despite the CP's far greater organisational and financial resources.) Both have won electoral success on the back of the SLFP's victories, dependent on no-contest pacts with the SLFP or joint pro-grammes. In turn, the SLFP under Mrs Bandaranaike has turned to the LSSP – and to a lesser extent the CP – when in power, though the 'coalition tactic' has been a troublesome one for all three. The inclusion of the LSSP in her Cabinet in 1964 led to her downfall in 1965, and the 1970 United Front broke up in 1975 with the expulsion of the LSSP. The *raison d'être* of their uneasy alliance lies in the SLFP's need to retain some sort of control over the urban population during periods of rising domestic inflation, and while following policies designed to boost rice production in the countryside at the same time as controlling consumer prices in the towns. The CP and the LSSP have many times shown their ability to call out the public sector trade unions (though clearly many trade unionists vote for the UNP or SLFP at elections) to put pressure on the government (without the necessity to use the strike as a 'political weapon' as such, for there have been compelling economic reasons why urban labour should protest at such measures as, for example, the attempt to cut the rice ration in 1962; the Finance Minister, Felix Dias Bandaranaike, was forced to resign and the full ration was restored). The LSSP and the CP, recognising their inability to form a government on their own, use the association with the SLFP as a means to obtain a share in government and policy-making, whilst reserving the 'right' to withdraw whenever they feel the need to maintain ideological purity or to contain criticism from the more radical of their own supporters over the direction of government policy.

The reasons why the lower castes of the highlands in some electorates vote left – an expression of anti-feudal sentiment and a demand for greater economic equality – have been indicated in previous chapters, and the radicalism of the south and west littoral will be taken up again in the chapter on the 1971 insurgency. Here just a few elaborations will be made to indicate the left's record as advocates of the 'working classes'. The early years of the CP and LSSP were characterised by the fissiparity most left-wing parties display (Dr Wickremasinghe began as a founder member of the LSSP), but they consistently put forward in pre-Independence days a programme of anti-colonialist measures and criticism of 'international capital'. Their conception of 'socialist democracy' was influenced by the teachings of Harold Laski, who had guided a number of future CP and LSSP leaders studying at the London School of Economics. Nationalisation of the 'commanding heights' of the economy was a major element, complemented by major land reform in the countryside. S. W. R. D. Bandaranaike began to carry out a number of their demands, but, as noted in chapter 1, his measures did not satisfy the left. Mrs Bandaranaike has been more amenable to their demands, carrying out the nationalisation of tea, rubber, and coconut plantations, and imposing a land ceiling on individual holdings of paddy and other agricultural lands since coming to power in 1970.[4]

Yet though promising a socialist revolution and the overthrow of the Colombo elites and feudal elements, by associating with precisely these people in government, the LSSP and CP have, over the last fifteen or so years, become compromised in the eyes of their 'natural' constituency among the young, and their percentage of the vote at general elections has declined. Furthermore, it has become evident that the rewards of government and the fruits of patronage, even under policies broadly designed to help the rural poor and urban labour, have been governed at the local level of distribution by the old considerations of influence and status as much as by need. In a reinforcing process, too few of the poor have believed that the secular ideology of the CP and LSSP would really break the traditional attitudes and relationships for the CP and LSSP nationally to carry sufficient weight to upset the control of the UNP and SLFP and their exploitation of traditional sentiment. And all the while, of course, both the left parties have been using exactly similar tactics to manipulate or capture lower-caste and anti-*Goyigama* feeling. The one instrument that they have eschewed so far is the deliberate founding of family networks and the use of kinship.

MPs and Cabinets

If behaviour at the constituency level has been as presented here, one might expect not only that consideration of the same factors occurs at the parliamentary and executive levels, but also that the consequences of such electoral behaviour should be apparent in the membership of parties, Cabinets, and lobbies.

TABLE 29   *Percentage distribution of caste among MPs, 1947–70*

Election year	Sinhalese castes							Tamils/ Moors/ Others	Total
	G	S	K	D	V	B	Other		
1947	50.5	4.2	9.4	1.1	1.1	1.1	4.2	28.4	100.0
1952	60.0	4.2	8.4	1.1	1.1	1.1	3.1	21.0	100.0
1956	58.9	5.3	8.4	2.1	–	1.1	3.1	21.1	100.0
July 1960	57.6	6.6	8.6	1.3	1.3	2.6	2.0	19.9	99.9
1965	61.6	3.3	7.3	1.3	2.0	4.0	2.0	18.5	100.0
1970	62.4	3.3	7.9	1.3	2.6	1.3	3.3	17.9	100.0

Source: identities supplied by politicians and party activists, and cross-checked by caste leaders.

The percentage distribution of caste among MPs since 1947 is as shown in table 29. This table charts a number of points of interest and confirms the processes outlined previously. The *Goyigama*, in an absolute majority, and unassailably the single largest community, appear to be somewhat over-represented in terms of their estimated population in the island as a whole. Note that the *Salagama* gain strength with the emergence of the SLFP in 1956 and 1960, but fall back sharply thereafter. The increased impact of the *Vahumpura* and *Batgam* and other depressed or numerically tiny castes after 1956 in the last three general elections is clear, too. Another major political change is shown in the sharp drop in the percentage under the 'Tamils/Moors/Others' heading, consequent on the removal of citizenship and hence voting rights from most of the Indian estate-labour population. Affecting most the up-country areas, the beneficiaries appear to have been the *Goyigama*.

TABLE 30   *Percentage caste distribution of candidates, 1947–70*

Election year	Sinhalese castes							Tamils/ Moors/ Others	No infor- mation	Total
	G	S	K	D	V	B	Other			
1947	46.2	4.5	12.3	1.4	3.1	2.2	1.7	27.5	1.1	100.0
1952	51.4	4.7	14.5	1.4	2.4	2.0	1.7	20.2	1.7	100.0
1956	52.6	3.2	11.2	1.6	1.6	1.9	1.6	19.5	6.8	100.0
July 1960	56.7	4.1	9.0	1.0	1.8	2.3	1.3	15.5	8.3	100.0
1965	52.9	3.6	8.4	1.3	5.6	3.8	1.3	22.6	0.5	100.0
1970	45.0	5.8	11.1	1.1	3.9	2.4	1.8	28.4	0.5	100.0

Source: identities supplied by politicians and party activists, and cross-checked by caste leaders.

If the caste distribution of candidates presenting themselves for election is percentaged, the picture in table 30 emerges. This is even more interesting. Note the number of 'unknowns' who emerged in 1956, encouraging more to enter the fray in 1960. By 1965 the number of those about whom nothing or very little is known begins to drop back, leaving the 1970 contest once more a contest between locally and nationally visible personalities. (It is not the case, either, that these 'unknowns' are largely members of the depressed castes, for these being so few, those that do stand are well known by their community, if not by others.)

But the major interest emerges if this table is compared to the caste distribution of MPs. The percentage of *Goyigama* being elected is decidedly higher than their proportionate distribution among candidates. (There were very few non-*Goyigama* Sinhalese in the State Council between 1931 and 1947. The proportion of non-*Goyigama* Sinhalese in the parliaments of 1947 to 1970 reflects the increase in the number, and reduction in size in terms of area, of electorates – as electorates become smaller it becomes easier to elect non-*Goyigama* candidates or at least to carve out electorates to accommodate them.) The proportionate number of *Sala-*

gama being elected was higher in 1956 and 1960 than their distribution among candidates, but their representation has fallen off since, with a relatively disproportionate number being elected in 1970. Very importantly, over the six elections the *Karava* have had proportionately more candidates than they have achieved representatives. Equally noteworthy is the comparative underelection of the *Vahumpura* and *Batgam* candidates.

The ebb and flow of caste voting, the attempts of castes to achieve representation, and the complaints of the non-*Goyigama* that the formal, procedural system, for various reasons, tends to operate against them – these trends and perceptions are reflected and summarised here in a most striking way.

The same patterns are to be found in the caste composition of Cabinets. The reliance on the *Goyigama* and Tamils of the Kotelawala Cabinets in the 1950s, and the total absence of Tamil members in the years of Sinhalese assertion, is marked, a Tamil returning to an SLFP government only in 1970. The sudden inclusion of *Salagama* members in S. W. R. D.'s Cabinets, the appointment of Asoka Karunaratne to the UNP Cabinets of 1965–70, and the reciprocal appointment of the *Vahumpura* member by the SLFP-led United Front after the elections in 1970, should also be noted.

Caste lobbies

The *Salagama, Karava,* and *Durava* representation in parliament deserves finer elucidation, for these three communities have come to operate recognised and consciously formed lobbies. Their political base extends beyond parliament to the spheres of commerce, the professions, and the administration, to form cohesive interest groups. Acting as representatives of their community interests, their alignments on matters of policy have at times cut across nominal party adherence; at the least they form points of access to the higher administration and other elite centres in national life for their community members.

Neither the *Vahumpura* nor the *Batgam,* for reasons mentioned previously, conduct their community life in this way; their leaders remain individuals operating in the higher *Goyigama* circles. In addition, the *Vahumpura,* who have a relatively close relationship with the *Goyigama* traditionally (for example, in most areas sharing the same seating), have preferred to operate, if at all, through the *Goyigama* at the elite level. The *Batgam,* on the other hand, who have a very distant traditional relationship with the *Goyigama* (still having to take a lower seat or remain stand-

TABLE 31 *Cabinet membership by caste and party, 1947–70*

Party	Year Cabinet formed	Sinhalese castes							Moor	Tamil	Other[a]	Total
		G	S	K	D	V	B	Other[b]				
UNP	1947	8	1	–	–	–	–	2	–	2	1	14
UNP	1952	10	1	–	–	–	–	–	1	2	–	14
UNP	1954	10	–	–	–	–	–	–	1	2	–	13
UNP	1955	10	–	1	–	–	–	–	1	2	–	14
MEP	1956	9	2	2	–	–	–	–	–	1	–	13
MEP	1958	10	2	2	–	–	–	–	1	1	–	15
MEP	1959	11	3	2	–	–	–	–	1	1	–	17
UNP	Mar. 1960	5	–	2	–	–	–	–	1	–	–	8
SLFP	July 1960	7	1	1	1	–	–	–	1	–	–	11
UNP	Mar. 1965	12	1	1	–	–	1	–	1	1	–	17
UNP	Jan. 1968	12	1	2	–	–	1	1	1	1	–	19
SLFP/UF	1970	13	2	2	–	1	–	–	1	1	1	21

[a] 1947: 1 Malay. 1970: 1 Burgher.
[b] 1947: 1 Hena, 1 Himna. 1968: 1 Himna, a sub-caste associated with the *Salagama*.

ing in the presence of the *Goyigama* in most areas), have not as yet successfully penetrated elite circles to any marked extent.

The *Goyigama* for their part obviously have no such pressure to generate lobby formation; they tend to divide among themselves at the elite level along the lines of family groups (with fluid shifts of partisanship within the kinship network), between the Kandyan and low-country interests on particular matters, and behind the personal authority of party leaders.

The *Salagama* community became prominent as a political lobby *pari passu* with the formation and growth of the SLFP. They turned to the SLFP partly because the UNP managed to affront three of the leading *Salagama* politicians of the 1940s: H. Sri Nissanka, QC, C. P. de Silva, and Sir Lalitha Rajapakse, QC. H. Sri Nissanka, ex-Buddhist monk, educated at Oxford, and a leader of the Criminal Bar in Lanka, entered politics as an ardent Buddhist–nationalist, which in Lanka is not incompatible with a profession of socialism of the 'welfare democratic' variety, successfully contesting Kurunegala as an 'Independent Socialist' in 1947. In no way a caste contest, Nissanka benefited from the split in the UNP vote between two formidable candidates standing under the UNP label. (None the less, considerable *Salagama* commercial interests in the field of bus transport in Kurunegala may have been of some influence.) He stood for the position of Speaker in the new parliament but was defeated by the UNP candidate, Sir Francis Molamure, who had the full backing of D. S. Senanayake himself.

C. P. de Silva was appointed Director of Land Development, as a trusted and loyal official under D. S. Senanayake who held the post of Minister of Agriculture in the 1947 parliament. He was transferred by Dudley ostensibly for failing to carry out Senanayake land policy; allegedly he was supposed, as director of the dry-zone colonisation schemes, to be bringing *Salagama* families from Balapitiya to the resettlement areas around Polonnaruwa. In this way, it was suggested, C. P. de Silva was easing the problems of landlessness for his own community. (C. P. de Silva had been very much D. S.'s man. When Minister he was largely instrumental in getting a statue of D. S. erected at the bund of Gal Oya tank. Dudley never got on particularly well with his father's trusted Civil Servants, partly because they constantly reminded him of his father's policies.) Sir Lalitha Rajapakse held the post of Minister of Justice under the first Senanayake Cabinets but was dismissed by Sir John Kotelawala in 1953.

These three turned to the SLFP and took with them the support of a large part of their community. At the 1952 elections Sri Nissanka lost his seat at Kurunegala, but C. P. de Silva successfully contested Polonnaruwa for the first time. The lobby was strengthened by the appointment of Gunasena de Soysa as Secretary to the Cabinet Planning Committee (subsequently Chief Planning Commissioner and later a senior Civil Servant in the Ministry of Defence and Foreign Affairs).

In the 1956 landslide the *Salagama* won seats for the MEP at Polonnaruwa, Ambalangoda–Balapitiya, Wellawatte–Galkissa, and Ja-ela. C. P. de Silva was made Minister of Lands and Land Development and Stanley de Zoysa became Minister of Finance. It was at this point that the lobby began to operate as an effective unit. It was most influential between 1960 and 1964, when nearly all the land-development projects – at the time the major development sphere – are alleged to have benefited *Salagama* interests. The lobby had ten members in the House of Representatives and four Senators in the Upper House, including an LSSP and a UNP member. It encompassed two puisne judges, and a Commissioner of assizes; the Deputy Inspector-General of Police, the Permanent Secretary to the Ministry of Defence, the Director of Irrigation, and the Ambassador to the United States; and in the commercial sphere, the owner/chairmen of three powerful trading and manufacturing companies.

Its political influence waned, however, when C. P. de Silva moved into opposition to Mrs Bandaranaike in December 1964, leading to her downfall in early 1965. Thereafter it re-formed less powerfully under the UNP. It remained extremely influential in key commercial areas of government with the chairmanship of two nationalised transport industries and retaining control of the Ministry of Lands and Land Development under C. P. de Silva. Sir Lalitha Rajapakse was appointed High Commissioner to the UK. The 1970 parliament held six *Salagama* MPs (three SLFP, two LSSP, and one CP) but the lobby itself has been cut off from positions of patronage and its commercial interests have declined somewhat.

The *Salagama*, unlike the *Karava*, are not divided on religious lines. For example, Stanley de Zoysa (Catholic) and C. P. de Silva (Buddhist), both members of the 1956 MEP Cabinet, voted consistently together, both assenting to the Buddhist Commission Report.

The *Durava* forms a small and compact business and commercial community. Its leader is generally held to be N. U. Jayawardene, the leading merchant banker in the island, with interests in textile manufacture, the coconut oil and fibre trade, real estate, tourism, and the import trade. Buddhist interest in the community is led by the Ven. Mädihé Pannaseeha, influential among the wealthy Colombo Buddhists who attend the Vajiramaya Temple in Bambalapitiya, and in his own sect, the *Amara-*

pura, as the *Maha Nayake Thero* (high clerical officer) of the *Amarapura Siri Dhammanrakshika Nikaya* (Mihiripenna). Parliamentary support since 1970 has been held by Bernard Soysa, LSSP MP for Colombo South, who, as Chairman of the Public Accounts Committee, has access to the higher administration and Civil Service.

Though the community is now important in the building and construction fields, its original caste occupation was toddy-tapping. Dr N. M. Perera's (LSSP) free toddy-tapping proposal in his 1964 Budget was one of the issues which split Mrs Bandaranaike's government; Bernard Soysa strongly supported the proposal against the opposition of the *Goyigama* and the *Karava* Buddhists.

In order to clarify the nature of caste lobby behaviour, it is worth while describing the 'Vavasseur Affair' which broke under the UNP government in 1968 following a Customs raid on one of N. U. Jaya-wardene's companies. The firm was heavily fined; the case was subsequently fought up to the Privy Council level.

It was an important affair, being the first time a Rs 5 million fine had been imposed, and usually it would be the LSSP who would raise the issue in parliament (see, for example, LSSP moves against the Associated Newspapers of Ceylon Ltd. They first aired allegations against the Group in 1969, forcing an Inquiry in 1971). But it was Ronnie de Mel, *Karava* and SLFP, who launched a lashing attack in the House against N. U. Jayawardene.[5] Bernard Soysa then spoke on N. U. Jayawardene's behalf, stating clearly the basis of his support: 'Now I want to make it quite clear to this House that the particular person (N. U. Jayawardene) who was named today by the Hon. Member for Devinuwara (Ronnie de Mel) happens to be by connection a kinsman of mine . . . on the basis of being a kinsman of mine he attempted to show some part of his case to me.'[6] Dr N. M. Perera intervened to check the debate.[7] On their return to power in 1970 an LSSP Inquiry Committee secured the transfer of the individual at the head of the Customs at the time of the raid. Finally, the Attorney-General moved to withdraw the case against N. U. Jayawardene, the Privy Council having held with N. U. Jayawardene on a technicality.

In such instances the nature of the caste lobby can be seen, functioning to protect its community interests, at times acting outside or across the party line, at times using party affiliation to secure protection. It is generally believed that the Vavasseur affair was instrumental in turning the *Durava* community against the UNP government for the 1970 elections. The affair evoked memories of the early 1950s, when Sir John Kotelawala, UNP Prime Minister, dismissed N. U. Jayawardene in 1953 from his position as Governor of the Central Bank. It was from this point that the *Durava* began to form and operate a lobby. The lobby in 1974 had two members in the House, three permanent secretaries, two additional permanent secretaries, and a senior assistant secretary in the higher administration, and the Managing Director of the nationalised textile corporation.

The *Karava* lobby is the most extensive, heavily involved in trade, commerce, and industry as well as in the professions and the administration. Unlike the *Salagama* and *Durava*, it is divided into Christian, largely Catholic, and Buddhist blocs.

The Christian bloc is, in general, the wealthier, better educated, and the more westernised. Their commercial and business interests tend to be powerful and extensive concerns dealing in the modern sectors of the economy, with strong traditions of enterprise in the technological and consumer sectors, and they seized the opportunities created under the UNP between 1965 and 1970 by the regulation of trading through the Open General Licence and Foreign Exchange Entitlement Certificate scheme. The 1970 Chamber of Commerce had as its President a *Karava* Christian and as its Secretary a *Karava* Buddhist married to a Christian. The Chairmen of Brown's Group Ltd, Mackwoods Ltd, Richard Peiris Ltd, the Yahala Group Ltd, and Pegasus Reef Ltd, five of the major commercial companies in Lanka, are *Karava* Christians.

The majority of the south-west coast fishermen, especially in the belt from Negombo to Puttalam, are *Karava* Catholics and 'other Christians' (the Buddhists having an aversion to the deliberate slaughter which fishing involves – though not necessarily to the eating of fish). It is no coincidence that the permanent secretaries to the Ministry in charge of Fisheries (and Trade and Commerce) usually have been *Karava* Christians. The religious support was commanded by Lakdasa de Mel, Metropolitan of Calcutta, and by Harold de Soysa, one-time Bishop of Colombo. (Lakdasa de Mel died in 1976, Harold de Soysa in 1971.)

The Buddhist wing of the *Karava* lobby is strong in the university, the professions, and the administration. Its outlook tends to be conservative, traditionalist, and narrowly nationalist. It has two strands of influence. One might loosely be termed the Buddhist intelligentsia, of immense influence in the early years of Independence, led by men such as N. Q. Dias, a Buddhist nationalist prominent in the 1956 campaign, Permanent Secretary to the Ministry of Defence and External Affairs 1960–4, and High Commissioner to India, 1970; the late Dr Ananda Nimalasuriya, Buddhist nationalist, member of the Public Services Commission 1960–4, and reappointed in 1970 till his death; and L. H. Mettananda, ex-principal of the eminent Buddhist school, Ananda College, and ardent publicist for the Buddhist nationalist cause. They have had great influence among the professional and administrative strata. Their spiritual home is Panadura/Ambalangoda, an area of strong Buddhist activism and *Sangha* dynamism.

The other strand relates to the *Karava* retail trading community who have outlets throughout the island. Usually small *mudalalis*, these indigenous traders rarely extend their operations beyond the accumulation of money to become commercial entrepreneurs on the scale of the *Karava* Christians. They tend to follow the lead of the *Karava* Buddhist intelligentsia rather than that of the Christian big-business circles. In favour of economic nationalism and austere living, they incline politically to the Buddhist–Marxist left. (Note that Panadura and Ambalangoda regularly return Trotskyists at elections though both electorates are strongholds of *Karava* Buddhist nationalism.)

The Christian/Buddhist division is reflected in the lobby's political inclinations, the Christians tending to be identified with the UNP and the Buddhists with the SLFP. Mrs Bandaranaike has relied heavily on the *Karava* Buddhists in her administration, as she has on the Kandyan *Goyigama*, while the *Karava* Christians and the low-country *Goyigama* have been identified with the UNP's administrations. For example, of the twenty-one appointments at the permanent secretary level made in 1970, seven went to Kandyan *Goyigama* and five went to the *Karava*. (The others went as follows: three to the *Durava*, one each to a *Salagama*, Burgher, and *Pannadura*, and three to Tamils.)

Since 1970 the *Karava* Buddhists have become prominent in the higher Civil Service with two High Commissioners, two ambassadors, the Director-General of Foreign Relations, the Chairman of the Public Services Commission, five Permanent Secretaries and two additional Permanent Secretaries, the Secretary to the Governor-General, and the Co-ordinating Secretary to the Prime Minister, the Auditor-General, five chairmen of nationalised enterprises, and the Additional Deputy-Governor of the Central Bank.

The simple enumeration of people in the various elite spheres of public life who happen, one might argue, to be nominally of one caste or another, in no way 'proves' the existence of a 'caste lobby', nor is it intended here to argue that every appointment has been to some degree a caste appointment. None the less, I have included mention of these groups, and adduced such evidence as I have for their existence, because both within the communities themselves and among the party elites, they are clearly perceived, identifiable by name, and their success in particular disputes closely followed and debated. As in the wider field of caste studies, often the most important revelation is that certain actions and attitudes are perceived as deriving from caste identities, loyalties, and antipathies, and that people in turn base their own actions and attitudes on these perceptions. In matters of appointment and recruitment, it is all too easy for a non-*Goyigama* to feel slighted on caste grounds if he fails to secure position or promotion against *Goyigama* competition; it is accepted that if a number of appointments appear to be given to one particular group of castes or bloc within a caste, the motivation lies in reward for past or future support, or to placate particular caste feeling. For example, since the victory of the United Front in 1970, members of the *Hena* community have been appointed to high administrative office. On many occasions these appointments were represented to me as an attempt to create a cadre of personally loyal administrative expertise.

It is recognised in turn that some communities consciously help their members to 'get on', providing financial and other aid, encouraging the younger members to compete for office where they might expect to be successful, offering in their own enterprises and via the patronage of their own professional careers channels of advancement, and in every way consciously strengthening their community.

6

The family in politics

A feature which is present in all castes to a greater or lesser degree is the *pelantiya*, or extended family group, which in turn forms a basis for cohesion and political support. In a traditional society it is neither surprising nor necessarily Machiavellian that families have used party to enhance their personal standing and influence, and that parties have relied on kinship structures in the place of binding ideologies and principles. Yet it is notable that despite universal franchise, parliamentary procedures, frequent transference of power at peaceful elections in an increasingly two-party system, and the emergence of the populist policies of post-1956, the grip of a few families on place and power in Sri Lanka has been diluted only marginally.

The case of Balangoda – an early example

The events surrounding a by-election in Balangoda in 1943 convey the flavour and the substance of the family rivalry that exists between the leadership of the UNP and the SLFP.

The by-election is a seemingly unimportant event in the years before Independence, yet it is illustrative of many of the interactions that continue to be powerful referents of political alignment and party allegiance.

Balangoda, in the Ratnapura District of Sabaragamuwa, lies in the heartland of the Ratwattes' territorial influence. The conduct of the 1943 campaign highlights the sensibilities of the Kandyan *Radala* (among whom the Ratwattes were eminent) and their reactions as urban politics came to their village for the first time. Mrs Bandaranaike, née Ratwatte, as a young girl and a new bride (she married S. W. R. D. Bandaranaike in 1940) would have learned many lessons from both the invective and the frenzied canvassing that surrounded the elections of the 1940s and 1943 in particular. The event shows, too, some of the problems S. W. R. D. Bandaranaike faced in building his Sinhala Maha Sabha into an effective counterweight to the politically established low-country families of the

Map 6   Sri Lanka, showing administrative districts

Senanayake clan. The story hints at broader Kandyan/low-country tensions and at sporadic attempts to win over the minority castes of the area to this or that elite cause.

It demonstrates clearly the political efficiency of the Senanayake caucus and their ability at the time to manipulate Ratwatte family divisions to their own advantage. In sum, it gets close to the substance of Senanayake–Bandaranaike/Ratwatte politics, the very personalised, family rivalry which is still at the core of UNP and SLFP competition at the elite level. National political leaders became involved in a local by-election because family pride and family loyalties were involved; and the success of an individual symbolised then, as now, the power and dominance of the clan and party as a whole.

Before sketching in brief the political background it is as well for the reader to bear in mind three characteristics of the times. First, he should be aware that Kandyan families are themselves closely interrelated by blood and marriage, and that the network reaches out beyond the highlands to the major families of other areas. Indeed, the Senanayake clan are related distantly in a number of lines to both the Bandaranaikes and the Ratwattes. (The Dias Bandaranaikes through the de Alwises for example; then the Eknaligodas are blood relatives of the Mahawelatennes and the Molamures; the Ratwattes are related on their side to the Mahawelatennes and Molamures; and Sir Francis Molamure married into the Wijewardene side of the Senanayake clan through the Meedeniyas.) First-cousin marriages are not uncommon. Even genealogically distant relatives are in moments of crisis drawn into the family circle and are expected to participate in and contribute towards family affairs.

Second, elections during the 1920s right up to the 1950s were conducted in a vituperative and defamatory manner. Scurrilous pamphlets distributed by the *kavi-kola-karayas* – libellous versifiers and political scandal-mongers – were much in evidence. A fictional description of their activities which refers to the Legislative Council elections of 1921 gives an idea of their usefulness:

On my father's side I was quite an aristocrat. My grandfather at the eighth remove was a Mudaliyar of high repute in the days of the Sinhalese Kings ... But my mother saved me from aristocratic isolation, for on my mother's side it was a downward relationship ... In a moment of youthful indiscretion he had lost sight of the blue blood that ran in his veins and against his parents' wishes and amidst the giggles of the ladies of his family had taken to wife a girl of nondescript origin ... It was not long before a scurrilous pamphlet was published with full details of my downward relationship. Part of the pamphlet was in prose but, off and on, the writer broke into verse ... I retaliated by hiring an expensive pedigree maker. He was an intellectual and made claims to be an historian. He completely rehabilitated my mother and faked on my father's side a pedigree even more illustrious than the family tradition. The scurrilous pamphlet was completely neutralised and equilibrium restored.[1]

It could be said that national leaders and municipal council members were accustomed to the mud-slinging. S. W. R. D. had had experience of this kind of campaign when he fought the radical and abrasive labour leader, A. E. Goonesinghe, in Colombo municipal politics and during the State Council elections of 1931 and 1936 (though he himself stood uncontested in both 1931 and 1936). But these tactics were rare in the secluded rural backwaters of the highlands and they burst upon Balangoda in 1943 with memorable venom.

Third, in those days the deference vote was a common and dependable feature. As S. W. R. D. wrote in his fictional story, 'The Mystery of the Missing Candidate':

'In most cases, if twenty-five per cent of the voters vote for the Party, seventy-five per cent vote for the individual candidate.'

'You must forgive my ignorance,' I apologised, 'I am new to this game. What do the people of this area think about our candidate?'

'Oh! The people here have a great regard for Mr Rajapakse,' Mr Wijesinghe replied with a laugh, 'He would be elected whatever Party he chose to belong to.'[2]

The history begins in 1931 when Sir Cudah Ratwatte, brother of Mrs Bandaranaike's father, was returned uncontested to the State Council for Balangoda. On 1 August 1933 he retired through ill-health. The ensuing by-election was won by Colonel T. G. Jayawardene with 6,763 votes to T. Walloopillai's 6,501 votes. The Colonel was J. R. Jayawardene's uncle. He had the support of the low-country politicians in the State Council and of some powerful low-country *mudalalis*. (Felix Dias Bandaranaike remarked as late as 1969 that the *mudalalis'* financial support of MPs rendered them nothing but 'puppets on a string'.)[3] All the *Radala* families of the area supported the Tamil, T. Walloopillai, who was a leading proctor and a resident of Balangoda and who had the support of the sizeable Indian (plantation) vote. Mrs Bandaranaike's father was one of his leading supporters and felt keenly the blow of an 'outsider' coming from the low country to defeat them on their home ground. Insult was added to injured pride when a bag of parippu was left on the Ratwattes' doorstep. (Parippu, a form of lentil, is a traditional food of the Tamils.)

At the 1936 State Council elections matters became more complicated. The results were as follows:

H. A. Goonesekera   14,539
Col. T. G. Jayawardene   10,360
E. W. Mathew   7,973

H. A. Goonesekera, a well-off low-countryman, came forward to contest Balangoda against the Colonel by virtue of his being married to
Mrs Bandaranaike's Mahawelatenne grandfather's sister. (H. A. Goonesekera's history is rather curious. He was adopted as a child by the
Mahawelatennes, who had no male heir, and was treated as one of the
family. He rose to be a *Rate Mahatmeya* in the Balangoda area – a post
usually reserved for the Kandyan *Radala*. He is generally referred to as
Mrs Bandaranaike's 'uncle', the usual Kandyan term for such relations
by marriage.) Originally the Ratwattes had asked E. W. Mathew to stand,
as the leader among the *Vahumpura* in the district, calculating that the
defeat of the Colonel by a non-*Goyigama* would be particularly satisfying.
However, when H. A. Goonesekera decided to contest, Barnes Ratwatte,
Mrs Bandaranaike's father, apparently felt obliged to support his 'uncle'
(actually, father-in-law's sister's husband). While, therefore, Ratwatte
prestige was restored by the Colonel's defeat, a bitterness developed
between the Ratwattes and Mathew's caste community, which was to
result in the latter's future electoral support of the UNP in the area.
H. A. Goonesekera was subsequently unseated for alleged bribery,
occasioning yet another by-election, which was held in October 1943.

At first there were no obvious candidates, and it seems that Barnes
Ratwatte was persuaded to come forward only reluctantly, believing himself to be uncontested. The campaign was planned in the traditional
dignified manner, with little personal canvassing among the electors by
the candidate, and electioneering was conducted on his behalf by the
village headmen and other village leaders.

Then, unexpectedly, Sir Francis Molamure came forward. It seems
clear that if he had indicated his intention in time, Barnes Ratwatte
would not have fought the election. Apart from anything else, the
Molamures were blood relatives of the Eknaligodas, a Ratnapura family,
and the latter of the Mahawelatennes. At one point a marriage alliance
had been contemplated between Sirimavo Ratwatte and a Molamure.

Sir Francis was from Ratnapura District but he had settled for a time
in Kegalle, where he practised as an advocate. He married in 1912
Adeline Meedeniya, daughter of Meedeniya, *Adigar* of Kegalle. He had
been returned uncontested for the Dedigama seat in 1931 and had been
elected the first Speaker of the State Council. He lost his seat in August
1935 after being charged on a technicality for contempt of court in a
testamentary case in which he was the beneficiary.

A notorious socialiser reputedly of great charm, on his return from prison he eloped with one of the most beautiful women of the day, settling to mining gems not far from Ratnapura town. His career was followed with great interest in the press and in no way diminished his popularity.

Not only did Sir Francis have personal and family backing. He was seen to be following family tradition by entering the politics of the area, for his cousin had represented Ratnapura in the days of the Legislative Council. There is no doubt that his entry into the contest posed a dilemma for all the influential families of the district.

It was decided that representation should be made to each so that the matter could be settled by the honourable withdrawal of Barnes Ratwatte before the election. Unfortunately these moves went disastrously awry, with accusations of humiliation from both sides. So divisive was the issue that in the ensuing battle, the family 'broker', related to both the Mola-mures and the Ratwattes, was obliged to uphold his pledged support for Barnes Ratwatte against his own uncle.

Thus far the contest stands as the expression and renewed cause of inter- and intrafamilial squabbles, significant enough in its context, but trivial in its detail and of no deep consequence. The profound and forma-tive aspects become apparent only as one ponders why Sir Francis inter-vened at Balangoda. On both sides national figures stepped in to support their candidate, and it is by considering the motives for their commitment that this question can be answered.

Behind Barnes Ratwatte, beyond his immediate family, were ranged S. W. R. D., Jayaweera Kuruppu, George R. de Silva, Bernard Aluvihare, D. M. Rajapakse, and H. W. Amarasuriya. Each proponent sheds light on the intricacies of political interaction, and I shall spend some time explaining their involvement.

S. W. R. D. Bandaranaike had married Barnes Ratwatte's daughter in 1940 and thus had a family obligation to support his father-in-law. Politically, he was anxious to extend and strengthen his Sinhala Maha Sabha. His own standing in Ratnapura was not such as to make him a natural leader in the district, but if his father-in-law were elected, his name would add weight and prestige to his own organisation.

He had few adherents to the SMS in the area, but of these, Jayaweera Kuruppu was undoubtedly the foremost. A founder member of the SMS, in 1936 he had been elected Member of the State Council for Ratnapura, defeating D. J. Vimalasurendra. (In 1951 he crossed the floor with S. W. R. D. and became a Minister in Bandaranaike's government.) Vimalasurendra was a member of the *Navandanna* community, of con-siderable strength in the electorate, and his defeat by one of Bandaranaike's supporters influenced his caste's future political alignments. Vimalasurendra had defeated George R. de Silva for the Ratnapura seat in 1931.

George R. de Silva had become the Member of the Legislative Council for Ratnapura on the death of his uncle, A. H. E. Molamure. (George R. de Silva's mother's younger sister was married to A. H. E. Molamure. The eldest sister was mother to the family broker who had tried to negotiate a settlement between Sir Francis and Barnes Ratwatte.) Defeated in 1931 at Ratnapura, in April 1942 he had been elected to Colombo North in a by-election. He had both a family and a political commitment to ensuring Barnes's success.

Bernard Aluvihare had been the member for Matale since 1936 and was a supporter of the SMS. (He held Matale till 1947. He had joined Bandaranaike's faction very early on and returned to parliament only in 1952 as one of the eight SLFP members who won at that election. He became a Joint Secretary of the SLFP.) At the 1936 elections he had faced the 'big guns' of Sir Oliver Goonetilleke and D. S. Senanayake who campaigned for one of his defeated opponents, Karaliyädde. He was bound to support S. W. R. D. in this contest and had a personal reason to oppose Sir Francis's supporters.

D. M. Rajapakse had represented Hambantota in the State Council since 1936. For local political reasons his family were generally anti-Senanayake and he was willing to lend his support to defeat their candidate. It is worth digressing here to comment on the careers of the Rajapakses for they illustrate the persistence of family electoral inheritance in Lanka. D. M. Rajapakse continued as Member of the State Council for Hambantota till his death in May 1945. His brother, D. A. Rajapakse, held the seat on D. M.'s death. D. A. Rajapakse went on to represent Beliatta under D. S. Senanayake, then resigned with S. W. R. D. to join the SLFP. Thereafter he contested Beliatta as the successful SLFP candidate till 1965 (except for March 1960 when he lost to Philip Gunawardene's MEP), when he lost to his UNP rival. He held office once as Parliamentary Secretary under C. P. de Silva in the MEP coalition. His brother's son, Lakshman, entered parliament in 1947 for his father's old seat, Hambantota, as an Independent. Thereafter he joined the Communist Party (Moscow) but contested the 1952 elections for the LSSP and lost. He won Hambantota for the MEP coalition in 1956 and held office as Parliamentary Secretary to the Minister of Trade and Commerce. In May 1959 he resigned when Philip Gunawardene left Bandaranaike's government; but in March 1960 he contested successfully the adjoining seat at Tissamaharama as a member of Gunawardene's MEP. Lakshman's brother, George Rajapakse, entered politics in March 1960 as successful MEP candidate for Mulkirigala. By July he had joined the SLFP and at every subsequent election he has held the seat for the SLFP. He was Parliamentary Secretary to the Minister of Finance till 1962 when he resigned over his Minister's proposal to cut the rice ration. In 1970 he was appointed Minister of Fisheries. George Rajapakse died in 1976 and his brother Lakshman, long alienated from Mrs Bandaranaike, if not the SLFP itself, was persuaded to return as the SLFP candidate; he held the seat for the SLFP at the by-election. D. A. Rajapakse's son, Mahendra (youngest member of the 1970 House till Rukman Senanayake's election in 1973), was in 1970 elected for the SLFP to his father's old seat at Beliatta.

Returning to Barnes's supporters at the Balangoda contest, we come finally to H. W. Amarasuriya. Like D. M. Rajapakse, his reasons for supporting the Bandaranaikes' candidate had their origins in the politics of his home area. He had been elected to the State Council in 1931 as the member for Udugama, standing as a Ceylon National Congress candidate.[4] In 1936 he had taken Galle, the seat being vacated by C. W. W. Kannangara, a protégé and relative of Sir Baron Jayatilleke who was identified with the Senanayake caucus in the CNC. C. W. W. Kannangara in 1936 took Matugama from the former member, D. P. Athulathmudali, who was a backer of S. W. R. D. (Athulathmudali's son, Lalith, one-time President of the Oxford Union, is pro-UNP, and was appointed Minister of Trade following the UNP's sweeping success at the 1977 elections.) Amarasuriya's commitment thus arose from factionalism within the CNC and the political manoeuvring around his own electoral area. His sympathies were the warmer because his brother Thomas had been defeated recently at the Galle Municipal Council elections by W. Dahanayake. (Dahanayake emerged in the Balangoda contest as a supporter of Sir Francis.)

In the 1930s and early 1940s the Amarasuriyas, a staunch *Karava* Buddhist family, were regarded as impregnable in Galle. They were wealthy planters owning large extents of coconut, tea, and rubber. Henry W. Amarasuriya stood under the UNP label and was defeated at Galle in 1947 by W. Dahanayake. He won Baddegama for the UNP at a by-election in 1949 but in 1952 he was defeated at Baddegama by Henry Abeywickreme and lost again at Baddegama in 1956. He increasingly turned his attention to the affairs of the Buddhist Congress. Of his three brothers and three sisters, Thomas, the second eldest brother, became the President of the Senate in 1956. Of Thomas's two daughters, one married M. R. P. Salgado, in 1970 the Additional Permanent Secretary to the

Ministry of Planning and Employment, and the other married Nihal Jayawickreme, in 1970 Permanent Secretary to the Minister of Justice. Nihal Jayawickreme is the nephew of Justice T. S. Fernando, in 1970 President of the Appeal Court. The brothers' uncle Edward's wife's sister married M. W. H. de Silva, 1956 Minister of Justice. H. W. Amarasuriya's UNP tradition was continued through one of his sisters, married to Major Montague Jayawickreme who has contested the Weligama seat for the UNP since 1947. In 1965 he became Minister of Transport and Works.

These six men were Barnes Ratwatte's most eminent political backers, men who had family obligations toward him, who were pledged to S. W. R. D. Bandaranaike's cause, or who had local political or personal reason to dislike or distrust the power of the Senanayake caucus in the CNC. Whom did Sir Francis marshal against them?

Sir Francis was supported by powerful national figures – the Wijewardenes and their Lake House Press, D. S. Senanayake and Sir John Kotelawala. His cause was upheld in the persuasive public oratory of W. Dahanayake and his campaign backed by formidable low-country *mudalalis*, not least of whom was the notorious 'Pavilion David' of Pavilion Hotel, Colombo, known for his alleged use of strong-arm persuasion common to the *chandiya*, or thug. Versifiers did not spare themselves on his behalf. Another UNP *mudalali* involved in the by-election was Leo Fernando, operator of the P.M.T. Company, one of the most powerful bus companies of the day. In 1943 he ran, with others, the important Panadura–Badulla and Hambantota-via-Pelmadulla lines, which ran across the district. (In 1947 and 1952 he held Buttala for the UNP.)

Dahanayake, at that stage of his flamboyant career, was Mayor of Galle, in his local politics virulently anti-Amarasuriya, and nationally a fiery left-wing anti-feudal radical.[5] His caustic invective against the aristocratic clans of the highlands, delivered in free and colloquial language, had earned him a reputation as a new kind of 'poor man's saviour' and he drew crowds unrivalled even by Bandaranaike. He turned his talents against Mrs Bandaranaike's father, who had been a *Rate Mahatmeya*, and publicly ridiculed the family and all they allegedly represented. Sir Francis, none the less, was somewhat unlikely company for Dahanayake. It was rumoured that perhaps Dahanayake was concerned to pay some debt of gratitude to Sir Francis. It is likely that his fight with the Amarasuriyas also played a part.

The Wijewardenes for their part had a long-standing social grievance to air at Balangoda. When Don Richard Wijewardene, founder of the Lake House Group, married in 1916 a daughter of Meedeniya, *Adigar* of Kegalle, not one of the Ratnapura *Radala* had attended the wedding (nor had they graced Sir Francis's marriage to another daughter, Adeline, in 1912). Politically, the Lake House newspapers supported the Senanayakes and, throughout the campaign, editorials and news comment covered Sir Francis at the expense of the Ratwattes. Bandaranaike was to remark in 1951, 'The English and Sinhalese papers that claim to be organs for the UNP have without restraint been attacking me bitterly from the start.'[6]

With such powerful, wealthy, and adroit support, coupled to his own local popularity, why was it thought necessary to bring in Sir John Kotelawala and D. S. Senanayake? The reason lies in the wider political calculations of the Senanayake caucus. Balangoda was seen as one element in the capture of a series of electorates stretching from Kurunegala District through to Ratnapura. The overall scheme had met with a temporary check, and Balangoda in 1943 provided a way clear. In 1931 Sir Francis had been returned uncontested at Dedigama. Following his legal difficulties he was unseated and in 1936 the caucus put forward Dudley to take the seat. He succeeded in doing so but in the face of considerably more opposition than Sir Francis had ever experienced. The problem was whether Sir Francis would demand his former seat at the next election, and if so, where Dudley could stand and be returned. It was felt Sir Francis's opposition to, or failure to support, Dudley at Dedigama would be disastrous. The solution was to offer Sir Francis another seat and to use the full influence of the caucus to ensure that he won it.

Why Balangoda? A number of electorates were considered. Kegalle was a possibility except that Harris Ratwatte, loyal to D. S. Senanayake, was entrenched there. The Senanayake–Wijewardene combine could hardly ask him to vacate his seat when their dealings with his brothers and other members of his family were so embarrassingly hostile. (Harris Ratwatte remained loyal to D. S. Senanayake and resisted family pressure to join S. W. R. D. in 1951. This caused a rift with Mrs Bandaranaike, to be healed only through his son, Anurudha, who was defeated as the SLFP candidate at Senkadagala in 1970.) S. W. R. D., commenting on the lasting bitterness which such family divisions could create, wrote:

Regarding the UNP of which I was a Vice-President, to give one example, Mr Harris Ratwatte, MP, was seen by an emissary of Sir (then Mr) U. A. Jayasundera, the Honorary General Secretary, with a view to having some UNP meetings in his constituency. When Mr Ratwatte was asked whom he would like to preside at these meetings, he replied that he would like me to preside. The answer he received was 'Mr U. A. Jayasundera will not hear of that name.'[7]

The matter was important strategically. In the adjoining Kurunegala District, Sir John held the north securely, but the south, at Naramala, which borders on Dedigama, had been a problem. G. E. Madawela had held it in 1931 and at the by-election following his death, Advocate W. M. de S. Jayasundera had been elected; neither was attached to the Senanayake caucus. In 1936 the caucus made a move to get the son-in-law of F. R. Senanayake (brother of D. S.) elected, and were successful. (On Siripala Samarakkody's death in 1944, R. G. Senanayake, brother-in-law of Siripala, son of F. R., nephew of D. S., and cousin of Dudley Senenayake, took over the seat for the UNP.) Kurunegala District was thus safe for the UNP, and their attention turned to Kegalle. It was determined that Dudley should succeed to the leadership in Kegalle District (via Dedigama) and Sir Francis should be persuaded to return to his home area of Ratnapura.

The by-election at Balangoda was the opportunity the caucus had been looking for; Sir Francis agreed to stand and the Senanayake–Kotelawala–Wijewardene clan threw their full weight behind him in furtherance of their geographic strategy. The contest had the not inconsiderable advantage, in their eyes, of forcing Bandaranaike, who would be bound to support his father-in-law, to share the humiliation of Barnes Ratwatte's defeat and would offer a sharp check to the success of the SMS. S. W. R. D. would be made to look the more ridiculous, politically, by supporting a representative of the old feudal order, defeated in the heartland of feudalism itself by the 'more enlightened' Sir Francis Molamure.

Two minor elaborations must halt the narrative here temporarily, for they give depth to the complexities and nuances which played such a vital role in 1943, and which remain as active memories and present forces in politics today.

It is significant that one major figure in the combine played no part at Balangoda in 1943, J. R. Jayawardene, though his mother was a sister of D. R. Wijewardene. The reason is that his base is in the maritime districts, and he would have been an utterly unacceptable figure in an up-country campaign. Feeling on such matters has been and still is very strong, reflected even in the terms used to address the Senanayakes, a lowland family, by the Kandyan *Radala*. D. S. Senanayake's father had been addressed by them as 'Senanayake *Appuhamy*', as if he were a well-off shopkeeper, definitely not one with whom the Bandaranaikes and Obeysekeres would be intimate socially. D. S. Senanayake, by the time he had gained distinction, had earned the respect of '*Hamuduravo*' (deferential form of address) from his followers and colleagues, but those in the Kandyan area who knew his family background rated him no higher than

'Senanayake *Unnahē*', a term used respectfully, but to craftsmen and others to whom one gave orders (though the *Batgam* and other social inferiors would address him if they dared as '*Hamuduravo*' without question). Dudley moved higher still in their vocabulary, to the affectionate abbreviation 'Dudley *Hamu*', in consideration of his mother who was a Dunuwille of aristocratic Kandyan heredity.

The second elaboration concerns the jockeying between D. S. Senanayake and S. W. R. D. for leadership at Independence. A number of ideas were aired before the formation of the UNP under D. S. Senanayake, assessing the various strengths and weaknesses of the SMS against the Senanayake caucus in the CNC. Two opposing legends persist in political tradition: one declares that S. W. R. D. could have led the new coalition but deferred to D. S. Senanayake's greater age and experience. A bolder elaboration of this asserts that Bandaranaike even then could have led the SMS into a new party in opposition to the Senanayake–UNP, but forbore in the interests of a peaceful and united entry into Independence. The alternative equally strongly declares that there was no credible opponent to D. S.; that he was beyond question the most authoritative political figure of the time, the natural leader. In this view, Bandaranaike's claims are hollow and inflated by his subsequent success.

This is not the place to discuss the rival traditions, but they enter the present history because the display staged by the Senanayake caucus at Balangoda undoubtedly gave Bandaranaike pause. Not long after, in 1946 when the SMS had joined the coalition grouping under the UNP label, he said at a meeting in Galle:

Some people think that the Sabha (as well as other parties) are now dead or dying, because they have joined the new party. This is not so, and the Sabha must continue its work as vigorously as possible, and increase its strength to the fullest ... If and when it is no longer possible for us honourably to continue in this party, we shall leave it ... Some people say the new party is merely Mr Senanayake's party, or that of a caucus. It is nothing of the sort. The party which was heralded some time ago by Col. Kotelawala at Kurunegala and Mr Molamure at Ratnapura, never came into being. On the contrary, Mr Senanayake consented to join the party formed by the various groups referred to above. From the personal point of view, I am satisfied, after many talks with Mr Senanayake, that he is not activated by petty or selfish motives, either with reference to himself or a caucus of his relatives and intimates.[8]

By 1951, on the occasion of the inauguration of the SLFP, Bandaranaike was saying:

Let it be remembered that a little time before the last General Election, Mr Senanayake, having earlier resigned from the Ceylon National Congress, had no party alignment at all and was just an individual, though no doubt power-ful, politician. There were at that time certain parties of which the Sinhala Maha Sabha was one of the most powerful. It would have been much more advantageous to me personally to have faced the elections through the SMS. Though it meant a personal sacrifice, I felt that it was in the interests of the country to combine with various other parties in the effort to secure the stability of Government which was needed at the beginning of the working of the Free Constitution. The Sabha agreed with this view and we joined in forming the U.N.P. It was on my proposal that Mr Senanayake was elected President of the Party.[9]

Whatever the subsequent estimates of rival strength, there can be no doubt that the by-election in 1943 at Balangoda turned out to be a triumph for the Senanayake caucus, with Sir Francis winning with a majority of over 17,000.

Naturally, allegations of large-scale impersonations and cash bribery followed the declaration of the result. Only a few months previously S. W. R. D. had spoken at the annual session of the SMS at Anurad-hapura of:

certain disquieting tendencies in elections. Although we have the widest possible franchise, certain malpractices that are being increasingly indulged in, such as bribery and corruption, intimidation, and impersonation, are prevent-ing a free and correct expression of the will of the people. A very unsatisfactory and dangerous situation is thereby created, and it is the duty of all political parties and leaders to take vigorous action to stop these evils.[10]

These 'tendencies' did not disappear overnight at Independence. In 1951, at yet another by-election at Balangoda, the *Samasamajist* – '*Voice of the LSSP*' – charged that the election was won by the UNP only by virtue of the withdrawal of the right to vote of 9,000 Indian estate workers in the electorate following the new citizenship laws, and by mass impersonation. The paper adduced 'two telling facts' in support of its accusations. In the 1947 general election 30,887 votes were polled out of a register of 63,000, less than 50 per cent. In 1951, 36,000 votes were polled out of a register of only 56,000 – 66.5 per cent. Moreover, in 1947 there were five candidates but in 1951 only two. Secondly, at most polling booths, polling was around 50 per cent of the electorate, but at those organised solely by UNP 'Bigshots' it was as high as 80 to 90 per cent. The article concludes by picturing LSSP supporters trudging to vote, courageously defying feudal arrogance, '*mudalali*–money–power', thug-gery, intimidation, and 'every weapon of the UNP'.[11]

Not surprisingly, the manoeuvring and manipulating that culminated in the bitter fight at Balangoda in 1943 continued after Independence.

Jayaweera Kuruppu, who had won Ratnapura as Bandaranaike's supporter in 1936, was persuaded to contest Nivitigala in 1947 under the UNP coalition label. He had won Ratnapura by a margin of nearly 8,000 votes, but lost at Nivitigala by a bare 24 to D. F. Hettiarachchi, then of the LSSP. This was a big upset for Bandaranaike for it deprived him of his principal organiser in the district. In 1947 at Ratnapura the UNP–Senanayake caucus put forward a family member, C. E. Attygalle, who won by a margin of 1,799. Attygalle's brother, Sir Nicholas Attygalle, organised his campaign for him. (John Kotelawala senior and F. R. Senanayake had married two of Nicholas Attygalle's aunts.)

Sir Francis continued to hold Balangoda till his death in 1951. His nephew, a proctor, sought the caucus's nomination, but the caucus by then was forced to concede to Bandaranaike's demand that his nominee, Jayaweera Kuruppu, take the UNP label. Kuruppu took the seat at the by-election in 1951 and two months later crossed the floor with Bandaranaike.

Though the Senanayake clan thus suffered a setback they had achieved a good deal. The Ratwatte family remained divided by the events of 1943 and the *Radala* remained isolated. Barnes Ratwatte, already a *Dissawe*, after 1943 was joined in office by the family broker and by Mrs Bandaranaike's maternal uncle, Sydney Ellawala. On the first occasion in the history of the Kandyan area that one province had three *Dissawes*, the appointments effectively circumscribed their party-political and family-factional activities and influence.

However, neither the Ratwattes nor the Molamures have abandoned the electorate. In March 1965 Clifford S. Ratwatte, one of Mrs Bandaranaike's brothers, won Balangoda for the SLFP. His election was contested and he was unseated. In the by-election which followed in 1966 his wife, Mallika, herself related to the Ellawalas, held it for the SLFP. In adjoining Pelmadulla Mrs Sita Molamure Seneviratne (daughter of Sir Francis by Adeline Meedeniya) fought for the UNP and lost to the SLFP candidate. She lost again at the by-election of 1967. And, in 1970, the 1943 Balangoda contest was refought by the younger generation: Mrs Seneviratne stood for the UNP at Balangoda and confronted Mrs Mallika Ratwatte for the SLFP, this time the Ratwattes had it.

These two ladies are in fact cousins by marriage (Mallika's father's sister married Sita's mother's brother). There is thus no neat division between the Senanayake clan and Mrs Bandaranaike's SLFP relations; from at least three generations back, intermarriage has taken place to produce a most complex social elite dominated by the 'aristocrats' of the low country and the Kandyan *Radala*, with deep fissions and subtle claims upon its members. It is more than an outsider can do to convey the full extent and every dimension of such relationships, but this section serves to illustrate certain of the political consequences.

The Balangoda by-election of 1943 provides an explanation of a kind for the spirited exchanges that many of the Bandaranaikes' actions and attitudes provoked; for example, S. W. R. D.'s takeover of the bus *mudalalis*, and Mrs Bandaranaike's continuing mistrust of capitalist private enterprise and her repeated attempts to curb the power of Lake House, culminating in 1973 in its acquisition by the state and the forced resignation of its Wijewardene chairman and family directors. (In protest, J. R. Jayawardene organised a boycott of Lake House newspapers and conducted house-to-house campaigns and rallies.)[12]

Family allegiance still influences the tone and direction of politics in Lanka: intrafamilial loyalties and fissions and family partisanship can determine political allegiance and party composition. Just two years after Independence, LSSP MP N. M. Perera wrote in an editorial of the *Samasamajist*: 'the same Senanayakes–Kotelawalas and Bandaranayakes have been ruling the roost for the last sixteen years under the Donough-more dispensation. Their record during this period has been one of abysmal reaction and utter indifference to the demands of the poverty-stricken masses.'[13] (Note that at this period the Bandaranaikes were classed with the UNP figures as 'reactionaries' by the left.)

The Senanayakes and Bandaranaikes have continued to dominate: a list of the Prime Ministers since Independence will serve to show the very narrow range of leadership:

D. S. Senanayake: 1947–1952
Dudley Senanayake (son of D. S.): 1952–1953
Sir John Kotelawala (nephew of D. S.): 1953–1956
S. W. R. D. Bandaranaike: 1956–1959
W. Dahanayake (caretaker): Sept. 1959–March 1960
Dudley Senanayake: March–July 1960
Mrs Sirimavo Bandaranaike (wife of S. W. R. D.): 1960–1965
Dudley Senanayake: 1965–1970
Mrs Sirimavo Bandaranaike: 1970–1977
J. R. Jayawardene: 1977 to date.

The Senanayakes and Bandaranaikes do, of course, personify the UNP and the SLFP; it is but a short step to see the two parties as the creations of the families – vehicles of their aspirations for power – and politics in Lanka as nothing but a veneer for a family struggle. This is a simplistic view and unconvincing, but none the less the personalities of the Senanayakes and Bandaranaikes have dominated and it is worth considering the extent of their influence.

The UNP family

The Senanayakes are of low-country descent. D. S. had been born in 1884 the third son of Don Spater Senanayake, landowner and plumbago merchant of Botale, near Mirigama.[14] One son, F. R., was groomed for public life and educated in England (Cambridge and the Inns of Court). On his return to Sri Lanka he became involved in the leadership of the Temperance Movement (a form of political protest under the guise of complaints over the arrack-renting policies of the colonial government). He died tragically young in 1926. One brother was destined for business and became a copra and graphite exporter in Colombo. D. S.'s lot was the management of the family estates and he was known to the public as 'Källe John' ('Jungle John'; F. R. had been nicknamed 'London John', and the business brother 'Colombo John'). As the Senanayakes became more wealthy and influential, an 'aristocratic lineage' became associated with their name, linking the heroic Sinhalese king, Parakrama Bahu the Great, who was born in Beligal Korale in Kegalle District, to their ancestry. The Senanayakes fostered the image by restoring the ancient temple at Mahiyangana in the eastern jungles, supposedly first dedicated by the famous Parakrama. (And at the by-election in June 1973 following Dudley Senanayake's death, posters were displayed showing the UNP candidate, Rukman, nephew to Dudley, overshadowed by D. S. Senana-yake and Parakrama the Great.)

The Senanayakes are related by blood and marriage to four other powerful families: the Wijewardenes, the Wickremasinghes, the Coreas, and the Kotelawalas. The chart in the appendix and the accompanying guide reveal how extensive the connections are, and how very successful and well placed the members are. The 'inner families' and their relatives hold high office in every sphere; in the administration, the judiciary, the armed services, in commerce and business, in the legislature; and until recently, in the Associated Newspapers of Ceylon Group, they controlled one of the largest newspaper and publishing concerns in Asia.

Though some of the family members, such as H. E. Tennekoon (see chart 4), have served under the Bandaranaikes, most are firm UNP sup-porters. (One of the notable exceptions is Hema Basnayake, who fell out with Dudley in 1969 and became a supporter of Mrs Bandaranaike.) Their extensive and entrenched position in public life and private business gives a strength and unity to UNP administrations noticeably lacking in

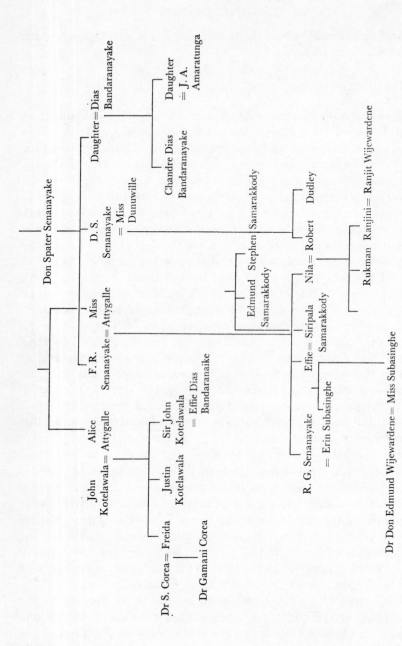

Chart 1   The UNP founding families: the Senanayakes and Kotelawalas

Note: Not all marriages, relationships, offspring shown.

the Bandaranaikes' more factional administrations, for at the very least, family members provide channels of communication and assistance over and above official paths, and facilitate co-ordination. For this reason, if for no other, as S. W. R. D. first discovered, the UNP's defeat at the polls, however overwhelming in terms of seats lost in the House, does not mean that their power is destroyed or their influence drastically curtailed.

Marriage alliances have been carefully arranged. For example, Ranjit Wijewardene, former Chairman of Lake House, was married to Robert Senanayake's daughter, Ranjini (niece of the then Prime Minister) at the parents' behest. D. R. Wijewardene's daughters were married with equal care. In the case of Nalini, married to Esmond Wickremasinghe (Joint Managing Director of Lake House, 1965), Sir Oliver Goonetilleke is said to have acted as broker. Marriage has served to forestall potential divisions, for instance by uniting up-country and low-country families. D. R. Wijewardene and D. S. Senanayake were following well-established custom in choosing Kandyan aristocrats as brides. As H. A. J. Hulugalle, himself a Kandyan aristocrat, has written, 'It was not uncommon for young men of wealthy low-country Sinhalese families to marry daughters of Kandyan chiefs. Three of the Wijewardene brothers and two Senanayakes did so.'[15] New blood and entrepreneurial talent is brought in at times. For example, Himali, the daughter of M. D. Gunasena, who began as a 'Norris Road *mudalali*' to become an important newspaper and publishing magnate, was married to Sinha Basnayake, the son of the sitting Chief Justice.[16]

Such conspicuous family structures naturally give rise to comment. The accusation that the UNP is the 'party of the *Goyigama*' is here given precise meaning, for the inner caucus is overwhelmingly *Goyigama*, and only a few of the relatives by marriage shown on the extended chart in the appendix come from non-*Goyigama* backgrounds. The matter of status, and the precise loyalties brought with marriage and descent, however, are less well defined by the association. Ananda Meegama's link with H. A. de S. Gunasekera, for example, seems to lie solely in the fact that they married the two daughters of a one-time lawyer practising in Kandy; but their importance to the UNP family lies in the fact that this association by marriage draws them, however peripherally, into the nexus of those whom the 'inner caucus' can approach and negotiate with, even though H. A. de S. Gunasekera himself has never been associated with the UNP. Again, though C. W. Amarasinghe was a distinguished Professor of Classics in Sri Lanka, his participation with the 'political family' was infrequent and he seems to have been regarded as an outsider by the Gomes family on account of his interest in converting his wife to Catholicism (the Gomeses come from a strong Buddhist background); none the less, it strengthened

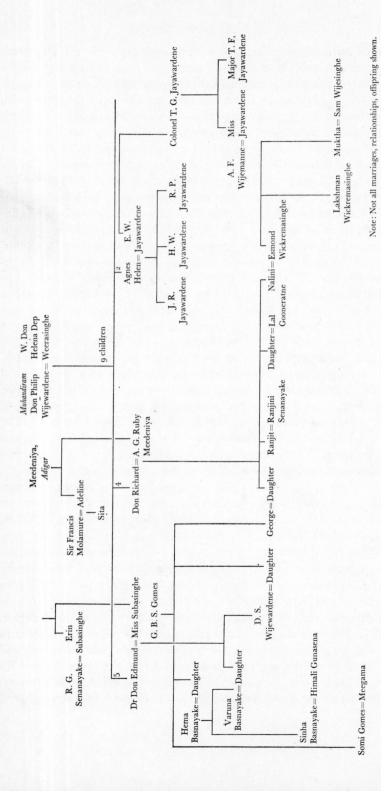

Chart 2   The UNP founding families: the Wijewardenes, Jayawardenes, and Wickremasinghes

Note: Not all marriages, relationships, offspring shown.

the caucus's image to be able to refer to their links with the academic hierarchy.

More particularly, the UNP has been charged with showing partisan patronage and nepotism. Sir John Kotelawala himself has commented: 'the party was accused of nepotism and called the "Uncle–Nephew Party" – the nephew being myself. The belief persisted among our political enemies that my only claim to distinction was the fact that D. S. Senanayake's brother had married my aunt.'[17]

One of the first uses of the taunt 'Uncle–Nephew Party' is recorded by the *Third Force* newspaper in 1948 in reference to the Jayawardenes. The member for Colombo South, UNP and a former Deputy Speaker, was deprived of his seat for 'fudging his election'. At the following by-election the UNP nominee was Major T. F. Jayawardene, nephew to E. W. Jayawardene whose brother-in-law was D. R. Wijewardene, and cousin to the then Finance Minister, J. R. Jayawardene.[18]

The SLFP family under Mrs Bandaranaike

In complete contrast, the SLFP was not moulded by S. W. R. D. around a family caucus, nor did he bring relatives into his government to consolidate his position; as the Bandaranaike chart and guide in the appendix indicate, the Bandaranaike 'clan' in public and political life originates with Mrs Bandaranaike.

S. W. R. D.'s position in the 'establishment' prior to Independence had been an uneasy one, as he belonged, by character if not by birth, to neither the new men of influence nor to the highest ranks of the Kandyan aristocracy. An experienced commentator over many years has written:

There seemed to be a conspiracy against him. In the struggle between the old Aristocracy of birth and breeding of Colonial times and the new 'temperance Aristocracy' of wealth and influence of later times Bandaranaike was caught like an areca nut in a cutter . . . There was in Ceylon higher circles an inner portal of politics to which he could not find the key . . . Even after he had become a Minister in the State Council, married into the Kandyan aristocracy, and had been included in the Cabinet in the new Parliament, he was at best tolerated as affectionately as toothache and as tenderly as a thorn.[19]

His relations with his political colleagues reflect the wider rivalry between the Senanayakes and the Bandaranaikes–Obeysekeres. The latter had been one of the chief Sinhalese Buddhist families in the nineteenth century by virtue of their Kandyan heritage and their links with the British government. Their position and influence had gradually been undercut by that of the Senanayakes who stole a march over the Bandaranaikes in

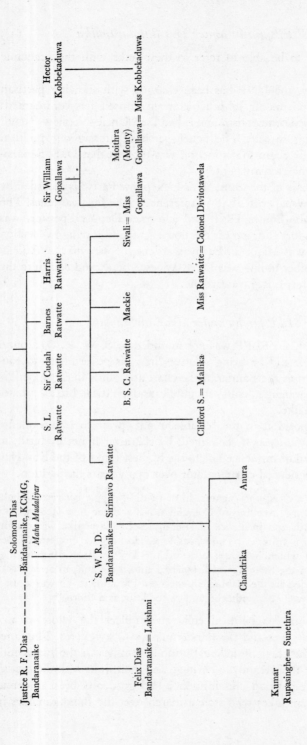

Justice R. F. Dias
Bandaranaike

Solomon Dias
- - - - - - Bandaranaike, KCMG,
Maha Mudaliyar

Hector
Kobbekaduwa

Sir William
Gopallawa

Moithra
(Monty)
Gopallawa Gopallawa = Miss Kobbekaduwa

Sivali = Miss
Gopallawa

S. L.
Ratwatte

Sir Cudah
Ratwatte

Barnes
Ratwatte

Harris
Ratwatte

B. S. C. Ratwatte

Mackie

Miss Ratwatte = Colonel Divitotawela

Clifford S. = Mallika

S. W. R. D.
Bandaranaike = Sirimavo Ratwatte

Felix Dias
Bandaranaike = Lakshmi

Chandrika

Anura

Kumar
Rupasinghe = Sunethra

Note: Not all marriages, relationships, offspring shown.

Cousins - - - - -

Chart 3   The Bandaranaikes/Ratwattes

the early twenties of this century by leading the nationalist and reform struggles (F. R. and D. S. Senanayake). Then S. W. R. D. in turn cut the ground from under the Senanayakes in the 1950s by which time they had themselves become the 'establishment' of post-Independence.

At the first election contested by the SLFP in 1952, only a limited number of seats were open to S. W. R. D. on the basis of family-territorial influence; in the Mirigama–Attanagalla area, in Colombo North, and in Weligama in the deep south. Of his Kandyan relations, only Bernard Aluvihare was interested in his political plans, and few of his wife's relatives supported him in their home district of Ratnapura. Of the four relatives who did stand for the SLFP, three were defeated. In 1956 itself, two of these four did not stand while the other two were returned. Again, few of Mrs Bandaranaike's relations actively supported her husband, and S. W. R. D.'s Protestant relatives were distressed at the MEP's Buddhist assertions and his association with the Marxists led by Philip Gunawardene. J. P. Obeysekere was perhaps typical of S. W. R. D.'s Kandyan relations in seeking to dissociate himself from their *Radala* connections as he knew only too well their unpopularity among the electorate S. W. R. D. was soliciting.

For the July 1960 elections Mrs Bandaranaike took over the leadership of the party from C. P. de Silva who had assumed the role as a founder member after S. W. R. D.'s death. Mrs Bandaranaike did not contest a seat at the elections and on her victory in July, she was elected to the Senate. In 1965 and 1970 she contested successfully at Attanagalla. (In passing, it is worth noting the allegation by some *Salagama* that C. P. de Silva was ousted because of his caste, which, it was felt, was inappropriate in a Sinhalese national leader, and would in any case antagonise the support of other castes.) Dr N. M. Perera, in a later acrimonious debate about a proposal to cut the rice ration, voiced what many have felt about Mrs Bandaranaike's politics:

are we all reactionaries in this House merely because we oppose a cut in the rice ration and because we oppose a reactionary Budget? Who is Mrs Sirimavo Bandaranaike to call us reactionaries? After all, she is a politician only by reason of the fact that she was the wife of Mr S. W. R. D. Bandaranaike. Apart from that, has she had any past with regard to politics?[20]

Two of her husband's relatives were re-elected and Felix Dias Bandaranaike, a cousin of S. W. R. D.'s, successfully stood for the first time. (The Dias Bandaranaikes are also distantly related to the Senanayakes through the de Alwis family.) Mrs Bandaranaike brought in two of her own relations, her uncle, who was defeated at Senkadagala, and her brother, Clifford S. Ratwatte, who was returned for Balangoda. From 1960 on, she has encouraged her family to enter politics, and has sought to build up a family caucus through entry to the legislature.

In 1965 five family members won seats and Mrs Bandaranaike herself stood for the first time, winning Attanagalla, part of the old Attanagalla seat won by her husband and divided at the 1959 Delimitation. In 1970 five more of her relations sought to enter parliament. Anurudha Ratwatte, son of her father's brother, was defeated at Senkadagala. Moithra (Monty) Gopallawa and Hector Kobbekaduwa, newly related by marriage, won at Laggala and Yatinuwara; Nanda Ellawala, related through Mrs Bandaranaike's uncle, Sydney Ellawala, won at Ratnapura; and Mallika Ratwatte, cousin to Nanda and married to one of Mrs Bandaranaike's brothers, Clifford, held Balangoda. Of these, only Nanda Ellawala had a background particularly fitting to a political career. Monty Gopallawa, Hector Kobbekaduwa's son-in-law, had a vaguely academic background and Kobbekaduwa himself had followed a modest career in the Kandy Municipal Council and the Public Services Commission. The strongest political qualification of the two Ratwattes was their relationship to Mrs Bandaranaike. Richard Udugama, a more distant relation, won Matale, his family's home area. Siva Obeysekere, Lakshman Jayakody, and Felix Dias Bandaranaike all retained their seats, and Pani Illangakoon finally regained Weligama, for the first time since 1956. (S. D. Bandaranayake, who had stood for the SLFP since 1952, stood as a China-wing CP candidate, forfeited SLFP support, and lost the seat.) Mrs Bandaranaike has succeeded in this way in encouraging quite a number of her family to enter politics, and through appointment, has begun to build a family political network.

Born in 1916 the eldest daughter of Barnes Ratwatte, *Dissawe*, she was educated at St Bridget's Convent, Colombo, and in 1940 married S. W. R. D., then Minister for Local Administration. One of her more enthusiastic biographers has described her welfare work with women's organisations amidst the 'lush feudal countryside of her native Balangoda',[21] and it is the feudal perceptions of family which she appears to have brought with her to government.

One of two sisters and four brothers, Mrs Bandaranaike has put her siblings to good use. Brother Clifford after 1970 became Chairman of the State Plantation Corporation, and brother Sivali the Director of the Export Promotion Secretariat. Mackie became the Prime Minister's Private Secretary, and S. C. Barnes became Public Trustee from the mid-1960s, and in 1974 was appointed a Supreme Court Judge. Her children have attained similar distinction. Anura, her son, seems to act increasingly as her adjutant, and heads the SLFP Youth League. Sunethra became Co-ordinating Secretary to the Prime Minister in 1970. Sunethra's husband, Kumar Rupasinghe, while acting as a gadfly to the left of Mrs Bandaranaike, in 1975 became a Working Director to the National Youth Council. Chandrika has been appointed successively as Settlement Planning Officer, Land Reform Commission (1970); Director, Land Reform Commission (1975); and most recently, has become the first woman chairman of a state corporation in charge of co-operatively run tea, rubber, and coconut plantations nationalised under her mother's recent land-reform measures.

But how powerful are they?

While it is relatively simple to describe the office and relationship of family members, it is more difficult to judge if family considerations influence political decisions directly, or to discern in a particular situation exactly how much emphasis should be given to familial ties.

Certainly kinship has been a useful political lever for the Senanayakes. For example, when the UNP was manoeuvring in 1964 to bring down the coalition, Dudley Senanayake won over two of his relations, formerly members of the coalition parties: Edmund Samarakkody, LSSP MP for Bulathsinhala, and SLFP Senator Sarath Wijesinghe. The Wijewardenes' Lake House Press group, at the time under the direction of Esmond Wickremasinghe, aligned itself powerfully behind the campaign. Again, in 1969 Dudley persuaded a distant relation, Jack Kotelawala, a founder member of the LSSP who had been at odds with the LSSP leadership for some time, to become his Ambassador to the USSR.

Nor have the Senanayakes been politically insensitive to the business interests of the family. When Dr N. M. Perera disclosed to the House allegedly fraudulent exchange control deals and income tax evasions by ANCL, Dudley Senanayake, then Prime Minister, conspicuously failed to appoint a Commission of Inquiry.[22] The *Young Socialist* deftly commented:

It would be well worth to take a look at the composition of the controlling interests of the Lake House group. The private capital of this group exists in the form of 36,000 shares, each valued at Rs. 70. 33,593 of these shares are owned by the Wijewardene family and their close relatives. The chairman of this group is Ranjit Wijewardene, who happens to be wedded to the daughter of Robert Senanayake, the brother of the Prime Minister, Dudley Senanayake – in other words, the Prime Minister's own nephew! The rest of the directorships of the company are distributed among the brothers-in-law of Ranjit Wijewardene. The country need not be surprised if the government makes no further moves in this matter. However shocking the scandal, whatever prominence it may have received in the international press, it must always be remembered that in UNP circles blood is thicker than water![23]

Family solidarity is no longer the prerogative of the UNP, however, and Mrs Bandaranaike has turned her family into a powerful instrument of government. Perhaps her earliest move came when in 1962 she advised the Queen to replace Sir Oliver Goonetilleke as Governor-General with Sir William Gopallawa. Sir Oliver had been closely identified with the UNP and was named in the initial investigations of the 1962 *coup* case.[24] Sir William Gopallawa's daughter is married to Sivali, a brother of Mrs Bandaranaike. In 1970, committed to the difficult programme of achieving agricultural self-sufficiency and far-reaching land reforms, Mrs Bandaranaike appointed Hector Kobbekaduwa as her Minister of Agriculture and Lands; his daughter is married to Sir William's son, Moithra (Monty), SLFP MP for Laggala. (It is perhaps important to note that when the estates were nationalised in 1975, the lands were turned over to the Ministry of Agriculture, not to the Ministry of Plantations held by the LSSP. This move indirectly led to the withdrawal of the LSSP from the United Front.) Again, when faced by the April 1971 insurgency, she turned to her relations and appointed Colonel Divitotawela, who is married to her sister, as Commander of the hastily raised Ceylon Volunteer Force.

The precise character of the complex political relationships involved in juggling the pressures of caste lobbies, family, and party obligations can be described by the following example. At the 1965 elections the *Karava* Christians had supported the UNP and it was necessary to find suitable ministerial compensation for them. The lobby put forward Hugh Fernando for the post of Minister of Commerce and Trade. He had not contested the 1965 elections and was at the time High Commissioner to Pakistan. In 1968, however, the seat at Nattandiya, won in 1965 for the UNP by Albert Pieris, fell vacant. Hugh Fernando was recalled from Pakistan to contest the seat for the UNP and won by a slender margin of 260 votes against the SLFP. The Cabinet was reshuffled, Dr M. V. P. Peiris (*Goyigama*) being moved from the Ministry of Commerce to become Ambassador to the USSR, enabling Hugh Fernando to take his place. Simultaneously, Mallory Wijesinghe, Sir Oliver Goonetilleke's son-in-law, retired as President of the Chamber of Commerce, and Eardley de Silva (*Karava*) took over the Presidency. By this time, the Permanent Secretary to the Ministry of Commerce, H. C. Goonewardene (*Goyigama*, and married to Mallory Wijesinghe's sister), had been replaced by P. A. Silva (*Karava*). The first appointment Hugh Fernando made as Minister of Commerce and Trade was G. V. S. de Silva (*Karava*) as Chairman of the Insurance Corporation, the only corporate appointment that came within his Ministry.

This sequence of appointments demonstrates very clearly the inner dynamics of elite politics. The UNP family network was broken and remade in different areas of the administration (Dr M. V. P. Peiris becoming an ambassador, and H. C. Goonewardene retiring to become Chairman of the Salaries Commission) in order to allow space for the *Karava* Christian lobby to operate, in a neat balancing of party, personal, and caste obligation.

It is no longer clear that the use of family and kinship is politically advantageous, however, at least electorally. While it is undoubtedly true that the election of Rukman Senanayake to Dudley's seat at Dedigama owed much to his membership of the UNP clan, it is also the case that Mrs Bandaranaike's inclusion of her close relations at the centre of her administration has aroused a great deal of dissatisfaction among the lower ranks of the SLFP, for it offends the party's essentially populist character. J. R. Jayawardene, who inherited the leadership of the UNP on Dudley's death, skilfully exploited voters' distrust of 'family politics' to his advantage in his widely publicised dismissal of Rukman from the inner workings of UNP councils some months after the by-election; though the affair was presented as an attempt to cleanse the UNP of 'family politics', it was aimed, too, at the Ratwattes – one stone, two birds.

7

Caste and the insurgency of 1971

Introduction

In April 1971 Sri Lanka faced an outbreak of violent insurgency that took many of its citizens and politicians by surprise. It swiftly became apparent that its supporters were mainly young, and that it drew on the frustrations of the rural unemployed and those with jobs they felt to be insufficiently rewarding either financially or in terms of status. School and university students from the three campuses of Peradeniya in the hills, and Vidyodaya and Vidyalankara, south and north of Colombo, where many from less wealthy and influential families attended, were also soon revealed as important contributors to insurgent support.

As the fighting continued, the movement was revealed as predominantly Sinhalese and Buddhist, at times strongly anti-Indian in sentiment; it was also widely reported as either an anti-*Goyigama* plot, or a movement of the low caste. The armed services were said to be rounding up the youth of known low-caste villages for detention, and it was rumoured that the low-caste insurgents were led by young *Karava* radicals. Were these reports true? And if so, what was their significance? This chapter attempts to set the caste dimension of the movement and its leadership against a more general description of the background and motives of the activists.

The Chairman of the Criminal Justice Commission appointed to enquire into the events of April 1971 and to establish the case against the alleged insurgents summarised the débâcle as a 'hopeless revolution'. Rohana Wijeweera, supposedly the supreme leader of the insurgent groups, countered swiftly that it was none the less a very successful political movement.

Both are right: it was a sadly bungled attempt to win power; ill-planned, badly directed (insofar as the fighting was directed at all) and in any coolly logistical calculation, hopelessly misconceived. Yet Wijeweera's defence of the Janatha Vimukthi Peramuna (JVP – People's Liberation Front) as essentially a political movement, embracing the aspirations and perceptions of those who felt they had no place and no future within the existing political parties, is valid, too.

Both its technical failure and its political success emanated from the same social roots. Neither pure class analysis nor the adapted Marxist reasoning of the left-wing parties adduced *ex post facto*, nor the materialist rebukes of the Prime Minister towards the '*no maga giya tharunayō*' – misguided or wayward youths – wholly or satisfactorily explain or describe the movement, its participants, or its influence.

A number of articles have appeared already which adequately describe the reaction of the CP and LSSP, who were faced with the embarrassing task of explaining why radical and revolutionary-minded youths broke away from their own Youth Leagues, and the charges and counter-charges which were bandied between the parties in vigorous attempts to link the movement to class, ideology, or the prevalent world-wide student unrest.[1] The events leading up to the insurrection, the socio-economic and the political background, have also been well enough presented to need no detailed repetition here.[2] What has yet to be produced to a wider public, other than the Sinhala pamphlets and flysheets issued by the insurgents themselves, is a description of the movement that places it within the dynamics of rural society in Lanka and explains how the universal analytic phrases such as 'generational conflict', 'frustration of expectations', 'educational dysfunctionalism', 'demographic imbalance' and the actual terrifyingly high youthful unemployment, precisely apply to the insurgent population in Lanka.

In other words, the nature of the insurgency is known, and its similarity to kindred movements overseas has been noted; the skeleton of events has been pieced together and the ideological outline roughly traced, yet what is lacking still is the flesh and blood. This chapter attempts to convey something of this inner vitality and tension and to show them as the product of the same forces that operate within the legitimate social structure.

As a preliminary I shall repeat the stark figures that define the common experiences of the young and pick out some of the more salient features which contributed to the way the movement was able to develop. In 1969 60 per cent of the total population of twelve and a half million were under twenty-five. Of the fourteen- to twenty-five-year age group, 45 per cent were out of school but unemployed. Approximately 74 per cent of the population were literate, the majority of the young in Sinhala or Tamil only, following the '*Swabhasha* Only' provisions of S. W. R. D. Bandaranaike's government. (Until then English had been the medium of instruction in educational establishments, and many of the older generation had at least some knowledge of English.) Despite the *swabhasha*, however, English has remained a mark of status; the educated young were beginning to suspect that a wholly *swabhasha* education was second-rate and denied them access to the outside world.

The role of English and the insurgents' understanding of its status is vividly revealed in the following passage from the statement made by one of the captured leaders: 'As soon as Osmund's brother said: "Here come the Police" everyone ran away . . . we were in the Burgher granny's house . . .Then when the Police came and questioned her she spoke at length, saying: "They ran away", "They ran away", "They did not come this way", etc. When she spoke in English they believed. Understand?'[3]

Approximately 72 per cent of the population is rural, with only 15 per cent residing in towns (the remainder is largely resident in the estate sectors). But it would be wrong to envisage the rural population as evenly distributed among the cultivable areas; approximately 75 per cent of the total population live within an eighty-mile radius of Colombo, the capital city. Because of this concentration and because of heavily subsidised public transport, many statistically rural residents live in areas which do not appear sharply urban or rural and they can and do pass easily to and from their more rustic family village to their urban place of work and their town relatives. More, perhaps, than the general population, the young seem accustomed to travelling frequently and extensively, for the purposes, for example, of attending school sports or of staying with relatives throughout the island in their search for employment. So for the mass of unemployed youth the common experience was of mobility, literacy, and familiarity with the opportunities and facilities offered by the urban jobs they so desperately sought.

A job in the bureaucracies or in teaching, white-collar, status work, was the ideal, and many thought that education qualified them for such employment as of right.[4] Education had seemed the path to full participation in Lanka's society and body politic, but for the poor and the unknown, with few or no contacts, somehow the rewards were not forthcoming. Educating a child was often a great sacrifice for the parents, for while tuition is free, books, shoes, clothing, and so on all had to be provided, and many could in any case ill afford to lose an immediately useful pair of hands to full-time education, however large the eventual promised return. By the late 1960s it had become apparent that the economy could not possibly absorb the huge numbers of school leavers and university graduates into clerical and administrative jobs in the towns to which they thought their education had entitled them. Acute frustration and a bitter feeling of having been let down became the common emotional experience of the young.

The condition of rural life for a large part of the young in turn exercised a strong 'push' effect, strengthening the desire for modern ways of life and new opportunities via education and non-manual employment. For though nearly three-quarters of the population live in rural areas, over half of these do not depend directly on agricultural income; by far the largest number are wage labourers. To use the language of the left, the last hundred years has seen the gradual 'proletarianisation' of rural families. (Rohana Wijeweera has characterised the unemployed young as those waiting to enter the rural proletariat; the movement was thus not among rural wage labourers, but characteristically, was the expression of those either waiting to sell their labour, or engaged in improving their saleability.)

There might be work enough in the Southern and Western Provinces, with their complex local economies and high population densities provoking a wide variety of secondary and tertiary economic needs, but the situation is very different in the remoter areas, and in the hinterlands of Sabaragamuwa, the North-Central Province, or the deep south, for example, conditions are little changed from pre-Independence days. Despite the increased political representation of the sparsely populated areas secured by the 1959 Delimitation, their needs seem to have been largely overlooked by politicians surrounded by the vociferous demands of the population of the capital. The *purana gam* (villages of the dry zone) scattered in the North-Central Province are still dependent on *chena* cultivation and the waters of a small local tank for their hard existence, cut off from towns accessible only by jeep. Barefoot children irregularly attend distant rural schools which are not infrequently ill-equipped and poorly staffed, certainly not able to offer opportunities comparable to those of the well-favoured schools of the towns. Men leave their families during the rice-cultivation seasons to travel across the island to Anuradhapura, hoping to gain sufficient money to return wearing shoes, maybe, or the 'shirt and trouser' or even perhaps a watch.

All these factors created an emotional ferment that was restless and dissatisfied. The insurgents' attempts to translate their feelings into logical analysis and political action can be traced in the histories and in the words of the participants themselves; here, in the next few paragraphs, we may conclude the preliminaries by crudely sketching their response.

The 'Government' had given them food, via the weekly household ration, so few were starving; the 'Government' had given them free hospital treatment and were justly proud of public hygiene standards, so few died because of neglect or insanitary squalor; the 'Government' had given them free tuition in the schools and universities, so few were illiterate and many were avid readers of the chatty, lively, and informed popular press – but the 'Government' had not given them jobs; had not given them a place in the power structure; had not found a way, via a growing, modernising economy to weaken the sometimes onerous social obligations upon the non-*Goyigama*.

The 'Government' was paternalist. Its activity was seen as something done by 'them' for 'us', rather than as something in which the ordinary individual could participate effectively. If one was of the wrong family, the wrong caste, and had no finances, there was no chance of standing for political office – except as the pawn of an elite clique. Since they could not change the system from within, because they could not enter it effectively, they would attack it from without. These ideas were circulated and discussed among the insurgents, each member contributing his own experiences. Rohana Wijeweera has described how Uyangoda, one of the main accused before the Criminal Justice Commission, pointed out that the SLFP members of the government were related by blood ties.[5]

Politically, the insurgents saw themselves as the socially oppressed and economically deprived striking the leading blow against a clique of elite families and their exclusive class interests. The personnel of the UNP government who they thought would try to hold onto power unconstitutionally if defeated at the 1970 general election, and the personnel of the popularly elected government of the United Front which won the 1970 election were seen as tarred with the same brush of elitism, whatever their party–economic identities as 'capitalist' or 'left wing'. Both came to seem essentially anachronistic, part of an exclusive system that left them with no effective role or reward. As for the Marxist CP (Moscow wing) and the Trotskyist LSSP, both were identified as bourgeois parliamentary parties irreversibly compromised by the 'coalition tactic', who had crept to power on the *saripota* or coat-tails of Mrs Bandaranaike.

In 1943 in Balangoda the Senanayake factions had displayed a masterly command of traditional social dynamics and had turned them to powerful and exact political advantage within the formal structure. In April 1971 the insurgents attacked the formal political structure as an inadequate parliamentary game played in the interests of elite families and bourgeois parties that had skilfully manipulated traditional social relationships to their own exclusive advantage. To a considerable degree the movement's own impulse sprang from the resentments created by the political manipulation of those relationships; it sought to translate its adherents from pawns at least into knights strong enough and near enough to the centres of power to cry: 'Checkmate!' As has been demonstrated in previous chapters, their analysis, though imprecise, was in many ways close to the realities.

The caste dimension

Nothing final and certain can be written of the involvement of certain castes in the movement. One insurgent imprisoned in Welikade prison has written a booklet on caste and the insurgency, arguing that certain of the higher castes manipulated the lower, depressed castes to their own advantage, making them fight for them without any intention of letting them be equals when they had achieved their aims. The LSSP Central Committee in 1972 discussed a brief outlining the role of caste in the insurgency. Many of the armed services took the view that the fighting was an expression of anti-*Goyigama* resentment and in certain areas went into low-caste villages and arrested all the youths regardless of any proof of participation.[6]

N. Shanmugathasan, the leader of the CP (China wing) splinter group, has analysed the appeal of the JVP thus:

The JVP tried a new mixture. They wrapped up a crude appeal to anti-Indian-ism (the plantation workers of Indian origin, who form a substantial portion of Ceylon's working class, were portrayed as pawns of Indian expansionism) with revolutionary phraseology. In this they seemed to be more successful. For additional measure they also subtly exploited an appeal to caste. Most of the leaders of the JVP belong to one caste.[7]

Shanmugathasan was right in alleging that the leadership was concentrated among one caste; of the forty-one alleged leaders appearing before the Criminal Justice Commission, fourteen belonged to the *Karava*, four were *Vahumpura*, and one *Batgam*. Only eleven belonged to the *Goyigama* community. And taking the 'inner circle' or 'politburo' of the movement, twelve out of the fourteen (or ten out of eleven, depending on whose list of politburo members one takes) were *Karava*.

What was the caste distribution among the movement as a whole? The government interrogated 10,192 suspected insurgents held in custody and obtained a breakdown of their age, race, years spent in schooling, and the number in employment. The data also yielded the breakdown for their caste as shown in table 32.

While the leadership appears to be concentrated among particular castes, principally the *Karava*, the mass of the insurgents do not appear to show any such bias. However, there are a number of reasons why these particular figures need to be treated with extreme caution as an index of caste membership. The tendency of the armed services to treat low-caste

TABLE 32   *Data on 10,192 suspected insurgents, by caste*

	Number	Percentage
Sinhalese castes		
Goyigama	5,962	58.5
Karava	636	6.2
Salagama	193	1.9
Vahumpura	1,038	10.2
Hena	204	2.0
Hunu	35	0.3
Batgam	944	9.3
Navandanna	159	1.6
Rodiya	2	0.0
Berawa	267	2.6
Kumbal	27	0.3
Tamil castes		
Paraiyar	17	0.2
Vellala	10	0.2
Hariyan	10	0.2
Panaduram	2	0.0
Kannda	1	0.0
Nadar	1	0.0
Unspecified	520	5.1
Omitted	164	1.5
Total	10,192	100.1

Source: data from government interrogations, circulated in mimeograph. Reported in Gananath Obeysekere, 'Some comments on the social backgrounds of the April 1971 insurgency in Sri Lanka (Ceylon)', *Journal of Asian Studies*, 33, 3 (May 1974), 367–84.

villages as insurgent strongholds has already been mentioned. This may be thought to introduce a counter-bias into the figures (i.e. that the low castes are, if anything, over-represented among the insurgents of the data sample), but, because of the treatment they received from the armed services, it is my impression that few of those arrested admitted to their correct caste identity if they could avoid it. Secondly, attempts have been made to verify the data by reference to the *gē* names of those arrested, as reported in the press and elsewhere. However, unless one knows with certainty the village and home area of the individual, *gē*-name identification can be perilous. As mentioned earlier, there is a distinct tendency for low-country immigrants to the dry-zone cultivation areas to adopt higher-caste identities. The same practice occurs in localised areas such as

Kuliyapitiya, too, a district of *Batgam* concentration, where a sizeable number have taken 'good *Goyigama*' names such as 'Mudiyanselagē'.[8] Thirdly, while a number of those arrested were not insurgents at all, a further unquantifiable number who were were not arrested. For example, in both Hiniduma, in the hinterland behind Galle and an area of low-caste concentration, and in Badulla, the local leaders were swept up in pre-5 April raids, and their followers never emerged as identifiable insurgents.

All these ambiguities make the sample data unreliable, both in terms of the population it purports to define, and in terms of the caste identities allocated to those arrested. None the less, despite the uncertainty it is notable that some of the heaviest fighting occurred along the south and west coast (*Karava* areas), and in a belt stretching south-east to north-west, from Tissamaharama, through Sabaragamuwa to Matale and the North-Central Province, touching the eastern jungles around Amparai and the western coastal jungles of the North-Western Province (areas of *Vahumpura* and *Batgam* concentration). In almost any district one cares to examine, the villages involved in the heaviest fighting appear to be of low caste: Wellawaya, and Warakapola in the south-east; the villages around Matale in the hill country, the thirty-two *Panne* villages around Kandy (*Pannadura*, a sub-caste of the *Batgam*); Paragamana, a large *Batgam* village one and a half miles from Marapone town on the Kandy road, where twenty-nine were killed trying to blow up a bridge; Damunupola, a large *Batgam* village in Galigomuwa (population of 1,506; the two other villages involved in that district, Getiyamulla and Kandegedera-Bakolamulla, were both *Goyigama*, with populations of 400 and 409 respectively).

The caste pattern of insurgent support and political activity among the young can be illustrated by looking at a specific locality. Pelmadulla, electorate number 140, in Ratnapura District, lies under the southern edge of the Adam's Peak Wilderness. It is cut to the north and south by low but precipitous hills, with river tributaries running through the rocky valley bottoms. Large areas are covered by scrub and jungle; the major cultivation is tea on the hill slopes with paddy fields extending across the narrow river plains. The chief, indeed practically the only industry is mining for gems, though toddy-tapping and illicit liquor-brewing provide secondary employment.

The electorate had many *Vahumpura* and *Batgam*. Though it is an area where traditional social norms are strictly observed (with the historic Sri Pada temple at nearby Ratnapura and a number of other powerful *vihares* within the electorate exercising discreet pressure), trading and the gemming business have enabled a number of persons to become very wealthy; for example, Bulath Mudalali and P. Pelendagama.

P. Pelendagama, with the support of the Mathew family, in 1970 stood for the UNP at Pelmadulla, and again at Ratnapura in a by-election in 1972. The *Vahumpura* in the area appear to be pressing not for structural change but for social acceptance. They are acutely aware of the place of caste in the politics of their area, alleging at the by-election in 1972 that George Rajapakse (SLFP MP for Mulkirigala and Minister of Fisheries in 1971), when sending colonists from the south coast into the Uda Walawwe, had given traditional *Vahumpura chena* lands and river-basin paddy to the colonists.

In terms of the established parties, the area was swept by the UF in 1970 and is greatly influenced by the politics of Nanda Ellawala, SLFP MP at Ratnapura, and Sarath Muttetuwegama, CP MP at Kalawana. In Ratnapura, where Muttetuwegama had stood in 1965, the influence of the CP (Moscow) has been very strong, apparently too strong for the JVP to break into effectively. (See, for instance, local sales of the CP tabloid, *Ginipupura*, against the JVP's *Ratubaleya*; nevertheless, the latter sold approximately 45,000 copies island-wide in its first issue; a tremendous achievement.)[9] However, a substantial number of CP Youth Leaguers in the district moved into the China wing, prior to 1970, and from there to Dharmasekera's group within the JVP. When Dharmasekera split with Wijeweera in March 1970, the Pelmadulla sympathisers stayed with Dharmasekera. It seems the China-wing leaders in any case did not allow much questioning of their policy, argumentative opinions being condemned as the 'upset-line'.

Four villages in Pelmadulla were particularly involved in the fighting of April 1971, most notably Bambarabotuwa on the edge of the Bambara-botuwa Forest Reserve. It is a very large *Vahumpura* village in the northern hinterland, off the Ratnapura–Mahawelatenne road (a minor road, not shown on map 7) running into the Central Province. (Note that it is close by Pelendagama, the home area of the UNP candidate.) Patakada and Sennasgama are both largely *Goyigama* villages off the Ratnapura–Pelmadulla road. Kehetenne, at the south-east border of Pelmadulla on the Ratnapura–Pelmadulla–Rakwana road, is a trading village: the fighting there seems to have centred on the activities of a few *Karava* leaders.

The reasons for the particular pattern of caste support and leadership described in this chapter are to be found in the political history of Lanka and the pressures imposed by changing economic circumstances on tradi-tional and social customs and attitudes. Despite twenty-five years or more

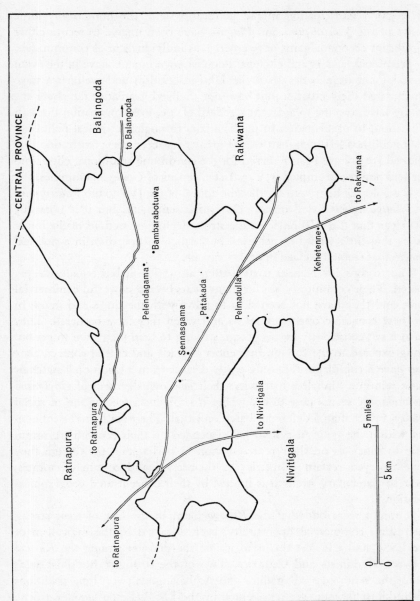

Map 7   Sketch map of Pelmadulla electorate, showing major roads

CENTRAL PROVINCE

Balangoda

to Balangoda

Rakwana

•Bambarabotuwa

Pelendagama•

Patakada •

to Rakwana

Sennasgama•

Kehetenne•

Pelmadulla•

Ratnapura

to Ratnapura

to Nivitigala

to Ratnapura

Nivitigala

5 miles

5 km

of electoral participation in the political system, the numerically large castes of the *Vahumpura* and *Batgam* have been unable to secure either significant economic gains or to emerge, as individuals or as communities, as prominent leaders and citizens. Populist governments have in the event served them little better than the UNP; socialism and welfarism have ameliorated their situation but have not changed it greatly: the closer the young have to come to a decent standard of life, to emancipation through education, to participation in public affairs through the radical politics of the established left-wing parties, the greater has been their frustration that the real fruits have been reserved for the continuing traditional elites, and the real power pre-empted by a restricted caucus of *Goyigama* families.

It would not be true to say that the appeal of the JVP to the *Vahumpura* and *Batgam* was based on anti-*Goyigama* sentiment, but it is none the less clear that the JVP reflected the strong feeling of sections of the lower castes that little would be achieved by further participation in a political system that seemed skewed in others' favour.

The reasons for *Karava* participation are different but equally deeply rooted. Their community has for many years been a powerful commercial force and they have not been slow to move with the times and invest in the new economic opportunities as and when they have occurred. They form a self-consciously aware group, striving to help their own to get on. Long exposed to the foreign influences of trade and coastal contact, they also have a confidence that only partly derives from a traditional status or place within a Sinhalese hierarchy; their acknowledgement of *Goyigama* 'ascendancy' seems now to be, where it is given, a recognition of social reality, rather than a deference based on ritual. Their ability to be influential within the political system has depended on their economic prominence as much as on their representation in parliament, for though they have reserved certain Ministries to themselves and certain electorates, their parliamentary strength is limited by their concentrated geographical location.

It might seem odd that the *Karava* have, in the face of their strong interest in commercial opportunity, been attracted by the radicalism of the LSSP and CP. Yet this is to ignore the division among the *Karava* between Buddhists and Catholics. Two of the strongest Buddhist areas along the south coast, Panadura and Ambalangoda, with long traditions of Buddhist fervour, are represented by the LSSP (Leslie Goonewardene and L. C. de Silva in 1970), and it is the *Karava* Buddhists rather than the Catholics who have been attracted by the left. The reason for this lies in the skilful weaving together by S. W. R. D. of Sinhalese Buddhist nationalist sentiment under the banner of 'democratic socialism': concern for the 'common man' and compassion for the depressed and unfortunate has provided a bridge to the economic policies of the Marxist left and the SLFP. Beyond the level of sentiment and belief, the *Karava* Buddhists have seen in the SLFP a way through the *Goyigama* supremacy represented in the UNP of D. S. Senanayake and Sir John Kotelawala. Mrs Bandaranaike has been inclined to respect the *Karava* Buddhist leaders of 1956 – N. Q. Dias was appointed Permanent Secretary to the Ministry of Defence and External Affairs, and Ananda Nimalasuriya was appointed Chairman of the Public Services Commission after her victory in 1960, though they were passed over by S. W. R. D. – and has continued to favour them since 1970. The UNP, in contrast, has tended to woo the *Karava* Christians.

The frustration of the young *Karava* insurgents thus had its basis in two forces: first, the experience of revolutionary left-wing electioneering and politicking which in practice had been realised in the 'coalition tactic' and the participation by the left leadership in the elitist manipulations of the SLFP and UNP rather than the promised fundamental social and political change; secondly, their membership in a community which was denied a political influence commensurate with its economic strength under the existing delimitation of electorates.

The top leadership

Marked differences in social background are apparent between the alleged leaders and those who were in the front line of the fighting. Within the leadership itself a number of ideological and personality differences which had considerable influence on its course and direction characterised the movement from the early days.

The forty-one main accused before the CJC have been identified by the state as the most important leaders of the insurgency, but not unnaturally they have sought to avoid individual responsibility for the events of April 1971. Crown witnesses have tried to describe the movement as a disciplined hierarchy with Rohana Wijeweera in overall command, seeking personal glory and acting through a few of his chosen followers in a thoroughly undemocratic way. It is clear, however, that the movement was not, and could not have been, a centrally organised body structured along the lines of the legitimate parties, nor could Wijeweera have hoped to retain sole authority over everyone who regarded himself as a member of the JVP. It was clandestine, fluid, and dispersed, with local groups coming into being and organising themselves long before Wijeweera's closest colleagues could approach them to discuss their political views, tactics, and organisation. Models for electing local leaders, structuring regional and district groups, and educating their members did exist, but in practice the local leader tended to be the most articulate and politically conscious member, the groups to emerge spontaneously before becoming part of a larger and more coherent structure, and their political understanding to be determined by the exigencies of their local situation. Indeed, few even of the forty-one main accused appeared to have a fully formulated political outlook, and amongst their followers, a wide range of views, aspirations, and political maturity is to be found.

No one in the JVP regarded it as a party; at most it was a *Peramuna*, or Front, but, more exactly, it was described as simply a movement designed to bring about the *rādical vādaya*, or radicalisation of the young.[10] The now-famous Five Lectures formed the chief instrument of mobilisation.[11] The first elaborated the nature of Lanka's 'Economic Crisis' – 'the crisis of the colonial and neo-colonial capitalist system which . . . is in the process of being transformed into a political crisis'; the second, entitled 'Independence – a Neo-Colonialist Strategy', argued that the 'so-called Independence was a neo-colonialist trick and an imperialist fraud'. The third, developed from Chinese arguments at the time of the 1962 Sino–Indian border conflict, claimed that the nature of Indian capitalism led it to seek domination over its smaller neighbours, and linked this drive to the actions of the Indian merchants and plantation labourers in Lanka (some members claimed that it was virulently hostile to the Indian minority in Lanka). The fourth, 'The Left Movement in Ceylon', denounced the 'politics and programmes of the Old Left Movement . . . from its inception to the present day'. The fifth and most important lecture, 'The Path the Ceylonese Revolution Should Take', was an attempt to counter Cuban, Russian, and Chinese models of revolution and to devise a suitable strategy for Lanka's particular circumstances. These lectures were not an exact formula, and considerable variation in content and conclusion seems to have existed, especially with regard to the final lecture.[12] They were not regarded by the JVP as composing a policy statement or manifesto, nor were they designed to create 'overnight Marxists'. As Wijeweera has put it, echoing a classic Buddhist analogy: 'These classes were only used as a bridge to draw people from the bank of capitalist thinking to our bank of Marxist thinking.'[13]

None the less, Wijeweera is acknowledged now as the 'leader' of the JVP though he himself claims never to have held any specific title or function within the movement. He was born in 1943 to *Karava* parents of middling status, living on the south coast. His uncle, Anonis Appuhamy, was a substantial local *mudalali* and a UNP supporter. His father had come from Baddegama, where he had been Church *Appu* (lay officer), then moving to Ambalangoda to become a cultivator. An active supporter of Dr Wickremasinghe, he had been crippled during a campaign in Matara and had become the owner of a small provisions store. His mother's father had been a big landowner in Tangalle. He received his early education at Godagoda High School through the medium of English. During the 1950s he became attracted to Dr Wickremasinghe's policies and became active in the Communist Party. In 1959 he moved to Dharmasoka College, Ambalangoda, to study for his science Ordinary-level examinations, and in the 1960 elections he campaigned for the CP and Aelian Nanayakkara. Though later the JVP were to regard the new generation of Communist Party MPs as 'false Marxists', in the early years of the 1960s Vasudeva Nanayakkara and S. D. Bandaranayake, though relatively obscure nationally, seemed to offer hope to the young for a renewed radicalisation of the left.

In October 1960 he went to Lumumba University in the Soviet Union, where he became increasingly dissatisfied with the international posture of Russian Communism and he began to study the experience of the Chinese. On his return to Lanka he met up with 'Sanath' and 'Karunaratne' (real names unknown), who were to become two of his closest associates. Sanath he met in 1964 at Anuradhapura where he was working as a cultivator and organising for N. Shanmugathasan's China-wing Communist Party. Karunaratne was then a pupil–teacher in Wattala and a member of the Moscow-wing Communist Party.

Mrs Bandaranaike rather unkindly called the top leaders a 'group of disgruntled and designing persons drawn from the rejects and the unwanted of practically every recognised political party'.[14] It is certainly true that most of the forty-one main accused followed Wijeweera's path through the left-wing parties to the JVP. Similar, too, are their social roots among the Sinhalese rural petty bourgeoisie, clearly the first post-1956 political generation, the offspring of the schoolteachers and minor officials who had voted Bandaranaike to power; Uyangoda, known in the movement for his agile mind and the elegance of his speech, is a good example. Distrusted by some as the confidant of Wijeweera and suspected of acting as Wijeweera's 'intelligence officer', he began his political career in the Moscow wing of the CP. Born Radalgē James Uyangoda, of the *Hena* caste, in Karandeniya, he campaigned in 1970 for Aelian Nanayakkara at Kamburupitiya. Until a few months before the insurgency he was employed as a clerk at the Urban Council at Kalutara.

Podi Athula, whose hands were severely damaged in an explosion whilst engaged in bomb-manufacture, was educated at the eminent

Catholic school of St Aloysius in Galle. Lionel Bopage had trained as an engineer, and Wiraj Fernando had studied engineering in London.

Two of the forty-one stand out: S. D. Bandaranayake and Susil Siriwardene (who had been educated at Oxford and Harvard), both related to Felix Dias Bandaranaike. Siriwardene had taken to teaching in Anuradhapura before being appointed to the elitist Ceylon Administrative Service. Both claim that their initial interest in the movement died when they discovered that it did not follow orthodox Marxism and that some of its adherents were advocating armed seizure of power.

The lower-rank leaders

The schisms between these alleged leaders will be discussed presently but first the case histories of four lower-rank leaders will be presented, because they describe the kind of young man who took authority in the movement, and, in the latter two cases, illustrate typically the political impetus towards the JVP and some of the varieties of opinion within it.

1

On 22 June 1971, while travelling on a bus on the Avissawella road, I witnessed a common feature of the post-April suppression of the insurgency. A police jeep had drawn up across the road in front of a garage and a crowd had gathered to listen to a young man, his hands and feet tied, confess his part in the fighting. He announced that he was a trained teacher, twenty-five years old, from Nawagamuwa near Dompe. He was, he said, the scion of a well-known and well-to-do family. He had taken part in the attack at Warakapola (one of the earliest incidents in the insurrection). He was the local leader of the Nawagamuwa area group and he had a large following of teenage rebels. After participating in various actions he had gone to Ratnapura to hide and had been captured there.

2

The Crown's case against the twenty-seventh accused in the Moratuwa area, Sunil Sisira Kumara alias Bandula, cited his activities as an insurgent leader whilst a student at Veyangoda Central School. His age at the time of arrest was twenty. Before the insurgency, it was claimed, he had installed himself at Katubedde Technical College (not far from Colombo town) and manufactured bombs. He had been the leader of the Moratuwa District.[15]

3

'L. F.' is a *Karava* from a Roman Catholic family living in Negombo. His father runs a tearoom. He was active for the LSSP. L. F. had become interested in the LSSP through the activities of his father and had begun to follow politics whilst still at school. At the time of China's split with Russia he joined N. Shanmugathasan's party. From there he got drawn into the JVP and began organising work for them in Colombo, Peradeniya, Kalutara, and Kegalle. He became a full-timer for the JVP. The organisers were all very poor and had no money, and he had to borrow trousers from school friends and money from his sisters.

In 1970 he felt that if the UNP were to stay in power it would be necessary to fight. He became aware at that time of the divisions between Wijeweera and some others, such as Dharmasekera and T. D. Silva. He became a local leader. He was later accused of trying to build up his own image, but, he says, because there was no leadership at the beginning, those who were most active became the leaders without any organised elections. This caused a great deal of mistrust and doubt in the movement. Though the emphasis was on the rural oppressed, the JVP had not lost faith in the urban working classes, and he himself had had contacts among them. He was aware that there were 'different levels of thinking' in the movement and many ideas as to the future though nobody had thought what they should do if they had gained power in April.

He had received no orders to attack on 5 April. Later, when the police were searching for him, he had surrendered, but he had been released without any charges being made. In the camp he had realised that the accused before the CJC could not be regarded as real leaders because they had not been elected and were fighting among themselves. He had met a deeper commitment to the movement in the camp than there had existed before the insurgency. They had realised, then, by discussing the events, that the JVP had not brought in the real rural oppressed except as fighters, only the rural petty bourgeoisie.[16]

4

Nimal Maharage gave evidence before the CJC on 17 October 1973. As a young man he had been a member of the Communist Party and had attended meetings held by Pieter Keuneman (founder member of the CP and leader of the Moscow wing) and party classes. In 1963 he had left school to become a full-time worker for the CP. He had gone to classes given by Bernard Soysa and Leslie Goonewardene. He had expected a social revolution to follow the coalition tactic of 1964 (when Mrs Bandaranaike took three members of the LSSP into her Cabinet) but it became apparent that the left leaders were interested only in their own class position. He saw then that the capitalist classes were under pressure and had two choices, to abolish democracy or to take in other interests. He had helped the United Front in 1965 but had been greatly disappointed that Philip Gunawardene's MEP had gone over to the right-wing forces of the UNP. This, and the Russia–China split, made him greatly disillusioned.

He met D. A. Gunasekera (a trade union leader in a leather factory, and until 1968, one of the Central Committee members of Shanmugathasan's party). Gunasekera had wanted to take him to China-wing classes. Thereafter he had become a member of the China-wing Communists. At that time he was working in a large factory in Colombo, where (he claimed) they demanded an eight-hour day and used sweated female labour. There was no security for the workers. He had tried to start a trade union but had been sacked. He became involved then with the JVP. He had gone to a camp where Shanmugathasan had given lectures. Many of the China-wing comrades at that time were also becoming members of the JVP.

Shan's trade union, the Ceylon Trade Union Federation, had about two thousand members then, and was trying to draw support from Bala Tampoe's Ceylon Mercantile Union. He had joined the Wellawatte Weaving and Spinning Mills (one of the largest textile concerns, then owned by N. U. Jayawardene) and had worked for the CTUF. The rank and file of the CTUF were disillusioned because the leadership did not allow the younger members to formulate policy. He carried out propaganda work for Marxist–Leninist policies and concluded that the younger members of the left had to remove the existing leadership before true left leadership could be achieved. At that time Shan suggested he leave the factory and he was removed from China-wing membership.

He wanted then to launch his own Marxist–Leninist party but he had no resources. He discussed the matter with D. A. Gunasekera and he met Wijeweera for the first time. In 1969 he went to another camp and received instruction on Indian expansionism, proletarian leadership, the classless society, and common land ownership. In December he attended a discussion about Dharmasekera and his allegedly anti-JVP views. The JVP leaders were trying to unite all the different viewpoints. Dharmasekera said that the Cuban model was the path that Sri Lanka should follow. The JVP felt that the UNP would not hold elections or would not surrender power. Even if the UF came to power, it would not be able to solve the problems because it was not a proletarian party and its support was dependent on the continuance of the capitalist system. In 1967, 1968, and 1969 Dudley Senanayake had hinted at youth rallies that it would be necessary for the UNP to remain in power if his rice programme was to be successful. In 1970, therefore, he felt they were faced with Hobson's choice. He chose to work for the UF and he instructed his JVP comrades in the Kotte area to work for the UF.

After the elections the JVP began to be harassed and he worked to help members who got into trouble. Early in 1971 the district leaders met at Hikkaduwa and discussed what to do about Loku Athula who was saying that members should be prepared to fight. He returned to the Colombo area and continued his propaganda work. He was searched by the police and the army. He and his brother were briefly taken into custody. His father, his brother, and he were brought before the Court. He met D. A. Gunasekera again after 5 April. His mother and father were harassed by the police, his brother was assaulted, and they threatened to shoot his young sisters. He was re-arrested and sent to Vidyodaya camp. Before he was arrested he gave Rs 2,000 to Loku Athula to spend on ammunition. Loku Athula had said that he had given this to him but he, Maharage, had never received any of it. He had thought before he met others in the camp that he had known what was happening in the movement, but after what he heard there, he realised that though he had been a leader, he knew little of what had been going on.[17]

Clashes among the top leadership

Part of what was 'going on' was the result of clashes among the most important leaders. It is difficult to discover any fundamental ideological basis for their disputes, however. Undoubtedly Rohana Wijeweera was the chief theoretician and the most mature political mind among them. His masterly presentation of his case before the CJC interpreted his life and times almost wholly in impersonal analytic terms, relating his own deepening understanding to the political evolution of his country. His rivals, in contrast, seem to have been those who were jealous of his political stature and those who questioned his tactical judgements.

In the first category may be included Loku Athula and his supporter T. D. Silva. Loku Athula before the CJC has accused Wijeweera of building an ego-centred movement with a secret politburo of Wijeweera's cronies, and has charged him with the responsibility of issuing orders for the movement to arm in 1970 (i.e. before the final police clamp-down which provoked the attacks of 5 April, implying an aggressive intent rather than a defensive reaction), and of giving the order for the 5 April attacks. In turn Wijeweera and his supporters describe Loku Athula as politically immature, seeking to win converts to his own person by aggressive calls for immediate action.[18]

Early in March 1970 Podi Athula told Wijeweera that Loku Athula was carrying on a campaign against him and was urging comrades to arm and to attack the government. Wijeweera at that point told Podi Athula that he knew of Loku Athula's activities and was taking steps to minimise them.[19]

During May, June, and July of that year Wijeweera was in prison, leaving Sanath, Karunaratne, and Loku Athula to carry out JVP activities. In July a big student meeting was held for the first time at the Vidyodaya campus of the university. Mahinda Wijesekera, the articulate student leader who had led a large part of the campus from the CP into the JVP and who became head of the united student front associated with the JVP, issued a booklet of the speeches made at that meeting. He explained: 'Why have we come out into the open now? We are ready to tell them we are not conspirators, we are not having revolutions in secret. We are not eight or ten people plotting revolution in secret to appear as heroes later. Revolution comes from the people.'[20]

On 1 August the JVP issued the first edition of their paper the *Deshapreemi* and on 10 August held a public meeting at Hyde Park, a big public garden in the heart of Colombo. Loku Athula disapproved of all the public meetings, saying that it exposed the JVP unnecessarily to political repression. Wijeweera in turn was unhappy at Loku Athula's leadership role. His supporters felt that Loku Athula took the line he did because he did not have a good grasp of political affairs and that this would be revealed at open meetings.[21]

(At this point in the proceedings the Chairman of the Bench intervened to ask: 'Is it the normal practice to kick down the ladder on which you rose up?' Wijeweera replied: 'It is not like that. In a Marxist revolutionary party individuals are not important, hierarchy and seniority are not important. It is a political understanding that determines leadership and mass consciousness.')

In July 1970 T. D. Silva had held a meeting at his home to discuss these matters. The evidence presented before the CJC concerning this occasion is curious. T. D. Silva had been a Linotype operator for Lake House for twenty-four years and was Secretary of the branch of the CMU at Lake House. (The CMU – Ceylon Mercantile Union – is affiliated to Bala Tampoe's tiny party, the LSSP–R) (Revolutionary section.) His house was often used for JVP meetings and his wife had come to hear of the movement. She consulted a light reader (clairvoyant) about its possible success. Apparently satisfied with what she had learned, she seems to have decided that Wijeweera would be a good match for one of her daughters. Wijeweera's break with T. D. Silva was partly the result of this foolishness.

Loku Athula alleges that Wijeweera gave orders to arm at a meeting in Ambalangoda in September 1970.[22] Wijeweera denies that he did so, saying that he lost control of the adventurists in the movement whilst he was in prison. See, for example, the following exchange:

BENCH: Do you agree that there were members of your movement who were collecting arms before November 1970?
RW: Yes, I have said so.
BENCH: But without your knowledge?
RW: Yes.
BENCH: Thereafter you approved of the action they had taken earlier?
RW: I instructed the District Committees to collect arms.[23]

And again, under examination by Podi Athula:

RW: From February 1971 I admit I gave instructions to arm. I have admitted all that you have admitted [sic] on this point.
PA: Is it a good legal point to admit that you gave instructions after February 1971 to arm the JVP else it would be massacred?
RW: Not a good legal point but a political reality.
PA: I'm inclined to agree with you![24]

Rohana Wijeweera's split with Dharmasekera in March 1970 was more intellectually profound. In January of 1970 the leaders had held a meeting at Kamburupitiya to discuss organisational matters, international communism, the organisation of leadership training, and the problem of Dharmasekera's tactical line. Another meeting was held at Dondra in March after Sanath had had information that a member of Dharmasekera's group had been sent to kill Wijeweera.[25]

Since 1968 Dharmasekera, as a member of Vidyalankara University, had been leading the campaign on the campus. Known as 'Castro Dharma' for his advocacy of Cuban-style revolution, his approach, it is alleged, had got the JVP labelled 'Che Guevarists', first by the China-wing press, which was then taken up as a common description. Considerable behind-the-scenes manoeuvring appears to have occurred at that time between student members of the CP, the China wing, and the JVP, with the JVP successfully infiltrating the inner circles of the CP (Moscow). Allegedly, Dharmasekera revealed the JVP members to the CP hierarchy (to facilitate his own claim to leadership) and thereafter he was distrusted by the Wijeweera group.[26]

Subsequently, Wijeweera alleges, Dharmasekera 'betrayed the JVP to the capitalist regime' by telling T. B. Illangaratne, pro-China sympathiser and MP for the SLFP, in March 1970 about the movement. In April Illangaratne apparently met J. R. Jayawardene to pass on the information and J. R. Jayawardene instructed the Criminal Investigation Department 'to enquire into the leaders of the Che Guevarists'.[27]

From the time that Dharmasekera was 'expelled' from the JVP the two factions continued their political activities separately, each staking out areas of control and allegiance. (Dharmasekera's group allegedly was responsible for the attack on the American Embassy during which a police inspector was killed on 6 March 1971.)[28] It is an interesting comment on the nature of the movement that Dharmasekera's expulsion by Wijeweera was considered legitimate even by Dharmasekera's own supporters.[29]

But personality and ideology were not the only reasons for the rift. It became clear during the CJC proceedings that Dharmasekera (who is *Goyigama*) was aware of the predominantly *Karava* character of the leadership; since he was in no position to challenge Wijeweera directly as figurehead, he sought to remove himself from what he plainly regarded as a stifling *Karava* clique. Thus even the factional splits at the core of the JVP had their caste aspect.

The fighters

The circumstances and role of many of those actually involved in the fighting were clearly very different. Many seem to have got caught up in the excitement of events and the large prospects generated by the relief from frustration involved in having something concrete to do that, they were assured, would change their lives radically and at once for the better. The four cases presented here vividly illustrate the pressures that led them to the attack and emphasise the minimal contribution political analysis made to their participation.

1

He joined the JVP as a schoolboy. Before that he had no politics. On 5 April he was asked by Sarath to be ready. He thought it was to stick posters, as before. He had been taken to Karandeniya school by tractor and told to assault the police station. He was threatened that he would be shot if he did not do so. He threw some bombs and went home. The next day, Sarath came and took him to a camp where he had to work as a cook. He was given lessons in how to shoot. Later he escaped and went to his sister's house in Colombo. He was arrested at Wellawatte (a suburb of Colombo).[30]

2

He had been interested in politics from childhood. His father was a labourer and his mother worked coir. He had studied for his Ordinary-level examinations and then for his Advanced-level examinations. He had failed his examinations. He had been twenty-three years old when he was arrested. His village was LSSP and his father also. He himself had been introduced to the JVP at his classes. They had told him that even if he went to the University and passed out, he would not be able to get a job. His sister and brother had wanted to be educated too, but the family was too poor for them to be schooled. He thought that he would be able to get the best out of his education under a socialist government. He had been prepared to fight for it. He thought it would help his whole family. He had been useful to the JVP because he could write well and draw posters. They held classes but did not tell him how to make ammunition or that he would have to throw bombs. He thought the JVP would help him to get out of his abject poverty. 'When they told us of the attack we had no idea how it could be done. They told us that the people and the army would support us . . . I never once stole and never robbed. The villagers even said that I had a "silver mouth" and would do all right in the world. Please let me continue to help my family. Let me continue my education . . . I renounce these politics and this adventurism I have been thrown into.'[31]

3

Until he was fourteen years old he had led a quiet life. He had three brothers and three sisters. His father was dead and his mother had brought them up. He had been a student at Galewala Maha Vidyalaya, and then became a student at the *pirivena* (centre of Buddhist learning) studying for his Ordinary-level examinations. He had no special knowledge of social matters. The leaders of the JVP had brought social problems before them. 'They misled us in such a way that they have blasted our whole future. They have made catspaws of us. The JVP ultimately led us to attack the government and government institutions.'[32]

4

The Crown presented evidence of 'conspiracy to commit murder'; their case was that Tennekoon had admitted he was involved with the insurgents and had accompanied them up to a point (but Tennekoon claimed he took no part in the attacks though he was informed of them). He had gone with the insurgents to the jungles and had helped them to search houses in the villages for guns and crowbars. He had broken into the house of the headmaster and into a shop.

Tennekoon had surrendered to the army at Kekirawa in June. He explained that he was the eldest in the family of ten. His father was an alcoholic. He had taken his Secondary School Certificate exams and had had to pay for his schooling by doing manual labour. Because his birth certificate did not have his father's name on it he found he could not get employment. He became involved with the JVP, hoping for relief. He had been asked to go for guerilla training and had gone to camps in the jungle. He heard that the leaders were putting small people like himself to the front. That had angered him and his friends but they had been told that they would be shot if they tried to run away. After he had been taken by the army he learned the real nature of the movement. He had been taught agriculture whilst at the detention camp and had earned some money. 'The leaders said all these things. We were just camp followers. The family is dependent on me. I must help my family and my younger brothers and sisters else my father will drink and the family will go under. I must fulfil my duties to my parents.'[33]

Here we catch a glimpse of the desperation of these youngsters and are able to realise both the potency of the JVP's message and its calamitous naivety. It was a successful movement because it articulated in a recognisable message the reality of their problems. It was a hopeless revolution because it relied on the romanticism and frustration of those who had little political awareness of the overall situation. It is not surprising that many of those who entered the camps after the insurgency began to reject the leadership of the JVP and to feel that they had been betrayed. But the experience does not appear to have led all of them to forgo political activism; the frustration and resentment is still present, and employment prospects are no better. Instead, many of the insurgents and their sympathisers have been provoked to study more carefully the reality of their situation and to consider more appropriate and effective action, not excluding further violence.

In the cases that have come before the courts and the CJC, and in talking to students, it becomes clear that many had believed that the village would be behind their actions, ready with material support and willing to join in the fighting. The youthful context of the insurgency raises interesting and perplexing questions as to the relationship between parents and their children and the abandonment of traditional norms of respect and filial duty. It is my own experience that few of the older generation really grasped the extent and the nature of the movement before April 1971. A number were then ready to agree with the emotional truth of the JVP's analysis, but few in the villages considered 'those youngsters' capable of actually dealing with the complexities of government, and could not visualise raw village lads giving orders to their traditional social superiors. None the less, a residual pride exists, that they should have committed themselves to action – 'even if they have gone to prison, it's not for stealing chickens'.

The role of the monks

Another aspect of the insurgency which has been scarcely touched upon as yet is the role of the Buddhist monks in the movement. Given the experience of the 1950s it was predictable, *a priori*, that some monks should be participant. However, after the events of April there appeared to be an official tendency on the part of the establishment to minimise the role of the monks (perhaps to give shape to their apparent wish not to face the suggestion that the insurgents had legitimate grievances which the government had failed to deal with – and with which the monks could identify; and in support of the line that the majority had been led astray by the corrupt and the power-seeking). The official figure given by the Ministry of Cultural Affairs of the number of monks arrested was fifty-six.

Yet members of the *Sangha* who had been arrested while disrobed and who had given false identities to the police have put forward a much higher figure, running into the hundreds. One monk claimed that he knew of 115 held in 1971 in the Magazine Prison, Colombo, alone.

The attitude of the insurgents towards the *Sangha*, insofar as it was articulated at all, was somewhat hostile, the impression being that resentment grew in proportion to the onerousness of temple service and the power of the local temple to exact observance of traditional respect. Along the south coast, where huge garishly painted Buddha-images stand alongside the roadway, slogans criticising the inactivity of the *Sangha* were painted on the statues, to the effect that the Buddha had been sitting long enough and it was time that he got up and did something in the here and now. Some insurgents apparently thought temple land would be divided among them after the insurrection.

The response of the *Sangha* establishment was generally muted. The *Siyam Nikaya* condemned the movement for its waste of life and neglect of the Buddhist precepts as much as because it represented an attack on the established hierarchy to which it is firmly linked. The *Ramanya Nikaya* rather studiously made no critical comment.

The attitudes of the monks who did become involved can be illustrated by the case of one who was a leader in Sabaragamuwa. Arrested on suspicion before the fighting broke out, he spent twenty months in prison before being released. In the absence of his leadership little fighting occurred in his area. A member of the *Siyam Nikaya*, he was a Peradeniya graduate and in 1971 a teacher at a *pansala* (compound where *bhikkhus* live). He said that many of the younger monks no longer took orders from their *nayakes* (clerical officers within Buddhist sects) and were disrespectful towards their seniors, having taken robes to get an education and to be provided for. (It was certainly noticeable that a number of the younger monks at the university campuses wore their hair to the limit of the length laid down in the *vinaya* – rules for members of the *Sangha* – and even took to wearing incipient moustaches.) At the Vidyodaya and Vidyalankara *Sangharamayas* (places of study belonging to the *Sangha*) they had been told by the other students that they were leading useless lives. They felt that they ought to be heroic leaders of their people as in the past. (He pointed out that the JVP was strongest at the campuses which had *Sangharamayas* – Peradeniya, Vidyodaya, and Vidyalankara, though there are other reasons for the Colombo campus's relative lack of sympathy.) They were opposed to the LSSP and the CP because they were pushing foreign ideologies and were opposed to Shanmugathasan's group because he was a Tamil and a Marxist (i.e. against a nationalism dominated by Sinhalese interests). Some of the Sinhalese JVP had accused Shan of giving the Jaffna organisers more money than party organisers in the Sinhalese areas. The established left took the line that it was the worker who led. The JVP took the line that it was the *bhikkhus* and peasants who should lead. Wijeweera had told them that the Tamils were anti-nationalist and might have to be pushed out of Lanka. They were not concerned with the future, only with the immediate revolution. They expected everyone to have jobs or land within twenty-four hours.

They used the imagery of the purge; the sudden seizure of power which would wash away the bad problems. The notion also had a tactical connotation: in a sudden movement they would seize arms, Colombo would surrender, the workers would go on general strike led by Bala Tampoe's supporters, and the army would join them.[34]

In essence, the JVP presented their case to the monks in the light of the Duththugamunu tradition, emphasising the monks' strong traditional role in national regeneration, and citing historical precedents of monks disrobing to participate in military affrays. *'Maubima nätnam Maranaya'* – the Motherland or Death! – was a slogan which had deep emotional reverberations for the younger monks.

In the practical development of the insurgency the monks could play an important part, for the *pansala* provided an ideally secure place to hide arms, leaflets, and wanted comrades, whilst the *bhikkhus* themselves could travel freely about the island, passing messages and running errands. In at least one instance known to me in a village near Ambamala–Bulathkohapitiya in Sabaragamuwa, a young monk fulfilled this role, then becoming a leader among the local insurgents, caching bombs in the *bana* hall and instructing the local youth in social and political matters under the guise of evening Buddhist studies.[35]

8

Conclusion

This book has focused on the relationship between Sinhalese social structure and the Sinhalese political parties. The analysis of both parties and
individuals in terms of their caste identities and familial relationships indicates the nature of the relationship between the parties and the wider
society. The personal lives and histories of the politically important and
the socially visible are of interest in their own right, but their study, in
addition, implicitly assumes that once we know who such people are, and
how they came to be so, then we have a reliable pointer to what they
believe and do politically. The caste and family identities of individuals
within the parties and the image and composition of the parties themselves
are in fact consonant, to the extent that the Sinhalese themselves take the
correspondence to be valid and meaningful.

A theme common to modern socio-political analysis, that of patron–
client relationships, also runs through the book; it is here subsumed
within the hierarchical structure of caste and the complexities of lineage
networks. Sri Lanka at Independence was a society in which the main
social links were not those of class, but of vertical relationships linking the
village to the rural elite, the lesser members of a community to the greater,
and the smaller political families to those who dominated national life and
public affairs.[1] At Independence, despite a wide franchise and democratic
forms and procedures, the active participants in the political order were
members of a recognised and oligarchic elite. The situation was not dis-
similar to late-nineteenth-century Britain where two major parties, led by
homogenously middle- and upper-class elites, contended for the votes of a
working class which was itself more or less excluded from political participation at elite level. Insofar as the Sri Lankan contending parties were
based on a form of patron–client network, political competition displayed
a factional quality rather than the ideological confrontation of opposed
parties.

The networks were rooted in traditional caste relations which were
given a new dimension under a parliamentary constitution in which

numbers mattered. Localism, and the geographic concentration of particular communities, allowed constituency leaders to be used as vehicles of
expression for caste-specific aspirations, though a distinction must be
drawn here between those communities who sought to operate through
their own caste elites, and those, generally lower in status, who sought or
accepted the leadership of their caste superiors.

The subtle interaction of such relationships was made the more complex by virtue of kinship and lineage networks operating within the caste
communities. Among the *Goyigama*, especially within the hill areas of
the former Kandyan kingdom, family pre-eminence was related to a
territorial-based deference that continued to exert a strong influence.
Elsewhere, among the coastal castes, the dominance of a few families
within the caste leadership was related to their newly emergent control of
mercantile and commercial resources as much as to traditional (ritual)
status or to landlord–tenant relationships. Among the lower castes of the
Vahumpura and *Batgam*, however, though kinship linkages appear to
have been of some importance locally, they did not form the basis of an
effective community leadership or of an elite structure recognised as representing the communities' interests as a whole.

Alternative linkages and networks were available, sometimes based on
class interests, such as those which developed among the professional
members of the administration, or within the education and medical
services; the trade unions formed alternative networks among the urban
employed. However, such networks offered only limited and partial
alternatives and membership in them was complementary to, rather than
exclusive of, caste/kinship ties which cut across recognition of broad
class or professional identities. (Much work remains to be done to clarify
the precise circumstance in which such alternative networks come into
play, and how, and in whose favour, conflicts of identity and loyalty are
resolved.)

In addition, other networks of a kind were offered in the organisations
of the political parties themselves, most notably in the left-wing LSSP and
CP. The relatively disciplined organisations of the ideologically committed parties of the left did offer an avenue of political advancement
avowedly free of consideration of caste or kin. Even within the UNP (and
later the SLFP) new demands for, and the exercise of, party-political skills
began to offer to relative 'nobodies' access to (limited) position and
(some) influence.

Such upward mobility as these avenues afforded was consolidated by
the ambitious by marriage into the local elite or into the lesser families of
the ruling lineages. Commercial parvenus married into the decaying

gentility or the professions; sons and daughters of 'good' families seized opportunities to buttress declining status by new wealth. None the less, since kinship ties effectively never extended across caste, caste identities served as an absolute check to ambition. *Goyigama* dominance limited the commercial coastal castes to roles as participators in elite influence, position, and power, denying them the right or chance to compete as equal contenders for political control and national leadership. At the bottom end of the status scale, low-caste ranking denied access to, let alone participation in, nearly all political processes except the act of voting.

The role of the MP at Independence was primarily that of a figure working and moving in national or local elite circles, concerned neither with *hoi polloi* in his constituency nor, more generally, with the mass as participators in public affairs. His role was legislative and such services as he delivered were paternalist in character and most often negotiated and delivered through intermediaries. S. W. R. D.'s campaigning style and the victory of the MEP in 1956 signalled a change. The new MPs elected from the rural hinterland on a 'popular vote' came to power not just as parties to an electoral programme but to secure, as individuals, direct benefits for those who had elected them. Over the next twenty years, MPs have increasingly expressed their role as largely, if not wholly, relating to the satisfaction of their supporters' demands, the solution of their problems with the bureaucracy by personal intervention, and the securing of tangible benefits for their constituencies. It would perhaps be exaggerating to say that, except in matters of specific personal interest, in more recent years their legislative presence has been marked only in their vote, but many have been content to leave the manipulation of parliamentary affairs to the party managers, and to accept the determination of policy by the party leaders.

Insofar as their interests reside in the satisfaction of *local* demands, their representational role has been as delegates of local groups, often specifically of local caste-community interests, or of the party faction within that community. Their usefulness to the party leadership resides, in turn, precisely in their links with the 'grass roots' of the caste/kinship structures and in their ability to speak for, or commit the support of, this or that numerically or commercially significant faction.

The populist approach of S. W. R. D.'s MEP in 1956 was translated into effective electoral support via, for the first time, incorporation of local, petit-bourgeois village networks within a nationwide movement, and secondly, via the exploitation of traditional deference under radical banners. The mass of the population for the first time was made to feel that it formed part of the politically relevant public. But the campaign was not simply that of a national elite utilising party politics to incorporate local influentials, together with their followers, into its political power base; rather, the 1956 contest marked the appeal of an elite faction to the lesser and the humbler over the heads of the members of the established national caste and kinship elite network in an attempt to mobilise a rush of popular support which would give the MEP sufficient power to break into, or altogether destroy, the established UNP ties at national level.

The attempt failed, and S. W. R. D.'s successors, abandoning the attempt to confront the national elites by popular arousal, have instead sought to build up caste and kinship networks parallel to the UNP's. Party-political competition in the event thus has initially strengthened the importance of caste and kinship identities and loyalties. Though proving a powerful instrument of securing mass support, enforcing party cohesion, and building party loyalty, the resulting limitations to advancement within the parties, the restriction of access to positions of influence within them to relatively few caste-acceptable supporters or to proven kin, also carries political risks. The 1971 insurgents' frustrated rejection of party politics was aimed, at the non-ideological level, precisely at the pernicious manipulation of caste and family ties within them.

To put it another way, S. W. R. D.'s populism had a perhaps unforeseen consequence. By opening up the political process to effective mass participation, he aroused aspirations among the hitherto excluded to join the elites in political leadership; his assertion of village values, his praise of the 'common man', roused hope among the lower castes and the socially depressed that the social structure, too, would somehow become more flexible and open. Their disillusion was the greater when, under Mrs Bandaranaike's rule, the SLFP began to adopt the conservatism of the UNP in its choice of leaders and supporters. The 1971 insurgents' bitterness towards establishment politics was strongly associated with their sense of having no place in, of being excluded from, a party that once prided itself on being the party of the 'common man'.

It was not only the political parties which found it expedient to manipulate traditional deference, status, and client relations, however; administrators found such linkages and relations effective instruments for extending central control over scarce resources. In an associated, somewhat overlapping process, the organs of the state – not only the bureaucracy but including the increasing numbers of state-controlled economic enterprises – used the dynamics of caste and family in their command of the patronage afforded by the allocation of those resources.

The operation of such networks and linkages gives to political and

public life in Sri Lanka an extremely personalised character. The significance of personal-dependency relations across the range of organisations is
apparent at many levels; the composition of the national leadership
exemplifies its central importance. What is the benefit of such relationships to the parties involved? What are the limits of flexibility and why
are they preferred to more straightforward political bargaining between
MPs and voters, MPs and party leaders?

In a rural society where class differentiation is, in many situations, only
partial and community of class interest is often weak, it is not surprising
that politicians should seek an alternative means of commanding votes
that invokes a wide, overarching attachment capable of rendering the
mass of individual voters amenable to manipulation in its simplifying
appeal. Furthermore, the hierarchical nature of caste relations means that
strong caste support at constituency level carries advantages beyond the
local base: caste members at higher levels are in a position to assist the
MP in recognition of his services to his constituents.

Caste provides the MP (and candidate) with an identity that in a sense
does away with the need for him to develop and present a political philo-
sophy: his social background, and, by association, that of his party's
leadership and allies, tells the voter all that he needs to know concerning
the MP's likely usefulness. On the voter's part, it is precisely this anti-
cipated usefulness – in concrete terms, the provision of goods and services,
the assistance in securing access to opportunity – that sways allegiance.
Usefulness is assessed not only or even primarily in material terms, however, but in social affinities. Those attributes which strengthen the
reciprocity of the relationship between the voter and the MP are highly
valued, in expectation that outsiders cannot be relied upon to recognise
their local responsibilities as strongly. If the constituent votes for someone
he 'knows', in the sense of knowing how he fits socially into the inter-
dependent caste/kinship structures, he does so in the expectation that a
common identity gives him some claim upon the MP, and in recognition
that the MP will, in turn, feel obliged to benefit and assist his own community. If no caste-compatible candidate presents himself, then the voter
chooses the party whose identity, reinforced by its ideological proclama-
tions and actions when in power, declares its interests to be closest to his
own. Faced with a choice between *Goyigama* candidates, for example, he
is likely to be influenced in the first instance by the reputation of the
major parties for looking after the interests of the voter's community;
only subsequently are modifying factors, such as the personality of the
candidates or their personal abilities, taken into account, though they
might, in the event, prove decisive. In other words, though caste identities

are not always sufficient conditions for electoral success, they do appear to be nearly always a necessary consideration for voter, party manager, and candidate alike.

Another reason why personalised relations are maintained is that, though the state has increasingly assumed responsibility for employment, welfare, and the relief of distress, it appears to the Sinhalese less likely that the state will recognise its responsibility to an individual in these respects than will kin. The state's provisions are generalised, and neither as specific in application nor as timely as the help one can receive from, or demand of, kin or other patrons. The very uncertainty and arbitrariness of state provision reinforces the perceived need to strengthen personal ties of obligation and reciprocal assistance.

In addition to individually rendered services, MPs share in the collective services expected of patrons: supporting charities, celebrations, and rituals, as well as other functions specifically concerned with the advancement of caste interest. The first category typically relates to village improvements, temple ceremonies, increasing local employment opportunities, and giving local support to national movements, organisations, and holidays. The latter, caste-specific patronage, typically relates to securing jobs for individuals, the provision of local schools and other educational opportunities, and the provision of local welfare facilities (either by encouraging state organisations to locate in the district or by assisting local groups to set up their own welfare provision).

The emergence of the MP as a new and additional patron (or, if in his person a traditional patron, with access to new resources) whose important contribution is his links with, and access to, the administration and the government, has provided constituents with an alternative to what was formerly often a single comprehensive tie to a locally dominant family. The skilful client has limited room to manoeuvre, to play off his patrons to his advantage. For example, a low-caste tenant on temple lands might enlist the support of his left-wing MP in an attempt to reduce his obligatory temple service (the more radical elements of the left have long proposed the nationalisation of temple lands); or he might encourage his friends to join with the temple monks in denouncing on temperance grounds a *Durava* MP's proposals to set up a toddy-distilling plant. The possible permutations are endless and pragmatically chosen. On the other hand, the client who finds his traditional patron (for some of the up-country areas one could write 'feudal patron') assuming the role of MP may not be in as strong a position; the combination of traditional status/deference with enhanced command over real resources may be so powerful as to leave the dependant more securely tied than previously.

Though politics are personalised, this does not seem to mean the same thing as individualised; neither the voter nor the MP is typically seen in isolation, as an independent entity capable of staking a claim on resources or winning votes solely in his own right. Events since 1970 have drawn attention to two aspects of this perception of individuals as operating within a social nexus. One of the criticisms of the young insurgents of 1971 by older inhabitants in the village was that, as individuals, they had no influence, could command no respect within existing structures. It was not just their youth which roused their elders' scepticism about their governing capacity, but their deliberate rejection of the structure of existing governing networks and alliances.

Another aspect has been revealed under pressure from the supposed recent devolution and democratisation of planning and administration to the 'grass roots'.[2] Insofar as the government MPs post-1970 represented the political authority of the centre in local areas, their role as agents of the devolutionary process, which by and large by-passed the regular administration, has tended to cut across established local networks and alliances. In order to secure access to resources, voters have had to lobby government MPs as wholly political representatives of the centre for the first time, and other contacts and linkages have become of less importance in securing a ration book or fertiliser quota than declared party allegiance. Although very little research has been carried out so far in this field, it would seem that the assertion of the MPs' political authority (i.e. that which they derive from being of the party in power) has not been wholly welcome, for the following reasons.

It reduces the effectiveness of the voter's claims upon the MP (except at election times) and adjusts the balance of the relationship in favour of the MP's discretionary favour and patronage. However limiting the customary relationships were in cutting off access and opportunity and in setting ascriptive boundaries to obligation, responsibility, and upward mobility, at least they provided known and accepted avenues of advancement, ways of securing benefits and of solving problems. A 'nobody' might stand even less chance under the MP's new authority than under the old dispensation, having little to offer the MP politically in return for favours except his vote. In short, it seems to have reduced the importance and usefulness of the caste-based, local community/centre relationships, and is seen as a threat to the social nexus established at local level. This, presumably, has been the government's intention.

Shifting balances in the constituencies have done little to upset the dominance of kinship groups and caste alliances at the national level; if, under Mrs Bandaranaike's recent leadership, the MP became more an agent and a tool of the party-political centre and less a representative of local community interests to the national elites, the grip of a few linked kin groups under the Kandyan *Goyigama* influence of the Prime Minister's family tightened. It remains to be seen whether the attempt to change the character of MPs' relations as intermediaries between government and the electorate will survive the 1977 general elections, or whether the shift was very much a function of the SLFP's overwhelming command of seats after 1970. It is not at all clear at present that the post-1970 administrative changes would not, in time, themselves have become susceptible to the temptations of caste and family, and restored the role of MPs as representatives of local social-group interests.

The years after Independence saw the emergence of three important processes inducing structural change, underlying the shocks of 1956 and 1971 and the kaleidoscopic patterns of political mobilisation and leadership of the next quarter century: rapid population growth, the expansion of state power, and the gradual commercialisation of agriculture. These three factors have had contrary and probably unequal effects on the strength of caste and family as instruments of political mobilisation, leadership formation, and party cohesion.

Rapid population growth has begun to weaken local ties and parochial attitudes, and to expand family structures beyond the point at which they can be effectively commanded by dominant kin. On the other hand, under a system of elective procedures and universal franchise, parties, administrations, and the organs of the state have been driven to seek, or have purposefully sought, greater access to numerically significant or commercially important local communities via the manipulation of caste and/ or kinship networks; numbers, both absolutely and relatively, matter.

The implications of the extension of state power are many and contradictory. Three may be indicated here. Insofar as daily life has become increasingly politicised, the expanding range and penetration of central government into what were formerly private concerns has tended to carry political cleavage and factionalism into new areas, intensifying both party rivalry, and, by extension, community and family competition. Secondly, the state's attempts to control and direct economic resources under the harsh necessity of maintaining viability, encouraging growth, and promoting development, has enabled it to gather in major new sources of patronage which governments of all political complexions have been tempted to use to enhance and strengthen the social ties and networks underpinning their political achievements. On the other hand, any attempt to make MPs act more like agents of central government, their authority derivative of the party in power, seems likely to encapsulate the local dimensions of

caste and family relationships within the political imperative (of supporting the governing party).

The third structural change – the gradual commercialisation of agriculture – received fresh impetus under the UNP from 1965 to 1970. The
UNP's attempts to launch a 'green revolution' in the countryside, assisted
by extensive agricultural inputs from overseas and domestic price adjustments, had more than economic objectives. Though in its own structure
and relationships heavily dependent on the manipulation of caste and
kinship ties, its social objectives, though not clearly stated, were not those
merely of attempting to create, in the long run, employment opportunities
for the rural young. UNP leaders of the 'inner core' were certainly aware
that a strongly modernising economy would increasingly liberate the
young from ascriptive status and from those identities which could be
enforced only as long as strong links were maintained with local traditions
and the communal awareness of a person's place in his 'home area'.

The agrarian programme of the SLFP-led United Front after 1970,
concentrating chiefly on redistribution and nationalisation of assets rather
than on production, had rather different implications. It seems likely
that, though the agricultural organisations created post-nationalisation
have been mostly nominally co-operative or collective in form and
avowedly neutral to caste or kindred, the actual beneficiaries have been
members of factions and communities ready to express their gratitude in
continuing support for the SLFP. It is, more than ever, hard to disentangle
conscious policy from implicit social manipulation: the turning over of
nationalised estate land to landless labourers in areas of *Batgam* concentration is, after all, of direct benefit to them and can quite legitimately be
so expressed in economic and party-ideological terms. On the other hand,
the government's measures gathered into its hands important and scarce
resources which enormously enhanced its powers of patronage; it would
be unsurprising if some of that patronage were used to strengthen and
extend existing caste and family power bases.

One need not impute conscious manipulation to the ruling elites, however, to predict that the actual outcome of the land-reform measures will
be to replicate existing patron–client, caste and kin relationships. Previous
settlement schemes have reverted to a pattern of high-status landowners
farming the settlement lands with lower-status landless labourers; the
Paddy Lands Act of 1958 failed as an instrument of tenancy reform as the
larger landowners took over the Cultivation Committees set up to imple-
ment the Act. The ceiling on landholdings is set high enough (25 acres of
paddy or 50 acres of other cultivated land) to allow families nominally to
subdivide holdings among individual members, or to resume personal

cultivation, effectively turning tenants into cultivators, or in other ways to retain control of the land, and, with the land, patronage and dependants.

Caste and kinship are functional to the party-political game in Sri Lanka; strong hierarchical linkages from the centre to the constituencies are created through caste and family networks and patron–client relationships, while strong horizontal ties between MPs, between voters, and between the ruling elites are also predicated on caste-community membership. The fact that such traditional loyalties and identities are operative within the constitutional framework does not necessarily imply that political life in Sri Lanka since Independence has been regressive, that there has been some falling away from the intended Westminster model. The procedures and institutions of a parliamentary democracy of the Westminster type have largely survived and, more than that, have allowed voters real choice between ideologies, economic programmes, party leaders, precisely because such a framework could encompass existing social forces while allowing them room to exercise and to develop. The constitutional inheritance has not been a dead-weight, nor become an irrelevance, but plays an integral part in a dynamic political process incorporating the essential elements of Sinhalese social structure, changing as that structure itself faces stress and transformation.

Appendix

The full UNP chart and guide and a guide to the SLFP family under Mrs Bandaranaike

Vernon Dissanayake
  Son-in-law of Sarah Wijesinghe. One-time Senator.
G. B. S. Gomes
  Son-in-law of Don Richard Wijewardene. One-time Joint Managing Director of the Lake House Group.
Lal Gooneratne
  Son-in-law of Don Richard Wijewardene. One-time Director of the Lake House Group.
Sir Oliver Goonetilleke
  Father-in-law of Mallory Wijesinghe. Distinguished Civil Servant before Independence; Governor-General, 1954–62.
H. C. Goonewardene
  Brother-in-law of Mallory Wijesinghe. One-time Permanent Secretary.
C. T. Goonewardene
  Brother of H. C. Goonewardene. One-time Surveyor-General.
[H. A. de S. Gunasekera
  Brother-in-law of Ananda Meegama. One-time Permanent Secretary. Not associated with UNP political party.]
Sepala Gunasena
  Brother-in-law of Sinha Basnayake and P. R. Anthonis. One-time Chairman of Independent Newspapers of Ceylon Ltd.
E. W. Jayawardene
  Father of J. R. Jayawardene; brother-in-law of Don Richard Wijewardene.
J. R. Jayawardene
  Son of E. W. Jayawardene; cousin of Ranjit Wijewardene. Minister under the UNP and present leader of the UNP; Prime Minister, 1977; President, 1978.
H. W. Jayawardene
  Brother of J. R. Jayawardene. Queen's Counsel.
R. P. Jayawardene
  Brother of J. R. and H. W. Jayawardene. Medical specialist.
Colonel T. G. Jayawardene
  Brother of E. W. Jayawardene; father of T. F. Jayawardene; father-in-law of A. F. Wijemanne.
Major T. F. Jayawardene
  Cousin to J. R. Jayawardene. One-time MP.
John Kotelawala, sen.
  Father of Sir John Kotelawala.
Sir John Kotelawala
  Nephew of D. S. Senanayake; uncle of Dr Gamani Corea. Prime Minister, 1953–6.
Meegama
  Brother-in-law of Hema Basnayake. One-time municipal engineer, Colombo.

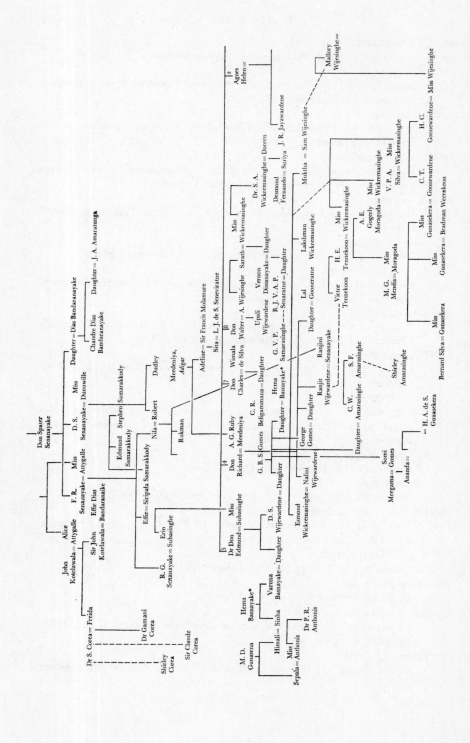

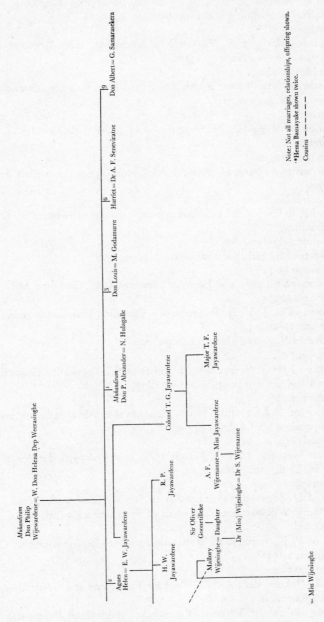

Chart 4   The UNP family: the Senanayakes, Wijewardenes, Wickremasinghes, etc.

Note: Not all marriages, relationships, offspring shown.
•Hema Basnayake shown twice.
      Cousins – – – – – –

Ananda Meegama
> Son of Meegama; nephew of Hema Basnayake. Economic Adviser, Ministry of Planning and Employment, 1970.

M. G. Mendis
> Brother-in-law of A. E. Gogerly Moragoda. CP (Moscow) MP for Ratgama, 1970. Trade unionist.

Sir Francis Molamure
> Brother-in-law of Don Richard Wijewardene. One-time Speaker of the House of Representatives.

Sita Molamure
> Daughter of Sir Francis; married to L. J. de S. Seneviratne. One-time Senator.

A. E. Gogerly Moragoda
> Married to a cousin of Esmond Wickremasinghe. Permanent Secretary, 1970.

Siripala Samarakkody
> Brother-in-law of R. G. Senanayake. One-time Member of the State Council.

Edmund Samarakkody
> Brother of Siripala Samarakkody. One-time MP.

Stephen Samarakkody
> Brother of Siripala and Edmund Samarakkody. One-time MP.

G. V. P. Samarasinghe
> Cousin of B. J. V. A. P. Senaratne. One-time Permanent Secretary.

Don Spater Senanayake
> Father of F. R. and D. S. Senanayake.

F. R. Senanayake
> Father of R. G. Senanayake. Member of the Legislative Council in the 1920s and leading politician of his day.

D. S. Senanayake
> Father of Robert and Dudley Senanayake. First Prime Minister of Independent Sri Lanka, 1947–52.

Dudley Senanayake
> Prime Minister, 1952–3, March 1960, and 1965–70. Leader of UNP. MP for Dedigama. Died 1973.

Robert Senanayake
> Son of D. S. Senanayake; brother of Dudley Senanayake; father-in-law of Ranjit Wijewardene. Chairman of Freudenberg's Ltd, 1970.

R. G. Senanayake
> Son of F. R., nephew of D. S., cousin of Dudley Senanayake. Cabinet Minister, 1953–9.

Rukman Senanayake
> Son of Robert. Became UNP MP for Dedigama at a by-election, 1973.

B. J. V. A. P. Senaratne
> Brother-in-law of Vernon Dissanayake. Additional Permanent Secretary, 1970.

L. J. de S. Seneviratne
> Son-in-law of Sir Francis Molamure. One-time Permanent Secretary.

Bernard Silva
> Brother-in-law of C. T. Goonewardene. One-time Government Printer.

V. P. A. Silva
> Brother-in-law of H. E. Tennakoon. Senior Civil Servant.

H. E. Tennekoon
> Married to a cousin of Esmond Wickremasinghe. Governor of the Central Bank, 1970.

Victor Tennekoon
> Brother of H. E. Tennekoon. His wife is a cousin of Ranjit Wijewardene and the sister of Ainsley Wijewardene. (Ainsley Wijewardene is married to a daughter of Sir Cudah Ratwatte; see p. 165.)

Bradman Weerakoon
> Brother-in-law of C. T. Goonewardene. One-time Secretary to the Prime Minister.

Esmond Wickremasinghe
> Son-in-law of Don Richard Wijewardene. One-time Joint Managing Director of the Lake House Group.

Lakshman Wickremasinghe
> Brother of Esmond Wickremasinghe. Bishop of Kurunegala.

Dr S. A. Wickremasinghe
> Brother-in-law of Sarath Wijesinghe. CP (Moscow) MP for Akuressa, 1970. Communist Party President.

A. F. Wijemanne
> Brother-in-law of Major T. F. Jayawardene. One-time Cabinet Minister.

Dr S. Wijemanne
> Son of A. F. Wijemanne; married to a daughter of Mallory Wijesinghe.

Sarath Wijesinghe
> Brother-in-law of Don Albert T. Wijewardene and Dr S. A. Wickremasinghe. One-time Cabinet Minister.

Mallory Wijesinghe
> Son-in-law of Sir Oliver Goonetilleke; cousin of Esmond Wickremasinghe. Company chairman.

Sam Wijesinghe
> Brother-in-law of Esmond Wickremasinghe. Clerk to the House of Representatives, 1970.

Dr Don Edmund Wijewardene
> Father of D. S. Wijewardene. Medical doctor.

D. S. Wijewardene
> Married to the daughter of G. B. S. Gomes. (His sister married Varuna Basnayake.) Advocate.

Dr Don Richard Wijewardene
> Father of Ranjit; father-in-law of Esmond Wickremasinghe, George Gomes (son of G. B. S. Gomes), and Lal Gooneratne. Founder of ANCL.

Ranjit Wijewardene
> Son-in-law of Robert Senanayake. One-time Chairman of the Lake
> House Group.

Don Charles Wijewardene
> Brother of D. R. Wijewardene. (His wife, Vimala, was one-time
> Cabinet Minister.)

Don Albert T. Wijewardene
> Brother of Don Richard Wijewardene.

Upali Wijewardene
> Son of Don Walter Wijewardene (brother of Don Richard); nephew
> of Sarath Wijesinghe. Chairman of Upali Group of Companies.

Guide to members of the Bandaranaike/Ratwatte family
(alphabetical by surname)

W. Neale de Alwis
> One-time member of the general committee of the Ceylon Planters'
> Association; one-time Chairman of the Southern Province Planters'
> Association. LSSP MP for Baddegama, 1970. Parliamentary Secretary
> to Felix Dias Bandaranaike. [Not shown on family charts.]

W. Neale de Alwis's nephew
> Married to a sister of Dias Bandaranaike. [Not shown on family
> charts.]

W. Neale de Alwis's sister
> Married to Sir Arthur Ranasinghe, who was Governor of the Central
> Bank, 1959. [Not shown on family charts.]

Felix Dias Bandaranaike
> Minister of Public Administration, Local Government, and Home
> Affairs, 1970. SLFP MP for Dompe from 1960.

Lakshmi Dias Bandaranaike
> Wife of Felix Dias Bandaranaike. Private Secretary to him, 1970.

S. D. Bandaranayake
> Related to the Bandaranaikes. Won Gampaha for the SLFP 1952–65;
> lost the seat for the CP (China wing) in 1970.

Sunethra Bandaranaike
> Daughter of S.W.R.D.; married to Kumar Rupasinghe. Co-ordinating
> Secretary to the Prime Minister, 1970.

Chandrika Bandaranaike
> Daughter of S. W. R. D. Settlement Planning Officer, Land Reform
> Commission, 1970. Director, Land Reform Commission, 1975. Chair-
> man, Co-operative Plantation Corporation, 1977.

Anura Bandaranaike
> Son of S. W. R. D. Head of SLFP Youth League.

S. W. R. D. Bandaranaike
> Prime Minister of Sri Lanka, 1956–9. Founder of the SLFP.

Mrs Sirimavo Bandaranaike
> Wife of S. W. R. D. Bandaranaike; daughter of Barnes Ratwatte. Prime Minister, July 1960–5, 1970–7. SLFP MP for Attanagalla from 1965.

Colonel Hector Divitotawela
> Married to Mrs Bandaranaike's sister. Appointed Commander of the Volunteer Force, 1971.

Nanda Ellawala
> Related to Mrs Bandaranaike through her uncle Sydney Ellawala; cousin to Mallika Ratwatte. Held Ratnapura for the SLFP, 1970.

Sir William Gopallawa
> Governor-General from 1962; President under the new constitution, 1972–7.

Moithra (Monty) Gopallawa
> Son of Sir William; married to daughter of Hector Kobbekaduwa. SLFP MP for Laggala, 1970.

Lakshman Jayakody
> Related by marriage to Mrs Bandaranaike. Has held Divulapitiya for the SLFP since 1965.

Hector Kobbekaduwa
> Related by marriage to Mrs Bandaranaike. Minister of Agriculture and Lands, 1970. SLFP MP for Yatinuwara, 1970.

M. B. W. Mediwake
> Related to Sir William Gopallawa. Minister of Local Government and Housing, 1959. SLFP MP for Minipe, 1970.

J. P. Obeysekere
> Related to S. W. R. D. Bandaranaike. Held Attanagalla for the SLFP in 1960. [Not shown on family charts.]

Siva Obeysekere
> Wife of J. P. Obeysekere. Won Mirigama for the SLFP, 1965 and 1970. [Not shown on family charts.]

Barnes Ratwatte
> Father of Mrs Bandaranaike. Contested Balangoda unsuccessfully in 1943.

Sir Cudah Ratwatte
> Uncle of Mrs Bandaranaike. Pro-UNP. Son, A. C. L. Ratwatte, Ambassador to Ghana and Malaysia under the UNP.

Harris Ratwatte
> Uncle of Mrs Bandaranaike; father of Anurudha Ratwatte. Supporter of D. S. Senanayake.

S. L. Ratwatte
> Uncle of Mrs Bandaranaike. Lost Senkadagala for the SLFP in 1960.

Clifford S. Ratwatte
> Brother of Mrs Bandaranaike. Won Balangoda in 1960 and 1965 for the SLFP. Chairman, State Plantation Corporation, 1975.

Anurudha Ratwatte
> Cousin of Mrs Bandaranaike. Lost Senkadagala for the SLFP in 1970.

Mallika Ratwatte
> Married to Clifford S. Ratwatte; cousin to Nanda Ellawala. Took Balangoda in 1970 for the SLFP.

Sivali Ratwatte
> Brother of Mrs Bandaranaike; married to a daughter of William Gopallawa. Executive in Lever Brothers, Ceylon, Ltd. Director, Export Promotion Secretariat, 1975.

Mackie Ratwatte
> Brother of Mrs Bandaranaike. Secretary to the Prime Minister, 1970.

S. C. Barnes Ratwatte
> Brother of Mrs Bandaranaike. Public Trustee from mid-1960s. Supreme Court Judge, 1974.

Kumar Rupasinghe
> Married to Sunethra Bandaranaike. Working Director, National Youth Council, 1975.

George R. de Silva
> Related to S. W. R. D. Bandaranaike. Joined S. W. R. D. from State Council where he sat under the UNP label. Was defeated at Colombo North for the SLFP, 1952.

Walter Thalgodapitiya
> Related to Mrs Bandaranaike. Commissioner of Assizes, 1957.

Richard Udugama
> Distantly related to Mrs Bandaranaike. SLFP MP for Matale, 1970.

Notes

PREFACE

1 V. Samaraweera, 'Sri Lanka's 1977 general election: the resurgence of the UNP', *Asian Survey*, 17, 12 (December 1977), 1195–206.
2 K. M. de Silva (ed.), *Sri Lanka: A Survey* (London, 1977).
3 Janice Jiggins, 'The nature of state power in Sri Lanka', paper presented to Conference on the Nature of State Power in South Asia (Institute of Development Studies, University of Sussex, October 1977).

CHAPTER 1. INTRODUCTION

1 Sir Charles Jeffries, *Ceylon, The Path to Independence* (London, 1962), p. 126.
2 Quoted in Jeffries, *O. E. G.: A Biography of Sir Oliver Goonetilleke* (London, 1969), p. 164.
3 For a revealing discussion of Theravada Buddhist notions of kingship, see S. J. Tambiah, *World Conqueror and World Renouncer: A Study of Buddhism and Polity in Thailand against a Historical Background* (Cambridge, 1976).
4 *Census Returns 1971: Preliminary Report* (Colombo, Dept of Census and Statistics, 1972). Forty-five per cent of the 14- to 25-year age group were out of school but unemployed in 1969. International Labour Organisation, *Matching Employment Opportunities and Expectations: A Programme of Action for Ceylon* (2 vols., Geneva, 1971).
5 The United Front consisted of the Sri Lanka Freedom Party, the Lanka Sama Samaja Party, and the Communist Party (Moscow). Though the UF took over two-thirds of the seats, it polled less than an absolute majority of votes, and the SLFP won fewer votes than the major opposition party, the UNP.
6 '... big money, diabolical minds, and criminal organisers'. Sirimavo Bandaranaike, 'A broadcast message to the nation by the Hon. Prime Minister' (Dept of Information press release, Colombo, 9 April 1971), and 'A notice issued to misguided youth' (Dept of Information press release, Colombo, n.d.).
7 Jiggins, 'Dedigama 1973: a profile of a by-election in Sri Lanka', *Asian Survey*, 14, 11 (November 1974), 1000–14.
8 One of the best introductions to the early years of Independence remains: W. H. Wriggins, *Ceylon: Dilemmas of a New Nation* (Princeton, N.J., 1960). See also A. J. Wilson, *Politics in Sri Lanka 1947–1973* (London, 1974); R. N. Kearney, *The Politics of Ceylon (Sri Lanka)* (London, 1973); C. A. Woodward, *The Growth of a Party System in Ceylon* (Providence, R.I., 1969).
9 H. A. J. Hulugalle, *Don Stephen Senanayake* (Colombo, 1975), p. 159.
10 P. E. Pieris (ed.), *Notes on Some Sinhalese Families, Part III, Being the Diary of Adirian de Alwis, Goonetilleke Samaranaike, 'Mudaliyar' of Salpiti Korale, for the Years 1777–1795* (Colombo, 1911).

11 Jiggins, 'Dismantling welfarism in Sri Lanka', *ODI Review*, no. 2 (1976), p. 85.

12 'Text of broadcast to the nation', 29 May 1970 (Ceylon Broadcasting Corporation, Colombo, 1970).

13 In conversation, 30 January 1971.

14 *Times of Ceylon*, 4 October 1959.

15 Convocation Address to the University of Sri Lanka, 1957; quoted in full in S. W. R. D. Bandaranaike, *Speeches and Writings* (Colombo, 1963), pp. 331–9. See also his prophetic speech during the debate on the Address of Thanks for the Throne Speech, at the first session of the First Parliament of Sri Lanka. November 1947; quoted in Bandaranaike, *Towards a New Era* (Colombo. 1961), p. 763; also his comments during the debate on the Address at the first session of the Third Parliament, April 1956: *Towards a New Era*, pp. 781–2.

16 The Official Language Bill, making Sinhala the one official language, was passed in 1956. After a *satyagraha* (non-violent campaign for reform), widespread riots, and the declaration of a State Emergency, the Tamil Language (Special Provisions) Bill was passed in 1958.

17 In conversation, 30 January 1971, G. V. S. de Silva (originally a CP member who left the party on the language issue and joined Philip Gunawardene, becoming his Private Secretary, 1956–9) claimed that only one portfolio was offered to the VLSSP (Viplavakari Lanka Sama Samaja Party: a Marxist offshoot of the LSSP) in the first Bandaranaike Cabinet. This was the Ministry of Industries and Fisheries, which Philip Gunawardene said should be offered to P. H. William de Silva. The VLSSP then demanded that the VLSSP should receive two Ministries. P. H. William de Silva returned after a second interview with the Prime Minister to tell his party that Bandaranaike had agreed and had offered both Ministries to himself, which he had accepted. The party then went in a body to Bandaranaike and demanded that William de Silva should keep Industries and Fisheries, but that the second Ministry, of Agriculture and Food, should go to the leader of the VLSSP, Philip Gunawardene. Bandaranaike accepted this demand, as a clever manoeuvre by the VLSSP to obtain two portfolios.

18 Speech made as Prime Minister, 4 June 1958, to the House of Representatives, meeting on the Governor-General's proclamation after the Declaration of the State of Emergency: *Towards a New Era*, pp. 450–1.

19 *Times of Ceylon*, 4 October 1959.

20 D. K. Rangnekar, 'The nationalist revolution in Ceylon', *Pacific Affairs*, 33, 4 (Winter 1960), 368.

21 Bernard Aluvihare, Collected Diaries (BA 1954 10/A), University of Sri Lanka Library, Peradeniya.

22 I do not intend to describe these in detail here, though reference will be made to them in the text; readers seeking an overview of the opposing approaches to economic growth and development are referred to my article, 'Dismantling welfarism'.

23 Jiggins, 'Dedigama 1973'.

24 For constitutional changes since 1972 and a discussion of their implications for politics, the administration, and the judiciary, see de Silva (ed.), *Sri Lanka*, pt III, pp. 281–375.

25 André Béteille, 'The future of the backward classes: the competing demands of status and power', in P. Mason (ed.), *India and Ceylon: Unity and Diversity* (London, 1967), p. 97.

26 M. Weiner, 'The politics of South Asia', in G. A. Almond and J. S. Coleman

(eds.), *The Politics of the Developing Areas* (Princeton, N.J., 1960), pp. 153–246.

27 M. S. Robinson, *Political Structure in a Changing Sinhalese Village* (Cambridge, 1975), pp. 247, 275.

28 W. H. Morris-Jones, *The Government and Politics of India* (3rd edn, London, 1971), p. 173.

CHAPTER 2. DESCRIPTION OF CASTES

1 See, for example, Wilson, *Politics in Sri Lanka*, p. 183, and Kearney, *Politics of Ceylon*, pp. 181–7.

2 Bryce Ryan, *Caste in Modern Ceylon: The Sinhalese System in Transition* (New Brunswick, N.J., 1953), pp. 4–5.

3 The three sects, the *Siyam Nikaya*, the *Amarapura Nikaya*, and the *Ramanya Nikaya*, are divided on caste rather than doctrinal lines. The *Siyam Nikaya* admits only *Goyigama*. The *Amarapura*, founded in the early nineteenth century as a protest against the caste exclusiveness of the *Siyam Nikaya*, admits monks of other castes, chiefly the *Karava*, *Salagama*, and *Durava*. The *Ramanya*, the more recent creation of some members of the *Siyam Nikaya*, is most catholic in its recruitment and is active in promoting both greater discipline and the Buddhist doctrine.

4 Louis Dumont, *Homo Hierarchicus* (London, 1972), pp. 262–3.

5 See, for example, M. N. Srinivas, *Caste in Modern India and Other Essays* (Bombay, 1962), pp. 6, 72.

6 For further discussion of Sinhalese caste divergence from the Indian 'model', see N. Yalman, 'The flexibility of caste principles in a Kandyan community', in E. R. Leach (ed.), *Aspects of Caste in South India, Ceylon, and North-West Pakistan* (Cambridge, 1969), pp. 78–112; Bryce Ryan, L. D. Jayasena and D. C. R. Wickremasinghe, *The Sinhalese Village* (Miami, Fla., 1958).

7 For a description of the British administration, see general histories such as: G. C. Mendis, *Ceylon under the British* (3rd edn, Colombo, 1952); for *rajakariya*, see Mendis (ed.), *The Colebrooke–Cameron Papers: Documents on British Colonial Policy in Ceylon 1796–1833* (2 vols., London, 1956).

8 Don Spater Senanayake became a *Mudaliyar*, the first member of his family to achieve this distinction. S. W. R. D. Bandaranaike's father had been a *Maha Mudaliyar* (high-ranking traditional officer), and the family had held such titles for generations. The British used both the indigenous elites and the rising men of wealth to gain access to the local administration.

9 E. F. C. Ludowyck, *The Modern History of Ceylon* (London, 1966), p. 115. Ludowyck comments, perhaps with some exaggeration: 'It was only the support of the senior civil servants that prevented the Governor withdrawing the appointment in the face of outraged Goyigama opinion.'

10 See Michael Roberts, *Facets of Modern Ceylon: History through the Letters of Jeronis Pieris* (Colombo, 1975), for a detailed description of one family's ventures.

11 Ludowyck, *Modern History of Ceylon*, p. 154. He comments: 'The racial bias which the election aroused was overlaid by caste prejudice: that was all.'

12 S. W. R. D. Bandaranaike (ed.), *The Handbook of the Ceylon National Congress, 1919–1928* (Colombo, 1928), pp. 608–9. The CNC asked all candidates to the Legislative Council to adopt publicly a resolution 'condemning the introduction of religious and caste considerations into elections'. The CNC subsequently

appointed a sub-committee 'to give wider publicity in the constituencies to the Congress principles and policy bearing on the elections'.

13 'Fisheries interest' here stands for the *Karava* caste.

14 Agriculture is the traditional occupation of the *Goyigama*, who are generally agreed to be the highest in status.

15 Sir Frederick Rees, 'The Soulbury Commission, 1944–1945', *Ceylon Historical Journal*, D. S. Senanayake Memorial Number, 5, 1–4 (1955–6), 43–4.

16 Ludowyck, *Modern History of Ceylon*, p. 281.

17 M. A. Singer, *The Emerging Elite: A Study of Political Leadership in Ceylon* (Cambridge, Mass., 1964), pp. 56–60.

18 J. A. Halangoda, *Kandyan Rights and Present Politics* (Kandy, 1920), p. 5. See also S. W. R. D. Bandaranaike (ed.), *Handbook of the Ceylon National Congress* for details of presidents of the CNC. The first president was a Tamil, and, over the next ten years, low-country *Goyigama*, *Salagama*, *Karava*, and *Durava* shared the presidency.

19 Woodward, *Growth of a Party System*, p. 33.

20 *Nindagam*: land granted at the king's pleasure under the Kandyan kingdom. The land reform Acts of Mrs Bandaranaike's United Front government have, at least on paper, radically altered the pattern of land-ownership in the country.

21 '*Mudalali*' means literally 'an elephant among those who have money'. The term refers to indigenous accumulators of wealth, largely through trading and associated activities, rarely through manufacturing and industrial entrepreneurship. The economic position of the *Goyigama* in the villages remains dominant: the *Goyigama* are rarely the tenants of a lower caste; most low castes are the tenants of the *Goyigama*. See S. J. Tambiah, 'Ceylon', in R. D. Lambert and B. F. Hoselitz (eds.), *The Role of Savings and Wealth in Southern Asia and the West* (Paris, 1963), pp. 44–125: 'The actual fact is that the high caste of the Goyigama are in any village economically differentiated and large numbers are economically depressed, being themselves landless tenants. But this does not negate the fact that that land is still virtually controlled by a minority of the high caste, so that the economic dominance of the high caste is rarely in practice violated' (p. 69).

22 Panchikawatte is an area of Colombo where particular types of economic activity are concentrated, thus giving the generic name to the group of businessmen involved in these activities.

23 Referred to as ANCL, and by the site of its major newspaper publishing business, Lake House. ANCL was taken over under the Associated Newspapers of Ceylon Ltd (Special Provisions) Act of 1973; the existing (private) shareholders were limited to a 25 per cent stake in the new company, the remaining shares being vested in a Public Trustee who was entrusted with their sale to the public, no one individual being permitted to own more than 2 per cent. All the independent newspapers have been taken over by Mrs Bandaranaike's post-1970 government.

24 These groups are distinguished by their gradual diversification into the modern sectors of the economy following the stimulation given by the UNP's administration of 1965–70.

25 M. D. Rhagavan, *The Karava of Ceylon: Society and Culture* (Colombo, 1961).

26 Tambiah, in Lambert and Hoselitz (eds.), *The Role of Savings and Wealth*: 'It is interesting to note that the most vital part of the entrepreneurial energy came from the coastal communities ... who were traditionally lower than the "good" Goigama caste, and whose fortunate commercial experience by virtue

of coastal trading contacts combined with the incentive to break through the strictures of the old feudal structure, enabled them to turn to new status avenues and eventually through wealth and education threaten the dominance of the farming Goigama caste. The significance of this entrepreneurial activity is that it set the path for the future investment activities of the middle-classes; a narrow segment made the leap from petty commerce to plantation enterprise; but the further leap from there to industrial investment has scarcely been made' (p. 57).

27 Roberts, 'The rise of the Karavas', Ceylon Studies Seminar, 68/69 ser., no. 5 (March 1969); see esp. pp. 6–8. Many *Karavas* have *gē* names with artisan connotations, the key component being *vadu*, meaning 'woodworker'. The article details the rise of a number of *Karava* and other castes of the south-west littoral during the nineteenth and early twentieth centuries.

28 A mark of their influence was the choice of W. A. de Silva as Urban Member for the Central Province to the Legislative Council in 1925. Roberts, 'The rise of the Karavas', p. 25.

29 John Clifford, a British sociologist working in Sri Lanka 1969–70, reports this in unpublished work for Polonnaruwa and Anuradhapura. See also John Clifford and H. P. Wimaladharma, 'Functioning of the Paddy Lands Act in a village of the North Central Province of Ceylon' (Mahaweli Development Board, 1971), pp. 6, 9 *passim*. Mrs Wimala Kannangara, ex-UNP MP for Galigomuwa, in conversation 21 February 1972, reports this for her area where a number of *Vahumpura* and *Batgam* have emigrated to the Southern Province. See also Robinson, *Political Structure*, p. 219: 'The dancing teacher, Appu ... announced that he had legally changed his name and that he was no longer Attapatugedera Appu, but was henceforth to be called Mudiyanselagē (a *vasagama* name) Appu. "That was the old way. Now I don't use that name" '.

CHAPTER 3. PRELIMINARY INVESTIGATIONS

1 *Statistical Abstract of Ceylon* for the years 1960–9 (Colombo, Dept of Census and Statistics, 1961–70), and *Statistical Pocket Book of Ceylon* (Colombo, Dept of Census and Statistics, 1966).

2 The number of youths aged 15–24 increased from 1,322,000 in 1946 to 2,610,000 in 1969–70. *Ceylon Year Book, 1960* (Colombo, Dept of Census and Statistics, 1961), p. 33; *Preliminary Report on the Socio-Economic Survey of Ceylon, 1969–70* (Colombo, Dept of Census and Statistics, 1971), p. 1.

3 Peter Newman, *Malaria Eradication and Population Growth* (Ann Arbor, 1965), figs. A1–A22, pp. 94–110, and p. 37.

4 Ryan, *Caste in Modern Ceylon*, p. 95.

5 Rees, 'Soulbury Commission', p. 44.

6 *Ceylon: Report of the Commission on Constitutional Reform* (Soulbury Report), Cmd. 6677, para. 278 (ii) (London, 1946).

7 Sir Ivor Jennings, *The Constitution of Ceylon* (3rd edn, London, 1953), pp. 74, 214, 52.

8 For example, Ambalangoda–Balapitiya, redistributed in 1959. See following pages.

9 The 1953 Commission, appointed following the 1953 Census, was wound up in 1954 with no major changes being made. In 1959 a further Commission was appointed though no new Census had been taken.

10 The proportion of low-country Sinhalese to up-country Sinhalese according to the Census of Population of 1963 was 3 : 2. This should entitle the low-country

areas to 76 seats as against 51 seats for the up-country areas. In fact, according to the division of seats adopted in 1959, the low-country areas got 54 seats and the up-country areas 73 seats. The up-country provinces in this calculation have been taken as Central Province, North-Western Province, Uva, and Sabaragamuwa, and the low-country as Western Province and Southern Province, giving a total of 127 seats after 1959. (Woodward appears to have removed 6 seats from his up-country calculation, possibly to exclude the plantation areas. He therefore arrives at the figure 47 as the up-country entitlement on a population basis. *Growth of a Party System*, pp. 255–69 *passim*, and p. 264 in particular.)

11 *Report of the Delimitation Commission*, SP xv (Colombo, The Government Press, 1959), para. 23.
12 Impressions recorded in conversation with prominent minority-caste figures. However, note that significant differences exist among the non-*Goyigama* in their precise attitudes to representation.
13 *Report of the Delimitation Commission* (1959), para. 24.
14 I. D. S. Weerawardana, *Ceylon General Election, 1956* (Colombo, 1960), p. 140.
15 *Ibid.* p. 138.
16 In 1964 C. P. de Silva, a leading *Salagama* politician, crossed the floor in opposition to Mrs Bandaranaike and in 1965 campaigned for the UNP.
17 Weerawardana, *Ceylon General Election*, p. 140.

CHAPTER 4. SABARAGAMUWA

1 *Report of the Delimitation Commission* (1959), Appendix VIII.
2 In terms of votes, this is generally true island-wide. The SLFP has relied heavily at election times on no-contest pacts or united programmes with the CP and LSSP. Its experience of government with these two parties has been less happy, however. The withdrawal of Philip Gunawardene's VLSSP from S. W. R. D.'s government in 1959 considerably weakened Bandaranaike's control; the inclusion of three members of the LSSP in the Cabinet in June 1964 led six months later to the defiance of the party whip by fourteen members of the SLFP and the downfall of Mrs Bandaranaike's government. And in the autumn of 1975 the LSSP withdrew from the United Front coalition of the SLFP, CP, and LSSP, leaving the government to face increasing opposition from the trade unions and urban labour. The SLFP has continued to tolerate the LSSP, however, precisely because of its strong influence in the south-western littoral and among sections of the lower castes, and its control over organised labour.
3 *Results of Parliamentary General Elections in Ceylon 1947–1970*, p. 6.
4 Jennings, 'The Ceylon general election of 1947', *University of Ceylon Review*, 6, 3 (1948), 133–95.
5 *Results of Parliamentary General Elections in Ceylon*, p. 6.
6 International Labour Organisation, 'A survey of employment, unemployment, and underemployment in Ceylon', *International Labour Review*, 87, 3 (March 1963), p. 251; *Preliminary Report on the Socio-Economic Survey of Ceylon*, pp. vi–vii. In the ten years between 1959–60 and 1969–70, unemployment rose from about 340,000 or 10.5 per cent of the labour force to 546,000 or 13.0 per cent of the labour force. By 1969–70, youths aged between 15 and 24 years accounted for 82 per cent of all unemployed persons.
7 Weerawardana, *Ceylon General Election*, p. 139.
8 Hulugalle, *Don Stephen Senanayake*, p. 159.

9 Ryan, *Caste in Modern Ceylon*, pp. 277–8; see also Kearney, 'The Marxist Parties in Ceylon', Ceylon Studies Seminar, 1973 ser., no. 6, pp. 8–9.

10 Robinson, *Political Structure*, p. 220.

11 While it is true to say that caste identity precedes class identity, not all of high status have commensurate economic standing, nor are members of the non-*Goyigama* unknown among the 'upper classes' nationally or locally. Landless *Goyigama* might conceivably align with *Vahumpura* (though not with *Batgam*) in an economic fight for better conditions; none the less, however wealthy, a *Batgam* would find it difficult, if not impossible, to pass beyond his traditionally inferior rank when in the company of the highest *Goyigama*; see Tambiah in Lambert and Hoselitz (eds.), *The Role of Savings and Wealth*, p. 73.

12 *Ceylon Observer*, 17 March 1974. Also recalled by D. L. F. Pedris in conversation, 30–1 March 1972.

13 The *Goyigama* UNP candidate, though well connected, did not have quite the same kind of local family status as the *Goyigama* SLFP candidate, who was related to the Dedigamas through his mother.

14 For the role of family inheritance in Lanka's politics, see Jiggins, 'Dedigama 1973'. For a contrary view, see Urmila Phadnis, 'Agalawatte by-election: a case study of the political behaviour of rural Ceylon', *International Studies*, 10, 3 (January 1969), 321–38.

15 In conversation, 21 February 1970.

16 Neither Keerthiratne in 1960 nor Karunaratne, who left the SLFP at the 1965 elections, was able to draw the majority of his caste in Rambukkana away from the SLFP.

17 A regular tactic in this area of Sabaragamuwa; *beedis* are a cheap cigarette and licences are issued for the cultivation of the leaf used to wrap the tobacco and for the wrapping. Typically, the licences are distributed to low-caste areas; see the SLFP candidate at the 1973 by-election at Dedigama: '... the largest number of beedi licences in the whole of Sri Lanka was given to the Dedigama electorate to encourage beedi cultivation ... Of the ninety-eight licences, twenty-four were given to the Dorawaka area' (UF meeting at Dedigama, reported in *Ceylon Daily News*, 3 July 1973).

18 A. E. W. Beligodapitiya is related to the Ratwatte family. Mrs Bandaranaike is also a Ratwatte but through her politics she has transcended her feudal identity to some extent, though exploiting it in certain contexts; see chap. 6.

19 In conversation, 12 February 1972.

20 It is my impression that migration in Sri Lanka is often associated with a search for status enhancement rather than economic betterment. Writing of the onerousness of caste obligation in the village, Tambiah notes: 'It is significant that in recent times one of the avenues of emancipation has been the recruitment and migration to government-sponsored colonization schemes.' (In Lambert and Hoselitz (eds.), *The Role of Savings and Wealth*, p. 73.) In Sri Lanka, townward migration has been slight, and a minor channel of status liberation, for even in the towns neither vocation nor ceremony has been dissociated completely from caste; see Morris-Jones, *Government and Politics*, p. 65, for Indian parallels.

21 This has remained true till April 1971, which marks a major departure from social acquiescence; see chap. 6.

22 In conversation, 30–1 March 1972.

23 Rees, 'Soulbury Commission', p. 44.

24 Note the variation to the similar verse quoted in the introduction. This variant I

heard spoken only by the *Batgam*, whilst *'Sirimā Ammā'*, is a widely used phrase.

CHAPTER 5. CONSEQUENCES AND IMPLICATIONS AT THE NATIONAL LEVEL

1 Press release, issued 25 May 1976 (Colombo, Ministry of Information, 1976); mimeographed, para. 22, p. 6.
2 Kearney writes: 'A new delimitation of parliamentary constituencies completed in 1976 created one new constituency in an area of *Vahumpura* concentration and another in an area of *Batgam* concentration, both scenes of heavy insurgent activity in 1971. Sources close to the Delimitation Commission, which prepared the new delimitation, suggested that these constituencies were created in the hope that enhanced parliamentary representation would draw youths from their castes away from politics of rebellion and violence and into the constitutional political process.' 'A note on the fate of the 1971 insurgents in Sri Lanka', Dept of South Asian Studies, Syracuse University, Syracuse, N.Y., November 1976.
3 Samaraweera, 'Sri Lanka's 1977 general election', pp. 1195–206.
4 For details of the land reform measures, see N. Sanderatne, 'Sri Lanka's new land reform', *South Asian Review*, 6, 1 (October 1972), 7–19.
5 Ceylon *Hansard*, cols. 1912–19, 7 September 1968.
6 Ceylon *Hansard*, cols. 1960–64, 7 September 1968.
7 Ceylon *Hansard*, col. 1918, 7 September 1968.

CHAPTER 6. THE FAMILY IN POLITICS

1 Fijik [pseudonym for N. E. Weerasooria], *Tales of Old Ceylon* (Maharagama, Sri Lanka, 1963), pp. 77–81.
2 Serialised in the *Sunday Times of Ceylon*, on 21 February, 28 February, and 1 March 1951.
3 At a Socialist Study Circle Seminar, reported in the *Ceylon Observer*, 12 December 1969.
4 The Ceylon National Congress by this time represented largely the low-country Sinhalese; the majority of the Kandyan elite in the 1920s had split away to form the Kandyan National Assembly. S. W. R. D. Bandaranaike's own Sinhala Maha Sabha, founded in 1934, had Kandyan support, but, although he was secretary to the CNC, the CNC did not regain influence among the Kandyans. At the death of W. A. de Silva, the leadership of the CNC passed to D. S. Senanayake and dissension between the Senanayake and Bandaranaike factions grew.
5 W. Dahanayake's career is worth repeating in outline here. On 11 March 1944 he stood against Simon Peeris of Badulla at Bibile by-election. Peeris, a wealthy bus *mudalali*, won the seat, but Dahanayake filed a petition against his election, argued his own case, and unseated Peeris. On 4 October 1944, Dahanayake won the by-election. In 1947 he won at Galle for the Bolshevik–Leninist Party of India. In 1952 he held Galle for the LSSP. He was shortly expelled from the LSSP for garlanding the UNP Prime Minister on his victory tour of Galle. He became an independent left-wing member, but in 1956 joined the Bhasha Peramuna of the Sinhala-Only protagonists. He held Galle for the MEP (it is

not entirely irrelevant that he had been to school with S. W. R. D. at St Thomas's, a leading establishment with status and function closely akin to British public schools), and became SLFP Minister of Education. He then joined a right-wing pressure group to oust Philip Gunawardene and P. H. W. de Silva in May 1959. After Bandaranaike's assassination he formed a caretaker government. On 7 December 1959 he resigned from the SLFP to form his own LPP; his resignation was not accepted and he was expelled promptly from the SLFP. Between December 1959 and March 1960 he dismissed his Cabinet and governed with the aid of his five LPP supporters. At the March elections he lost Galle by 483 votes. He held it for the opposition in July 1960, and in 1965 won Galle as a UNP supporter. He became Minister of Home Affairs under the UNP. In 1970 he won Galle as a member of the UNP, but he resigned from the UNP and till 1977 sat in the House as an Independent. (See Ceylon Daily News, *Parliament of Ceylon*, Colombo, ANCL, 1947–70.)

6 Speech made at the inauguration of the SLFP, 2 September 1951; quoted in *Speeches and Writings*, p. 144.

7 Speech made at the inaugural meeting of the SLFP; quoted in *ibid*. pp. 145–6.

8 Address delivered in Galle on 27 July 1946 at the Annual Session of the SMS; quoted in *ibid*. pp. 114–15.

9 *Speeches and Writings*, p. 143.

10 Reported in *The Nation*, 24 July 1943 (file in National Archives).

11 *Samasamajist*, 1 January 1951 (file in National Archives).

12 Reported in *The Sun*, 18 November 1973.

13 *Samasamajist*, 4 February 1950. See also A. R. Tyagi and K. K. Bhardwaj, *The Working of Parliamentary Democracy in Ceylon* (New Delhi, 1969), pp. 146–7: 'What strikes most to a political analyst about the Ceylonese political parties, is the fact that they are more a private affair than a public organisation. The leadership of the ruling parties has been more a family affair than a matter to be decided by their national executives or state-wide organisations.'

14 Among his rivals in the plumbago business were: Jacob de Mel, *Mudaliyar* D. C. Attygalle, N. D. P. Silva, D. D. Pedris, H. J. Peiris, M. A. Fernando, John Clovis de Silva, U. D. S. Gunasekera, H. Bastian Fernando. The spread of names indicates that opportunities in the nineteenth century were seized by many castes, not just the *nouveaux riches Goyigama* and rising families of the commercial coastal castes. All the above left considerable fortunes. The Senanayakes were luckier than most in having mines on their own land.

15 Hulugalle, *The Life and Times of D. R. Wijewardene* (Colombo, 1960), pp. 37–8. Whether the practice had been long established is not clear.

16 See chap. 2, n. 22. The indigenous businessman acquires the name of the site of his business, or the name of his company.

17 Sir John Kotelawala, *An Asian Prime Minister's Story* (London, 1956), p. 67.

18 *Third Force: The Voice of a Centre Democratic Group* (formerly *Straight Left*), 1, 3 (November 1948) (file in National Archives).

19 D. B. Dhamapala, *Among Those Present* (Colombo, 1962), p. 72.

20 Ceylon *Hansard*, col. 3180, 23 August 1962.

21 K. P. Mukerji, *Madame Prime Minister, Sirimavo Bandaranaike* (Colombo, 1960), p. 71.

22 Ceylon *Hansard*, 1 September 1959.

23 *Young Socialist*, 4, 4 (November 1969), 122.

24 Jeffries, *Sir Oliver Goonetilleke*, pp. 155–6.

CHAPTER 7.   CASTE AND THE INSURGENCY OF 1971

1 See, for example, Tissa Fernando, 'Elite politics in the new state: the case of post-Independence Sri Lanka', *Pacific Affairs*, 46, 3 (Fall 1973), 361–83; S. Arasaratnam, 'The Ceylon insurrection of April 1971: some causes and consequences', *ibid.* 45, 3 (Fall 1972), 356–86; F. Halliday, 'The Ceylonese Insurrection', *New Left Review*, 69 (September–October 1971), 55–93.

2 Kearney and Jiggins, 'The Ceylon insurrection of 1971', *Journal of Commonwealth and Comparative Politics*, 13, 1 (March 1975), 40–63.

3 Rohana Wijeweera, *Statement to the CJC* (official English text) (Colombo, Criminal Justice Commission, 1973), p. 259.

4 Tambiah has commented that the attraction of government office and the power it gives over the public is 'an historic legacy of feudal office and its privileges, and the nature of colonial administrative office, backed by status and power, is considered more attractive than sheer commercial wealth alone; in any case, persons in such office are in a position to command wealth by the institution of dowries by means of which status and wealth make a satisfactory exchange'. He remarks, too, on the 'conception of office, especially political office, not as welfare-minded public service, but as a leverage for accumulation of wealth by the distribution of favours and for demanding gratuitous favours from the public'. Tambiah in Lambert and Hoselitz (eds.), *The Role of Savings and Wealth*, pp. 60 and 64.

5 Wijeweera's evidence before the CJC on 22 October 1973. (Unless otherwise stated, the references are to my notes made in court.)

6 Interview with an officer of the Ceylon Volunteer Force, 5 December 1973.

7 N. Shanmugathasan, *April Bloodbath in Ceylon (Sri Lanka): A Marxist–Leninist Analysis* (London, 1971).

8 Kuliyapitiya in the North-Western Province; information supplied by local administrative officials.

9 Information supplied by local residents and checked with newsagents.

10 'Because of the traditional reformist, leftist influence, the members of the older generation who were sunk in reformism and were disillusioned and dispirited were drawn into the tide of the new radicalisation only in comparably [sic] small numbers. It was in such a socio-political situation where...under the UNP government the youth and student frustrations had increased and a general bitterness was being felt at the plight of the new generation, that the youth of this country including young workers, and students who had been caught in the wave of radicalisation had been showing signs of militancy were brought   to the position of demonstrating their hostility toward the existing conditions. While, under the UNP Government, unemployment was spreading more and more and the cost of living...was spiralling higher and higher, radicalism began to take hold of the young generation.' *Proceedings of the Criminal Justice Commission* (Colombo, 1971), vol. 19, 7588–9.

11 *Ibid.* vol. 19, 7576–82.

12 *Ibid.* vol. 7, 2106–7.

13 *Ibid.* vol. 19, 7576.

14 'Text of broadcast to the nation' by the Hon. Sirimavo Bandaranaike, Prime Minister, on 24 April 1971 (Dept of Information press release, 24 April 1971), p. 3.

15 Crown's case against the twenty-seventh accused, Moratuwa area, heard before the CJC, 2 August 1973.

16 Interviewed by me, 19 October 1973.
17 Evidence of Nimal Maharage, heard before the CJC, 17 October 1973.
18 Evidence before the CJC, 23 October 1973.
19 Wijeweera's evidence before the CJC, 24 October 1973.
20 Sinhala pamphlet, shown to me on the campus, and mentioned in the evidence before the CJC on 22 October 1973.
21 Evidence before the CJC, 23 October 1973.
22 Statement of B. A. R. Kurukulasuriya, pp. 34–6. See also *CJC Proceedings*, vol. 19, p. 7790. Wijeweera later claimed: 'While the State was openly repressing us outside there was Loku Athula and his followers brandishing their swords inside saying that only they were ready to face the repression.' 'Summary of written submission of 13th suspect, Rohana Wijeweera', p. 11.
23 During Piyasiri's (alias Kularatne Banda) cross-examination of Wijeweera before the CJC, 4 December 1973.
24 During Podi Athula's cross-examination of Wijeweera before the CJC, 22 November 1973.
25 Wijeweera's evidence before the CJC, 19 October 1973.
26 *Ibid.*
27 *Ibid.*
28 Uyangoda's evidence before the CJC, 7 August 1973.
29 Uyangoda's evidence before the CJC, 13 September 1973.
30 My summary of Statement of no. 45, Colombo, before the CJC, 19 October 1973.
31 My summary of Statement of no. 2, Ambalangoda, before the CJC, 19 October 1973.
32 My summary of Statement of one of the accused, changing his plea to guilty before the CJC, 2 August 1973.
33 My summary of Crown case and Statement of no. 66, Kekirawa, before the CJC, 19 October 1973.
34 Interviewed by me, 24 November 1973. See also the Statement of no. 108, Colombo (Mt Lavinia, Dehiwela, Moratuwa), before the CJC, 2 August 1973.
35 The village was known to me before the insurgency. On my return in June 1971, further details of its participation in the insurgency were given. See also Robinson, *Political Structure*, pp. 280–1, where she reports that one of the local temples was a centre of insurgent organisation and describes the monks' role in giving classes and acting as part of a communications network. The insurgents had attempted to bomb Alutgala police station.

CHAPTER 8. CONCLUSION

1 Readers are referred to James C. Scott, *The Moral Economy of the Peasant* (New Haven and London, 1976) for a provocative and thoughtful discussion of patron–client relationships in peasant societies and their relevance to political institutions and processes.
2 For the details of post-1970 administrative changes, see Samaraweera, 'The administration and the judicial system', in de Silva (ed.), *Sri Lanka*, pp. 353–75. For an analysis from the point of view of a district administrator, see B. Weerakoon, 'Role of administrators in a changing agrarian situation: the Sri Lanka experience', *Journal of Administration Overseas*, 16, 3 (July 1977), 148–61.

Bibliography

The reader is referred to the excellent and comprehensive bibliography by H. A. I. Goonetilleke, *A Bibliography of Ceylon: a systematic guide to the literature on the land, people, history and culture published in western languages from the sixteenth century to the present day*, 2 vols., Zug, Switzerland, Inter Documentation Co., 1970. Useful notes on further reading are to be found in R. N. Kearney, *The politics of Ceylon (Sri Lanka)* and C. A. Woodward, *The growth of a party system in Ceylon*. Additional material is to be found in the Sri Lankan publications *Marga* and *Modern Ceylon Studies*, and in the mimeographed *Ceylon Studies Seminar* series. The reader is also referred to the following articles and books not mentioned in the text:

de Silva, K. M. 'The formation and character of the Ceylon National Congress 1917–19'. *Ceylon Journal of Historical and Social Studies*, 10 (January–December 1967), 70–102.

Obeysekere, Gananath. *Land tenure in village Ceylon*. Cambridge University Press, 1967.

Snodgrass, Donald R. *Ceylon, an export economy in transition*. Homewood, Ill., Richard D. Irwin Inc., 1966.

Smith, Donald E. (ed.). *South Asian politics and religion*. Princeton, N.J., Princeton University Press, 1966, pt IV.

Yalman, Nur. *Under the Bo tree*. Berkeley, University of California Press, 1967.

The following lists in alphabetical order the sources referred to in the text:

BOOKS AND PAMPHLETS

Almond, G. A. and Coleman, J. S. (eds.). *The politics of the developing areas*. Princeton, N.J., Princeton University Press, 1960.

Aluvihare, Bernard. Collected diaries. In manuscript. Peradeniya, University of Sri Lanka Library, BA 1954 10/A.

Bandaranaike, S. W. R. D. *Speeches and writings*. Colombo, Dept of Broadcasting and Information, 1963.

Towards a new era. Colombo, Dept of Information, 1961.

Bandaranaike, S. W. R. D. (ed.). *The handbook of the Ceylon National Congress 1919–1928*. Colombo, H. W. Cave & Sons, 1928.

Ceylon Daily News. *Parliament of Ceylon* (issued after every general election up to and including 1970). Colombo, Associated Newspapers of Ceylon Ltd.

de Silva, K. M. (ed.). *Sri Lanka: a survey.* London, C. Hurst & Co., 1977.

Dhamapala, D. B. *Among those present.* Colombo, M. D. Gunasena & Co., 1962.

Dumont, Louis. *Homo hiearchicus.* London, Paladin, 1972.

Fijik [N. E. Weerasooria]. *Tales of old Ceylon.* Maharagama, Sri Lanka, Saman Publishers, 1963.

Halangoda, J. A. *Kandyan rights and present politics.* Kandy, Butler & Co., 1920.

Handbook of rupee companies, 1971. Colombo, Colombo Brokers' Association, 1971.

Hulugalle, H. A. J. *Don Stephen Senanayake.* Colombo, M. D. Gunasena & Co., 1975.

   The life and times of D. R. Wijewardene. Colombo, Lake House Press, 1960.

International Labour Organisation. *Matching employment opportunities and expectations: a programme of action for Ceylon.* 2 vols., Geneva, 1971.

Jeffries, Sir Charles. *Ceylon, the path to Independence.* London, Pall Mall Press, 1962.

   O.E.G.: a biography of Sir Oliver Goonetilleke. London, Pall Mall Press, 1969.

Jennings, Sir Ivor. *The constitution of Ceylon.* 3rd edn, London, Oxford University Press, 1953.

Kearney, R. N. *The politics of Ceylon (Sri Lanka).* London, Cornell University Press, 1973.

Kotelawala, Sir John. *An Asian Prime Minister's story.* London, Harrap & Co., 1956.

Lambert, R. D. and Hoselitz, B. F. (eds.). *The role of savings and wealth in Southern Asia and the West.* Paris, UNESCO, 1963.

Leach, E. R. (ed.). *Aspects of caste in South India, Ceylon, and North-West Pakistan.* Cambridge, University Press, 1969.

Ludowyck, E. F. C. *The modern history of Ceylon.* London, Weidenfeld & Nicolson, 1966.

Mason, P. (ed.). *India and Ceylon: unity and diversity.* London, Oxford University Press, 1967.

Mendis, G. C. *Ceylon under the British.* 3rd edn, Colombo, Colombo Apothecaries Co. Ltd, 1952.

Mendis, G. C. (ed.). *The Colebrooke–Cameron papers: documents on British colonial policy in Ceylon 1796–1833.* 2 vols., London, Oxford University Press, 1956.

Morris-Jones, W. H. *The government and politics of India.* 3rd edn, London, Hutchinson University Library, 1971.

Mukerji, K. P. *Madame Prime Minister, Sirimavo Bandaranaike.* Colombo, M. D. Gunasena & Co., 1960.

Newman, P. *Malaria eradication and population growth.* Ann Arbor, University of Michigan Press, 1965.

Pieris, P. E. (ed.). *Notes on some Sinhalese families. Part III, being the diary of Adirian de Alwis, Goonetilleke Samaranaike, 'Mudaliyar' of Salpiti Korale, for the years 1777–1795.* Colombo, Colombo Apothecaries Co. Ltd, 1911.

Rhagavan, M. D. *The Karava of Ceylon: society and culture.* Colombo, K. V. G. de Silva & Sons, 1961.

Roberts, M. *Facets of modern Ceylon: history through the letters of Jeronis Pieris.* Colombo, H. W. Cave & Sons, 1975.

Robinson, M. S. *Political structure in a changing Sinhalese village.* Cambridge, University Press, 1975.

Ryan, Bryce. *Caste in modern Ceylon: the Sinhalese system in transition.* New Brunswick, N. J., Rutgers University Press, 1953.

Ryan, Bryce, Jayasena, L. D., and Wickremasinghe, D. C. R. *The Sinhalese village.* Miami, Fla., University of Miami Press, 1958.

Scott, James C. *The moral economy of the peasant.* New Haven and London, Yale University Press, 1976.

Shanmugathasan, N. *April bloodbath in Ceylon (Sri Lanka): a Marxist-Leninist analysis.* London, Mao Tse-tung Thought Institute, 1971.

Singer, M. A. *The emerging elite: a study of political leadership in Ceylon.* Cambridge, Mass., MIT Press, 1964.

Srinivas, M. N. *Caste in modern India and other essays.* Bombay, Asia Publishing House, 1962.

Tambiah, S. J. *World conqueror and world renouncer: a study of Buddhism and polity in Thailand against a historical background.* Cambridge, University Press, 1976.

Tyagi, A. R. and Bhardwaj, K. K. *The working of Parliamentary democracy in Ceylon.* New Delhi, Sultan Chand, 1969.

Weerawardana, I. D. S. *Ceylon general election, 1956.* Colombo, M. D. Gunasena & Co., 1960.

Wilson, A. J. *Politics in Sri Lanka 1947–1973.* London, Macmillan Press Ltd, 1974.

Woodward, C. A. *The growth of a party system in Ceylon.* Providence, R.I., Brown University Press, 1969.

Wriggins, W. H. *Ceylon: dilemmas of a new nation.* Princeton, N.J., Princeton University Press, 1960.

ARTICLES

Arasaratnam, S. 'The Ceylon insurrection of April 1971: some causes and consequences'. *Pacific Affairs*, 45, 3 (Fall 1972), 356–86.

Clifford, J. and Wimaladharma, K. P. 'Functioning of the Paddy Lands Act in a village of the North Central Province of Ceylon', Mahaweli Development Board, 1971. Mimeographed.

Fernando, Tissa. 'Elite politics in the new state: the case of post-Independence Sri Lanka'. *Pacific Affairs*, 46, 3 (Fall 1973), 361–83.

Halliday, F. 'The Ceylonese insurrection'. *New Left Review*, 69 (September–October 1971), 55–93.

International Labour Organisation. 'A survey of employment, unemployment, and underemployment in Ceylon'. *International Labour Review*, 87, 3 (March 1963), 247–57.

Jennings, Sir Ivor. 'The Ceylon general election of 1947'. *University of Ceylon Review*, 6, 3 (1948), 133–95.

Jiggins, J. 'Dedigama 1973: a profile of a by-election in Sri Lanka'. *Asian Survey*, 14, 11 (November 1974), 1000–14.

'Dismantling welfarism in Sri Lanka'. *ODI Review*, no. 2 (1976), 84–104.

'The nature of state power in Sri Lanka'. Paper presented to Conference on the Nature of State Power in South Asia, Institute of Development Studies, University of Sussex, October 1977. Mimeographed.

Kearney, R. N. 'A note on the fate of the 1971 insurgents in Sri Lanka'. Dept of South Asian Studies, Syracuse University, Syracuse, N.Y., November 1976. Mimeographed.

'The Marxist parties in Ceylon', Ceylon Studies Seminar, 1973 ser., no. 6. Mimeographed.

Kearney, R. N. and Jiggins, J. 'The Ceylon insurrection of 1971'. *Journal of Commonwealth and Comparative Politics*, 13, 1 (March 1975), 40–63.

Obeysekere, G. 'Some comments on the social backgrounds of the April 1971 insurgency in Sri Lanka (Ceylon)'. *Journal of Asian Studies*, 33, 3 May 1974), 367–84.

Phadnis, Urmila, 'Agalawatte by-election: a case study of the political behaviour of rural Ceylon'. *International Studies*, 10, 3 (January 1969), 321–38.

Rangnekar, D. K. 'The nationalist revolution in Ceylon'. *Pacific Affairs*, 33, 4 (Winter 1960), 361–74.

Rees, Sir Frederick. 'The Soulbury Commission, 1944–1945'. *Ceylon Historical Journal* (D. S. Senanayake memorial number), 5, 1–4 (1955–6).

Roberts, M. 'The rise of the Karavas'. Ceylon Studies Seminar, 1968/69 series, no. 5, March 1969. Mimeographed.

Samaraweera, V. 'Sri Lanka's 1977 general election: the resurgence of the UNP'. *Asian Survey*, 17, 12 (December 1977), 1195–206.

Sanderatne, N. 'Sri Lanka's new land reform'. *South Asian Review*, 6, 1 (October 1972), 7–19.

Weerakoon, B. 'Role of administrators in a changing agrarian situation: the Sri Lanka experience'. *Journal of Administration Overseas*, 16, 3 (July 1977), 148–61.

PUBLIC DOCUMENTS

Bandaranaike, Sirimavo. 'Text of broadcast to the nation', 29 May 1970. Colombo, Ceylon Broadcasting Corporation, 1970.

'A broadcast message to the nation by the Hon. Prime Minister', 9 April 1971. Colombo, Dept of Information, 1971.

'A notice issued to misguided youth', n.d. Colombo, Dept of Information.

'Text of broadcast to the nation', 24 April 1971. Colombo, Dept of Information, 1971.

Census returns, 1971: preliminary report. Colombo, Dept of Census and Statistics, 1972.

Ceylon: Report of the Commission on Constitutional Reform (Soulbury Report). Cmd. 6677. London, HMSO, 1946.

Ceylon year book, 1960. Colombo, Dept of Census and Statistics, 1961.

Parliamentary debates (Ceylon *Hansard*), House of Representatives, 1947–1972; Senate, 1947–1971; thereafter National Assembly.

Preliminary report on the socio-economic survey of Ceylon 1969–70. Colombo, Dept of Census and Statistics, 1971.

Proceedings of the Criminal Justice Commission. Colombo, *CJC*, 1971– . Mimeographed.

Report of the Delimitation Commission, SP xv. Colombo, The Government Press, 1959.

Report of the Delimitation Commission. Colombo, The Government Printer, May 1976.

Results of parliamentary general elections in Ceylon 1947–1970. Colombo, Dept of Elections, 1971.

Statistical abstract of Ceylon. Colombo, Dept of Census and Statistics, 1961–70.

Statistical pocket book of Ceylon. Colombo, Dept of Census and Statistics, 1966.

Wijeweera, Rohana. *Statement to the CJC*. Official English text. Colombo, Criminal Justice Commission, 1973. Mimeographed.

Index